Raising Venture Capital

For other titles in the Wiley Finance Series
please see www.wiley.com/finance

Raising Venture Capital

Rupert Pearce
and
Simon Barnes

John Wiley & Sons, Ltd

Other Wiley Editorial Offices

John Wiley & Sons Inc., 111 River Street, Hoboken, NJ 07030, USA

Jossey-Bass, 989 Market Street, San Francisco, CA 94103-1741, USA

Wiley-VCH Verlag GmbH, Boschstr. 12, D-69469 Weinheim, Germany

John Wiley & Sons Australia Ltd, 42 McDougall Street, Milton, Queensland 4064, Australia

John Wiley & Sons (Asia) Pte Ltd, 2 Clementi Loop #02-01, Jin Xing Distripark, Singapore 129809

John Wiley & Sons Canada Ltd, 22 Worcester Road, Etobicoke, Ontario, Canada M9W 1L1

Wiley also publishes its books in a variety of electronic formats. Some content that appears in print may not be
available in electronic books.

Library of Congress Cataloging in Publication Data

Pearce, Rupert.
    Raising venture capital / Rupert Pearce and Simon Barnes.
        p.   cm.
    Includes bibliographical references and index.
    ISBN-13: 978-0-470-02757-8 (cloth : alk. paper)
    ISBN-10: 0-470-02757-6 (cloth : alk. paper)
    1. Venture capital.   I. Barnes, Simon, 1969–   II. Title.
    HG4751.P43 2006
    658.15′224—dc22
                                        2005034994

British Library Cataloguing in Publication Data

A catalogue record for this book is available from the British Library

ISBN-13 978-0-470-02757-8 (HB)
ISBN-10 0-470-02757-6 (HB)

Typeset in 10/12pt Times by Integra Software Services Pvt. Ltd, Pondicherry, India
Printed and bound in Great Britain by Antony Rowe Ltd, Chippenham, Wiltshire
This book is printed on acid-free paper responsibly manufactured from sustainable forestry in which at least two
trees are planted for each one used for paper production.

Contents

Preface   xiii

Part I   The Business of Venture Capital   1

1   Entrepreneurs and Venture Capitalists   3
   1.1   Introduction   3
   1.2   Entrepreneurs and business creation   3
   1.3   Why entrepreneurs need external capital   4
   1.4   Venture capitalists   6
   1.5   How to read this book   7

2   Other People's Money   9
   2.1   Introduction   9
   2.2   The fund-raising cycle   10
   2.3   Relationship with LPs   11
   2.4   Identity of the LPs   11
   2.5   Conclusions   13

3   The Limited Partnership   15
   3.1   Introduction   15
   3.2   The primacy of a limited partnership   15
   3.3   Facets of a limited partnership   17
   3.4   Partnership terms   19
     3.4.1   Life   19
     3.4.2   Capital commitments   20
     3.4.3   GP management   20
     3.4.4   Profit share   21
     3.4.5   Investment restrictions   21
     3.4.6   Transaction costs and fees   21
     3.4.7   Further funds   22
     3.4.8   Transfer of LP interests   22
   3.5   Conclusion: The venture capital business in a nutshell   22

4   The Competitive Environment   25
  4.1   Introduction   25
  4.2   Capital competition   25
     4.2.1   Vintage years   25
     4.2.2   Sector and geography   26
     4.2.3   IRRs and cash-on-cash metrics   27
  4.3   Deal competition   28
  4.4   Conclusions   28

5   The VC's Investment Model   31
  5.1   Introduction   31
  5.2   Fundamentals of VC risk   31
  5.3   Extreme caution over the act of investment   33
     5.3.1   Focus on proprietary deal flow   33
     5.3.2   Early exclusivity   34
     5.3.3   Due diligence   34
     5.3.4   Drip-feed approach to investment   35
     5.3.5   Syndication   35
     5.3.6   Internal investment process   36
  5.4   Exit obsession   38
  5.5   High reward for high risk   39
  5.6   Downside risk management   40
     5.6.1   Tranching of investments   41
     5.6.2   Price protection   41
     5.6.3   Follow-on capability   43
     5.6.4   Information and veto rights   44
     5.6.5   Special exit rights   45
  5.7   Dynamic capital allocation   45
  5.8   The human element   46
  5.9   Conclusions   48

Part II   Accessing Venture Capital   49

6   Introduction to Part II   51

7   Is Venture Capital the Right Option?   53
  7.1   Introduction   53
  7.2   What do I want my business to become?   53
  7.3   Can my business match those ambitions?   54
  7.4   How much capital does my business require?   54
  7.5   Do I want to control my business for a long time?   55
  7.6   What kind of life do I want to lead?   56
  7.7   Am I comfortable with an exit?   56

8   Choosing a VC Firm   59
  8.1   Introduction   59
  8.2   Substantial long-term resources   59

8.3   Long and relevant experience   61
8.4   A leader, not a follower   62
8.5   Scaling the business   62
       8.5.1   Powerful proprietary networks   62
       8.5.2   Portfolio community   62
       8.5.3   International capability   63
       8.5.4   Additional skills leverage   63
8.6   Successful reputation   63
8.7   Personal chemistry   63

9   **The Entry Point**   65
9.1   Introduction   65
9.2   Which qualified access route?   65
       9.2.1   A personal contact   66
       9.2.2   A portfolio company contact   66
       9.2.3   Industry gurus   66
       9.2.4   Professional advisors   66
       9.2.5   Professional intermediaries   66
       9.2.6   Cold calling   67
9.3   Generating a qualified access point   67
       9.3.1   Portfolio company access   67
       9.3.2   The great and the good   68
       9.3.3   Personal contacts   68
9.4   Communicating the initial message   69
9.5   What is the VC firm looking for?   69
9.6   Conclusion   70

10   **The Investment Process**   71
10.1   Introduction   71
10.2   Phase one – initial engagement with the VC firm   72
        10.2.1   The kick-off meeting   72
        10.2.2   The initial presentation   73
10.3   Phase two – preliminary due diligence to term sheet   74
        10.3.1   Preliminary due diligence   74
        10.3.2   Term sheet negotiations   75
10.4   Phase three – from term sheet to completed investment 76
        10.4.1   Final due diligence   76
        10.4.2   Legal documentation   77
        10.4.3   Syndication   79
        10.4.4   Special situations   79
        10.4.5   Internal approvals   80
10.5   Afterwards   80

11   **Preparing for the Investment Process**   81
11.1   Introduction   81
11.2   Timing   82

		11.2.1	Timing the approach	82
		11.2.2	Raising enough funds	82
	11.3	Valuation		82
		11.3.1	Introduction to valuation	82
		11.3.2	Valuation bases – the entrepreneur's perspective	84
		11.3.3	Valuation bases – the VC's perspective	85
		11.3.4	Why value is important	86
		11.3.5	Conclusions for an entrepreneur	87
	11.4	Choosing an investor		88
	11.5	Grooming the business		88
		11.5.1	Revisiting timing and value assumptions	89
		11.5.2	Ensuring management stability	90
		11.5.3	Spring cleaning	91
	11.6	Transaction structure		92
	11.7	Transaction logistics		95
		11.7.1	Confidentiality	95
		11.7.2	Non-solicitation	96
		11.7.3	Preparing for site visits	97
		11.7.4	Poison pills	97
	11.8	Conclusion		98

Part III   The VC Term Sheet   **99**

12   Introduction to Term Sheets   **101**
	12.1	Purpose		101
	12.2	What is a term sheet?		101
	12.3	Why have term sheets at all?		102
		12.3.1	Risk management	102
		12.3.2	VC policy	103
		12.3.3	Deal syndication	103
	12.4	What happens to a term sheet?		104
	12.5	Methodology of Part III		104
	Pro forma term sheet			106

13   Business Valuation   **121**

14   Investment Structure   **123**

15   Syndication   **125**
	15.1	Introduction to syndication		125
	15.2	Reward for syndicate leadership		126
	15.3	The entrepreneur's response		127

16   Investment Milestones   **129**
	16.1	Introduction to investment milestones		129
		16.1.1	Milestone definitions	129
		16.1.2	Milestone waivers	130

16.2 Attractions for the VC firm   131
16.3 Attractions for the entrepreneur   132
      16.3.1 Protected committed funding   132
      16.3.2 Guaranteed subscription price   133
      16.3.3 Fund-raising without milestones   133
16.4 Areas to watch out for   134
      16.4.1 Sizing each tranche   134
      16.4.2 Careful drafting of milestones   135
      16.4.3 Syndicate decision-making   135
      16.4.4 Enforcement teeth   136
      16.4.5 Negotiation approaches   137
      16.4.6 Earn-ins and ratchets as an alternative   137

17 Corporate Governance   **139**
17.1 Introduction to corporate governance   139
17.2 VC board representation   139
      17.2.1 Composition of the board   139
      17.2.2 Nominations to the board   140
17.3 Board process   142
      17.3.1 Regularity and quorum   142
      17.3.2 Committees   142
      17.3.3 Board veto rights   143
17.4 Shareholder information   144
17.5 Shareholder veto powers   145

18 Equity Participation   **147**
18.1 Introduction to equity participation   147
18.2 Voting rights   147
      18.2.1 Introduction to voting rights   147
      18.2.2 Attractions of voting rights to the VC firm   147
      18.2.3 Attractions for the entrepreneur   149
      18.2.4 Voting rights – areas to watch out for   149
18.3 Dividend rights   150
      18.3.1 Introduction to dividend rights   150
      18.3.2 Attraction of dividend rights to the VC firm   150
      18.3.3 The entrepreneur's response   151
18.4 The preference cascade   152
      18.4.1 Preference shares   152
      18.4.2 "Double-dipping" preferred shares   154
      18.4.3 "High watermark" preferred shares   157
      18.4.4 The best type of preference?   159
      18.4.5 Application of the preference   159
      18.4.6 Legal considerations   161
18.5 Redemption features   162
      18.5.1 Attractions of a redemption feature to the VC firm   162
      18.5.2 Events of default   163

18.5.3   Default   163
18.5.4   The decision-making process   163
18.5.5   Legal issues   164
18.5.6   Alternatives to redemption   164
18.6 Conversion rights   165
18.6.1   Voluntary conversion rights   165
18.6.2   Compulsory conversion rights   166
18.6.3   Adjustment to conversion rights   167

19 Share Incentives   **169**
19.1 Introduction to share incentives   169
19.2 Sizing of incentive programmes   170
19.3 Who bears the dilution?   171
19.4 Ratchets   172

20 Share Vesting   **175**
20.1 Introduction to share vesting   175
20.2 Attractions of vesting to the VC firm   175
20.3 The entrepreneur's response   176
20.4 Vesting – areas to watch out for   178
20.4.1   Pace and level of vesting   178
20.4.2   Good/bad leaver provisions   180
20.4.3   Acceleration on exit events   181
20.4.4   Treatment of vested shares   183
20.4.5   Repurchase mechanics   184

21 Pre-emption Rights on Securities Issues   **185**
21.1 Introduction to share issue pre-emption rights   185
21.2 Attractions of share issue pre-emption rights to a VC firm 185
21.3 The entrepreneur's response   186
21.4 Areas to watch out for   186
21.4.1   What triggers pre-emption rights?   187
21.4.2   Reference terms of pre-emption   188
21.4.3   Partial pre-emption?   188
21.4.4   Who gets pre-emption rights?   189
21.4.5   Pre-emption top-ups   189
21.4.6   Administration of pre-emption rights   190

22 Anti-dilution Rights   **191**
22.1 Introduction to anti-dilution rights   191
22.1.1   Full ratchet anti-dilution   191
22.1.2   Weighted average anti-dilution   192
22.1.3   Mechanism of action   192
22.2 Attraction of anti-dilution to a VC firm   193
22.3 The entrepreneur's response   194

	22.3.1	Fundamental unfairness	194
	22.3.2	Limitation of anti-dilution in practice	194
	22.3.3	Shareholder double advantage	195
22.4	Pay to play		196
	22.4.1	What is "pay to play"?	196
	22.4.2	Determining the amount to pay	196
	22.4.3	Consequences of not paying…	197
	22.4.4	New developments	198
22.5	Areas to watch out for		198
	22.5.1	Carve-outs	198
	22.5.2	Pricing considerations	199
	22.5.3	Proxies for value	199
	22.5.4	Price benchmarks	200
	22.5.5	Who squeezes who?	200
	22.5.6	Differential pricing	200
	22.5.7	Syndicate dangers	201
23	**Provisions Relating to Share Transfers**		**203**
23.1	Introduction to share transfers		203
23.2	Transfer restrictions		203
	23.2.1	General restrictions	203
	23.2.2	IPO restrictions	204
	23.2.3	Mandatory sales	205
23.3	Transfer pre-emption rights		205
	23.3.1	Nature of pre-emption	206
	23.3.2	Partial pre-emption?	206
	23.3.3	Who gets pre-emption rights?	207
	23.3.4	Pre-emption top-ups	207
	23.3.5	Buyer of last resort	208
	23.3.6	Administration of pre-emption rights	208
	23.3.7	Exclusion of certain transactions	208
23.4	Drag-along rights		209
	23.4.1	What are drag-along rights?	209
	23.4.2	Why is drag-along needed?	209
	23.4.3	Drag-along implementation	211
	23.4.4	Further issues to consider	212
	23.4.5	Enforcement of drag-along rights	213
23.5	Tag-along rights		214
	23.5.1	Introduction to tag-along rights	214
	23.5.2	Nature of tag-along rights	214
	23.5.3	Partial tag-along?	216
	23.5.4	Timing of subsequent sale	216
	23.5.5	Different classes of shares	216
	23.5.6	Who gets tag-along rights?	217
	23.5.7	Pre-emption top-ups	218
	23.5.8	Administration of pre-emption rights	218
	23.5.9	Exclusion of certain transactions	218

24   Deal Management Terms   219
  24.1   Introduction   219
  24.2   Conditions precedent   219
    24.2.1   VC firm's strategy   220
    24.2.2   Entrepreneur's strategy   220
  24.3   Exclusivity   222
    24.3.1   VC firm's strategy   222
    24.3.2   Entrepreneur's strategy   223
  24.4   Cost reimbursement   225
    24.4.1   VC firm's strategy   225
    24.4.2   Entrepreneur's strategy   226
    24.4.3   Financial assistance   228

Index   229

Preface

This book was inspired by the realisation that venture capital deals are best done when everyone around the negotiating table understands what the deal is about. An inexperienced entrepreneur with a great business idea, up against experienced venture capitalists who have negotiated dozens of deals is hardly a level playing field when it comes to striking an investment agreement that will define the relationship between entrepreneur and investor for years to come. But it is a myth that venture capitalists prefer it this way. Indeed, for reputable venture capitalists focused on backing and building high potential businesses, striking a deal with an entrepreneur who is inexperienced or lacks knowledge of venture capital is often an uphill battle that needlessly increases the already high transaction risk. The process of investigating, negotiating and completing a VC investment can be long and arduous as the entrepreneur and his or her advisors fight every step of the way in the dogged belief that the transaction is a fight to the death. In reality the deal is the beginning, not the end, of a process; it is the starting point for a relationship focused on building a valuable, successful company.

The aim of this book is to allow entrepreneurs and venture capitalists to understand each other, the deals they sign, and the way in which those deals translate into effective business relationships to build successful new ventures. Crafting a positive relationship at the outset is the basis for managing the unavoidable rough times ahead of the venture and ensuring that the relationship does not fracture and destroy value for both parties.

For an entrepreneur embarking on the process of raising venture capital finance, understanding the venture capital business model, the decision making process within a VC firm, and the forces that drive a venture capitalist's behaviour is fundamental to the successful outcome of the fund raising effort and to positioning the entrepreneur's business for future growth and success in the medium term. This book examines the very core of the venture capital business model, exploring how this impacts upon the twists and turns of the fund raising process, and ultimately poses the question – is venture capital the right funding option for the entrepreneur's new venture?

For venture capitalists in the business of backing high potential entrepreneurs, this book takes a fresh look at deal fundamentals and highlights where and when aspects of the deal are flexible, what really does or does not matter, and how the clauses in a venture capital term sheet are derived from the underlying exigencies of the venture capital business model. Moreover, the book examines how the process of dynamic capital allocation throughout the life of a VC fund can materially impact the performance of that fund, and how this, in combination with the investment terms can minimise the impact of poorly performing investments within any given venture capital portfolio.

This book is positioned as a professional text, written with a level of detail appropriate to professionals in the area – entrepreneurs, venture capitalists, bankers, lawyers, accountants, consultants, advisors and government policy makers. The book offers deep insights into the deal making process but is accessible to a wider audience via introductory sections for first time entrepreneurs, or those inexperienced in the venture capital field, and for MBA students aiming to embark on careers in entrepreneurship or venture capital. The venture capital business model is largely US-derived and the principles of venture capital deals remain largely the same regardless of geography. Where there are specific local differences we have pointed them out but the lessons we draw are applicable in the US, Europe and other regions.

HOW TO READ THIS BOOK

This book is structured in three parts: Part I deals with the business of venture capital, exploring initially why entrepreneurs and venture capitalists need each other. We examine how venture capital funds are structured, the dynamics of the venture capital business model, and the competitive environment within which venture capitalists operate.

Having explored the business of venture capital, Part II addresses the challenge of raising finance from a venture capital firm. It is here that we pose the question: Is venture capital the right option for funding the business, and if so how should an entrepreneur access venture capital? The venture capital investment process, deal selection and valuation issues are considered and we have provided a number of recommendations and tips for entrepreneurs preparing to embark on fund raising.

Part III of the book provides a blow-by-blow account of the structure of a venture capital deal by explaining the clauses of a venture capital "term sheet" outlining the key aspects of the proposed investment. Managing term sheet negotiations successfully can make or break the entire deal, and it is here that the true mettle of venture capitalist and entrepreneur is tested to the full.

Part III, therefore, draws together the principles of the venture capital business discussed earlier in the book, and explains how they are manifested in the terms of the deal. The example term sheet provided at the beginning of Part III is representative of those used today in most jurisdictions, and the chapters that follow illustrate why each clause is there and how it is driven by the fundamentals of the venture capital business model. This approach allows the reader to understand why venture capital deals are how they are, and why certain clauses are immovable objects (albeit with workarounds and different choices) whilst others are not.

Solutions to some of the most common sticking points in venture capital deal negotiations are suggested, with the goal of enabling deals to happen quicker and more effectively. Even in the most trying of negotiations, it is important to remember that this deal is the beginning, not the end of the entrepreneur-venture capitalist relationship and it is this theme that runs throughout the length of this book.

The process of raising venture capital finance is often considered – even by the professionals involved in the process – as a win-lose transaction ... one player's "win" on an issue must connote another player's "loss". But such an approach is needlessly confrontational, fails to recognise the long term nature of the transaction being entered into (essentially a marriage), and is often based on a prejudiced and uninformed starting-point. This book's goal is to seek to educate and inform the protagonists in such transactions – both principals and their advisors – to a level of strategic detail and understanding that will help them collaborate to produce win-win outcomes where each party recognises the fundamental fairness of the final outcome, providing a sound foundation for an honest, open and collaborative relationship between VC and entrepreneur going forward – an environment in which the newly funded business can go from strength to strength and deliver up the ultimate outcome sincerely desired by all: a truly successful enterprise.

Additional material is also available at www.wiley.com/go/raisingventurecapital.

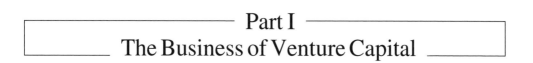

Part I
The Business of Venture Capital

1
Entrepreneurs and Venture Capitalists

1.1 INTRODUCTION

From early beginnings in the aftermath of World War II, and rapid expansion from the mid 1970s, the venture capital (VC) industry has evolved from an ad hoc collection of pioneering investors into a sophisticated, fast paced and highly specialised industry. During this period, venture capitalists (VCs) have provided the fuel for entrepreneurs to create a generation of companies that have changed the face of the planet. The exponential growth (and occasional dramatic decline) of the computing, communications, biotechnology and internet sectors has placed the VC industry firmly in the limelight, and subsequently under the spotlight, as volatile capital markets have taken their toll.

The question of how the VC industry works, however, remains a mystery for many novice entrepreneurs, and the dynamics of VC deals are challenging for those without first-hand experience. This book examines the fundamentals that drive the VC industry, explains how these fundamentals translate into investments, and culminates in a blow-by-blow account of how venture capital deals are structured.

Understanding the relationship between "entrepreneurs" and "venture capitalists" is at the very heart of this book, and is the key to structuring a win-win deal that creates value for both. The first step in beginning to understand this relationship is to take a look at exactly what entrepreneurs and VCs do, to examine what kind of people they are, and to establish why they need each other.

1.2 ENTREPRENEURS AND BUSINESS CREATION

Understanding what VCs do is best tackled by first considering the focal point of the industry – entrepreneurs who create businesses worth backing. Entrepreneurs have been creating opportunities, pursuing ideas, and starting businesses of one form or another since the dawn of time. But the precise question of what an entrepreneur *is*, what an entrepreneur *does*, and what characteristics he or she should ideally possess is something that has taxed economists and philosophers alike for the last 250 years. These may at first seem like obvious questions to answer, but the problem is the following: We all know a successful entrepreneur when we see one; we all have our own ideas about what they are like, but if you try to describe the characteristics that "make" an entrepreneur successful, it suddenly becomes very difficult. Successful entrepreneurs display a huge range of attributes – most of which apply to successful people in just about any walk of life. Copious amounts of research at business schools around the world have failed to develop reliable psychometric tests or even define specific personality profiles that predict who is likely to be a successful entrepreneur. The reality is that entrepreneurs come in all shapes and sizes, and from a variety of educational backgrounds, meaning that the task of picking the likely successes from a crowd of hopeful entrepreneurs is, by definition, extremely difficult. This, however, is the challenge faced by VCs on a daily basis as they witness a succession of hopeful entrepreneurs presenting their business ideas with the aim of securing much needed investment. For VCs the difficulty of trying to select management teams and business ideas they believe will evolve into successful high growth businesses means that in general they "hope for success but plan for failure" when they make investments. The resultant investment agreements between VCs and the entrepreneurs they back are structured to reflect this sentiment and, as we shall see later in the book, many of the deal terms are designed to minimise the VCs exposure in the event of financial failure of the entrepreneurial venture.

Text Box 1.1:   The Evolution of Entrepreneurs

The word *"Entrepreneur"* was first used in an economic context by the French philosopher Richard Cantillon in 1755. Cantillon's original definition of an entrepreneur was a simple trader, with an eye for opportunistic profit. Cantillon's entrepreneur "bought at a certain price and sold at an uncertain price, thereby operating at risk". Cantillon's entrepreneur was, by definition, an individual who specialised in taking on risk and lived on his wits.

The economic definition of an entrepreneur was modified a few years later by another French economist, Jean Baptiste Say. Say was the first recognised Professor of Economics in Europe and also ran his own business. His vision of the entrepreneur was of a more sophisticated individual able to identify an important market need and marshal the resources, including manpower, raw materials and the finance required to meet that need.

The economist Joseph Schumpeter advanced the concept of the entrepreneur yet further in the 1930s and 40s. Schumpeter stated that entrepreneurs were innovators and change agents who brought about "a gale of creative destruction". They change the way we perceive the world, live our lives and do business.

But is entrepreneurship all about the person or is it simply a process? This question is addressed in the definition of entrepreneurship put forward by Professor Howard Stevenson of Harvard Business School as "the pursuit of opportunity regardless of resources currently controlled". This definition captures very nicely the image of entrepreneurs being driven by the pursuit of opportunity and being able to muster the resources to do so on a flexible ongoing basis – perhaps using their networks to get things done when they don't actually own the resources to pursue opportunities on their own.

It is the last two definitions of entrepreneurship on which the VC industry focuses its attention. The personal computing, software and biotechnology sectors are prime examples of industries built via entrepreneurs who innovate, create and change the world. VCs look for businesses with the potential for global impact and they back entrepreneurs with just such a vision. VCs also appreciate that although a great deal of successful entrepreneurship is about having the right people, it is also a process in which businesses are built via the aggressive pursuit of opportunity, and in which their role is to provide the financial resources as the business grows.

1.3   WHY ENTREPRENEURS NEED EXTERNAL CAPITAL

A good starting point in any discussion of venture capital is to ask the question "why do entrepreneurs need to raise finance at all?". It probably sounds like there is an obvious answer too, but why don't all new ventures start up on a shoestring (i.e. with minimum finance) and simply grow as the cash flow generated from sales allows? Many successful businesses have been built this way and it is a formula that has worked for many types of start up. Indeed, Professor Ian MacMillan of Wharton Business School summed up this key virtue of many a successful entrepreneur with the following "Miser's Axiom".

Text Box 1.2:   The Miser's Axiom

Never buy new what can be bought second-hand

Never buy what can be rented

Never rent what can be borrowed

Never borrow what can be begged

Never beg what can be salvaged

This attitude to venture creation is at the core of what entrepreneurial management teams often do best – they manage very limited resources. They beg, borrow and salvage in order to propel a new venture as far as possible because they rarely have the resources to make it work.

The reality is, however, that most new ventures need a cash injection at some stage and many will require large amounts of cash before they generate revenue. In the biotechnology industry for example, it may take $100 M of investment before a company even gets close to launching a product. Other business models may require substantial early-stage funding in order to rapidly create and embed a viable market position for long-term return on investment and competitive positioning, which could not be achieved through cautious, organic growth.

External finance is needed, therefore, when the business is aiming to grow faster than cash flow generated internally will allow. External finance simply bridges the cash flow gap between the start up phase of a new venture and the point at which that new venture becomes self-sustaining via internal cash flows that are sufficient to maintain its optimum growth profile. This is the fundamental, and very simple reason that entrepreneurs need VCs. VCs will bridge the gap when, usually, no-one else will.

All new ventures undertake a journey from the "Valley of Death" to the "Promised Land". In other words the bank balance of a new venture declines to the point at which cash flow in

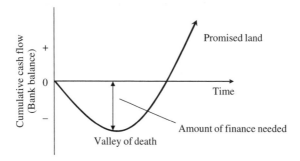

Figure adapted by kind permission of Prof. Sue Birley and Prof. David Norburn (*Mastering Entrepreneurship*) ed. Sue Birley and Daniel F. Muzyka, p. 159.

Figure 1.1   The Valley of Death

is equal to cash flow out. That turning point indicates the maximum negative amount the bank balance of the new venture will reach and hence the total amount of cash needed to "reach the Promised Land".

Many start ups fail not because the business proposition was fundamentally poor, but because the cash flow management just did not work out – in other words the business ran out of cash just before securing the first customer, or raising the next round of finance. Raising enough cash to cross the Valley of Death (with a little spare) is, therefore, the priority for most entrepreneurs and an enormous amount of time and effort is devoted to courting the VCs who possess financial resources to fuel this journey.

1.4   VENTURE CAPITALISTS

The modern VC industry is highly sophisticated and notoriously difficult to understand, but it's really very simple. VCs are aiming for one thing: capital gains. VCs are professional fund managers who invest cash in high risk start-ups, in return for equity (i.e. shares), with the aim of generating very substantial capital gains by selling those shares at a later date through some form of exit event, such as a trade sale or trading the shares on the stock market after an initial public offering (IPO). The golden rule of investment "buy low, sell high" is modified in the realm of venture capital to "buy *very* low sell *very* high" to account for the extreme risk profile of such businesses and, as we shall see later in this book, VCs employ a wide range of legal and financial instruments to manage the extreme investment risks they are taking.

Most novice entrepreneurs who deal with VCs, however, don't think of them as being in a business subjected to the same responsibilities and pressures that all businesses have – in other words providing a return to shareholders (as we shall see in Chapter 2, the "share-holders" for VCs are the so-called limited partners who provide the VC with funds to invest). Rather they think of them as a kind of giant cheque-book providing an endless supply of cash that must be coaxed across into the hands of the entrepreneur on the best terms possible; the entrepreneur must first stalk an unsuspecting VC, wrestle him or her to the ground, force a pen between their fingers, prise open the cheque-book and get them to sign. More experienced entrepreneurs take a different view – they regard a VC not just as a walking cheque-book, but also as a giant Rolodex, offering the potential to broaden their networking range, to open influential doors and ultimately to accelerate business growth. In the true spirit of "beg, borrow and salvage", VCs are not just a source of finance for entrepreneurs, they are business partners who can be drawn upon to provide advice, an email account, office space, meeting rooms and above all, the credibility that investment from a top quality VC bestows upon an otherwise unknown start up business.

These preconceptions are of course partly based in truth: from the entrepreneur's perspective the most mis-used word in the VC lexicon is probably "value-added" (as in "we are a value-added investor"), closely followed by "smart-money". Precisely how much value VCs bring to the business beyond the cash they invest has been the subject of extensive research and in some cases the jury is still out. The research has concluded that VCs add lots of value in some areas, less value in others and in some areas can even destroy value! While it is undoubtedly true that top quality VC firms can deliver significant added value to a business from time to time, it is overwhelmingly the case that the single most valuable service provided by VCs to the entrepreneurs they back is the investment of cold, hard cash. But for an entrepreneur to view this act in isolation is a grave error, which may indeed scupper the entrepreneur's hopes of successfully securing venture funding on attractive terms in the first place.

Although it is probably sound advice for entrepreneurs to assume that a VC will add negligible value to the venture beyond the act of funding it, it is equally true that unless they understand the nature and dynamics of the VC's business – essentially the context within which the interaction will take place – they will be unable to grasp the factors and resources that underpin the fundamentals of VC investing and will therefore be unable to turn these factors to their advantage. In such circumstances, either entrepreneurs will inadvertently present the investment opportunity to the VC in a way that leaves the VC unmoved, or (often worse) will secure investment from the VC on highly unattractive terms and embark on a deeply flawed relationship with their new "business partner" (after all the VC fund is now a part of owner of the business) in which they will not be able to leverage the relationship to its maximum potential. Even worse, by accepting a bad deal from a VC the seeds of eventual business failure may already have been sown for the fledgling business venture.

Therefore, before examining how to access a VC or differentiate between them, it is essential that an entrepreneur takes some time to understand the nature of the beast – the dynamics of the business model employed by most VCs, the marketplace in which they seek to compete, and the core business philosophies and mindsets that derive from these factors and which will dramatically influence the interaction of VC and entrepreneur.

VC investment in the early twenty-first century is undoubtedly a business, as opposed to philanthropy. It may as yet remain a "cottage industry" in many parts of the world, with question-marks regarding the ability of the sector to scale or leverage its traditional business model beyond small partnerships, but it is nonetheless an industry operating in an intensely competitive environment. As such, every VC firm will, to a greater or lesser extent, experience the same business and operational issues, the same market pressures and the same strategic constraints and these will in turn each drive the behaviour of every VC down very similar paths. As such, VC firms are no different from any other business operating in a mature and highly competitive industrial sector – and in many ways they are no different to the entrepreneurial ventures they back.

If the entrepreneur can come to understand these key dynamics of the VC's business, the tools of the VC trade and the way in which a VC strives to use them to manage risk, as well as the established business environment and process within the industry, then that entrepreneur will be best-placed to address two key issues: First, whether VC finance makes sense in the context of their own personal and business ambitions: and second, to obtain the best deal possible and structure a productive relationship which extracts maximum leverage from what the VC has to offer post-deal. When this is achieved, the chances of commercial success for the venture will often be dramatically improved.

1.5 HOW TO READ THIS BOOK

This book was inspired by the many entrepreneurs who struggle to understand the business of venture capital when they first encounter it. Although at first glance it may seem that entrepreneurs who understand VC deals must be a bad thing for VCs (aiming as they do to get the best deal) this is not the case. For a VC, doing business with an entrepreneur who does not understand the constraints and pressures of the VC model – and who accordingly does not understand the process he or she is entering or the legitimacy or otherwise of the key clauses in an investment contract – can be a long, uphill and often unproductive battle. By contrast, the engagement between a VC firm and an entrepreneur who knows the landscape he or she is entering and where and how an investment proposal may be flexed, is like a breath of fresh air for the VC firm and will mean that BOTH parties can set about reaching a fair, flexible and creative agreement in a calm and business-like manner. Deals are completed quicker, relationships are preserved and businesses are built faster when each side of the negotiating table understands what makes the other tick. This is the aim of the book.

Part I explores the business of venture capital, examining how the fundamental dynamics of the business drive the day to day behaviour of a VC, and concludes by examining the key criteria that a business must have in order to position itself optimally within the VC's own business environment – in other words, to be positioned attractively for VC investment.

Part II of the book examines in detail the process of raising venture capital finance, including a look inside the decision-making process for most VCs, how VCs value businesses, and how to get through the door for that crucial first meeting.

Part III of the book drills into the fine detail of what a venture capital investment proposal or "term sheet" looks like. We have included an example pro forma term sheet in Part III – which is derived from the industry standard or "boiler plate" term sheets that are now used across many jurisdictions including the USA, Europe and Asia. We have unpicked each clause in that term sheet so that entrepreneurs (or indeed VCs) engaged in negotiations can understand what the clause means, why it is there and how it may be flexed. Part III of the book need not be read "sequentially" and can be used as a reference source for addressing any aspect of a VC investment transaction at any time.

We hope that by the end of this book, entrepreneurs, VCs, investment banking professionals, corporate lawyers and MBA students engaged in the art of entrepreneurship will have a very clear handle on the nature of the entrepreneur-VC relationship, and more importantly, how to make it work.

2
Other People's Money

2.1   INTRODUCTION

The first point to note about VCs is that contrary to the belief of many novice entrepreneurs, VCs do not sit at the beginning of the capital supply chain. They are not playing with their own money, but in fact with someone else's. In simple terms VCs are professional fund managers who screen, evaluate, invest in and monitor entrepreneurial new ventures on behalf of the pension funds, banks and insurance companies who invest in the VC fund they manage. In other words, just like many other businesses, VCs are acting on behalf of their shareholders (referred to in this case as limited partners ("LPs") for reasons we shall explore below).

The theoretical role of VCs is to act as financial intermediaries providing sector-specific expertise in sourcing, assessing and investing in entrepreneurial new ventures that the limited partners would find difficult to carry out on their own. The specific expertise of VCs in evaluating new ventures allows them to invest profitably in projects that the less specialised investors who invest in the fund would otherwise reject. By becoming closely involved in the entrepreneurial venture, usually through taking a seat on the board of directors, VCs manage potential information asymmetries between limited partners and entrepreneurs to ensure that once entrepreneurs receive cash from the VC's fund, they continue to act in the interests of the shareholders in their business.

The fact that a VC firm is not playing with its own money, but with someone else's money is both a blessing and a curse for entrepreneurs. It's a blessing, because the partners in the VC firm will be much more likely to take investment risks with someone else's money

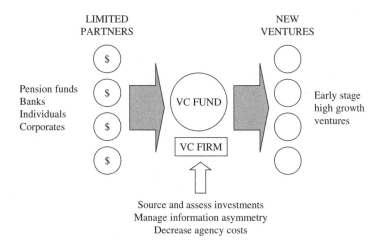

Figure 2.1   The fundamental role of venture capitalists as intermediaries

than they would with, say, their own savings allocated for the mortgage, retirement etc; but it's also a curse, because the nature of risk that a VC firm will take with its investment funds is, in reality, tightly defined by the circumstances in which those funds are made available to the VC firm and by the very fact that those funds are not its own. In short, a VC's entire business is operated in a fiduciary capacity with regard to the VC firm's financial backers.

Venture capitalists are essentially financial intermediaries whose role is to identify, evaluate and invest in high risk investments that the limited partners would otherwise find difficult to invest in directly. They manage the "information asymmetry" that exists between a potentially complex early stage company and the LPs who usually don't have the time or skills to overcome this asymmetry. Ultimately, the VCs "decrease the agency costs" of investing – meaning that the LPs would find it very costly to invest without the VC managing the investments for them – principally because of the greater number of wrong decisions they would be likely to make on their own.

2.2   THE FUND-RAISING CYCLE

Typically, a VC firm will raise funds for investment every two to three years. The fund-raising process will comprise a marathon self-promotion exercise not unlike the trials to which an entrepreneur is put when seeking to raise finance from the VC community. The VC firm will prepare a selling document known as a private placement memorandum (the "PPM") and the senior partners of the VC firm will then hawk this document (essentially a business plan) and themselves round the fund-raising community, selling their skills, experience, deal-flow network and, above all, their investment track record. Typically, this process can take between six months and a year from initiation of the fund-raising to the ink drying on the investors' cheques. Sometimes the VC firm will run the process itself; sometimes it will use a professional intermediary; sometimes it will do a bit of both. There is an important point to note at this stage – the completion of the fund raising process does not result in all the funds flowing into the VCs bank account. The LPs sign up to a commitment to make funds available when requested at regular intervals by the VC. In other words the VC draws down funds to invest on an as needed basis – helping to maximise the returns to LPs who can, therefore, hold onto their cash as long as possible.

For an established VC firm which is already in business, the process will typically commence with an approach to the existing investors in the firm's most recent fund, to seek their commitment to re-invest. The hope is, of course, that existing LPs will be keen to remain investors in the VC firm's business and can be successfully encouraged to make early commitments which will form the cornerstone of the VC firm's next fund. The firm will then seek to build further commitments from new investors around those cornerstone commitments. Again, this is not unlike the experience of an entrepreneur when seeking to raise subsequent rounds of development finance: the continued financial support of the existing shareholders will often be essential in terms of creating deal momentum, particularly in terms of setting the share price for the deal. Similarly a VC firm raising a new fund will usually begin with an intensive period of bringing the existing shareholders on-side.

Research into how LPs choose which VC funds to invest in has confirmed that existing relationships between LPs and VCs possess a great deal of longevity. Once the relationship is built around one or two successful fundraisings, then LPs tend to invest again and again in the same VCs. Research has also shown that LPs use not only objective measures of a VC firm's track record (such as the internal rate of return on previous funds) but also subjective views of the VC firm's reputation and track record. Criteria such as the VCs reputation amongst entrepreneurs, other VCs and even other LPs play an important role in the decision to invest. Hence the obsession that most VCs have with their own reputation – it is absolutely crucial in order to make sure the funds and the deals keep flowing.

2.3   RELATIONSHIP WITH LPs

A VC firm's existing investors (the LPs) are its very life-blood. VCs will meet each of those investors informally on a regular basis, will report to all LPs formally via written quarterly reports charting the progress of the fund, and will conduct at least one formal meeting with all LPs every year (often in a suitably impressive location). In addition, each fund managed by a VC firm will usually have an advisory board or committee composed of the senior LPs in that fund (usually the biggest investors) and this advisory board will meet quarterly or semi-annually to discuss the activities of the fund (such as investment strategy, fund terms, investment limitations and possible conflicts of interest). The LPs therefore play an important role in the management of the fund and exert a strong influence on the VC firm. This influence is apparent in the structure of the investment deals that VCs strike when they back entrepreneurs. The investment terms that VCs insist on are usually driven by the deal they have signed with the LPs in their own fund, and they cannot bend the deal terms outside the parameters set by their agreement with the LPs.

A VC firm will therefore be engaged almost constantly in an interplay of views with its LPs on all matters concerning the firm, its fund(s) and its investment activities. This open dialogue not only ensures that the firm's LPs are kept happy and that the firm has an early warning system for any upcoming concerns and issues, but also means that the fund-raising process (or at least the cornerstone formation part of it) effectively becomes a constant, gradual process through the life of an operative VC fund, rather than a madcap exercise from a standing start every three years or so at the end of the investment life of an operative VC fund.

At the same time, the VC firm will be conscious of not resting on its laurels and part of its ongoing investor relations activities will also involve sounding out potential new investors for its upcoming new fund, a process that will culminate in the eventual formal fund-raising exercise. Increasingly, this fund-raising and investor-relations activity has been professional-ised in recent years, with personnel appointed at a senior level within the VC firm to work full time on this important activity (often recruited from professional intermediaries such as investment banks, corporate finance boutiques and fund managers) and with significant investment in administrative infrastructure (e.g. portfolio reporting software) to support this team's activities. "Dazzling the LPs" has become a full time occupation of the VC community.

2.4   IDENTITY OF THE LPs

Who are these LPs? The typical investors in a VC fund include many types of financial institution, but predominantly insurance companies, pension funds, life assurance companies, public and private trusts, as well as some high net worth individuals. A significant constituency of the LP community is now made up of "funds of funds" – these are themselves managed investment funds, which raise money from their own investors solely for the purpose of investment in other funds, such as VC funds.

So, it is immediately obvious that the vast majority of investors in a VC fund are highly sophisticated professional investors, who are themselves being paid to manage the money of other people. Therefore, even those making decisions to invest in a VC fund are subject to their own market pressures and performance benchmarks, which will directly influence their behaviour as LPs in a VC fund and indeed, taken together as a community, the shape and terms applicable to VC funds generally. These "upstream" factors have become extremely important for the VC community, particularly in recent years as the LP community has generally become more risk-averse (owing to the market correction in 2000) and suffered from a technical over-allocation to the VC "asset class" (only ever a very small component of overall investment activity) caused by subsequent volatility in the public markets. For example, if an investor had a requirement that its private equity investments would amount to no more than 4% of its funds under management, then a fall in world public equity markets could cause that restriction to be breached, because the value of the public market assets would fall while the investor's commitment to the VC asset class would often remain unchanged because much of its commitment would be just that (a commitment that has not yet been drawn down by the VC firm) and because the VC assets would not be required to be marked to market in the investor's books as rapidly as publicly traded assets). In other words, the valuations of venture capital investments are much stickier than those on the public markets and therefore technical imbalances can occur in times of market volatility. It has also become the case that, whether or not the VC's fund itself performs above or below expectations, it is possible that poor decisions taken elsewhere by an LP (for example a fund of funds) may mean that this LP is out of business by the time the VC's next fund is ready to be raised, creating a potentially significant hole in the VC's planning for its next fund.

VC firms also typically run a separate side-by-side fund for people in its business network (often called an "Entrepreneurs' Fund") – essentially individuals with whom the VC firm has a particularly close and value-added relationship. These will include entrepreneurs, business angels (wealthy private individuals, often successful entrepreneurs themselves), CEOs and other senior executives from the firm's portfolio, industry contacts, scientists or "thought leaders" in the relevant investment sectors favoured by the VC firm, as well as key contacts from the financial community. Because investing into VC funds is generally not open to most individuals (not least because the minimum investment level in a VC's main fund would typically be in the range of $1–5 M) and because the sector historically has performed extremely well in investment terms (see below), the chance of participation in a side-by-side Entrepreneurs' Fund can be used to reward financially those who are prepared to help the VC firm in a material way – for example by sourcing investment opportunities, vetting an investment opportunity, serving as an interim manager or non-executive director of a portfolio company, or serving on an advisory board brain-storming sector developments, etc. The capital commitments involved will rarely be more than a small fraction of the amounts committed to the main fund (typically a few thousand dollars per individual), but this is money that is very much value-added for the VC firm and its eventual investment portfolio.

To complete the picture, many of the more sophisticated LPs in VC funds will now demand co-investment rights – comprising the right to invest additional capital directly into selected entrepreneurial businesses alongside the VC fund on a case-by-case basis. This, clearly, deepens the VC's relationship with any such LP and illustrates the web of financial relationships that an entrepreneur enters when dealing with the VC industry.

2.5 CONCLUSIONS

So, a VC's business is operating in the middle of a highly complex capital supply chain. Indeed, this supply chain may well be circular, such that in some small way the entrepreneur may well be funding the VC indirectly out of the revenues from his or her own business. For example, the entrepreneur may make employer contributions to a pension plan for employees and will most likely be paying insurance premia (e.g. for patent litigation insurance, etc): those contributions/premia will be made to the operator of the plan/scheme, e.g. an insurance company, which will invest the contributions/premia in a variety of asset classes, including perhaps a modest allocation (typically in the range of 3–5% of assets under management) to the venture capital asset class, either directly or through a fund of funds. Part of this asset-class allocation might be committed to an investment in the VC's fund – the VC will draw down committed capital on an as-needed basis, including for investment into the entrepreneur's business … and hey presto, the cycle of cash is complete!

As we will see below, the VC asset class has performed consistently strongly against other investment asset-classes over the medium and long term. As we discussed earlier, it is also the case that many top tier VCs have over the years developed a dedicated following of investors who invest again and again. This has both restricted access to these top tier VCs by new LPs looking to invest in the VC asset class for the first time, and has also made it difficult for new VCs to raise a first fund. The VC-LP relationship is, therefore, surprisingly conservative from both directions! Top tier VCs are therefore able to raise new funds very quickly and are in the business of turning away or scaling back investment interest, rather than soliciting new investors at any price. For the most distinguished VCs, this has continued to be the case even through the difficult years of 2000–2005, when virtually every VC's returns turned negative and they struggled even to return the initial capital committed for investment, let alone make a profit. The same cannot be said for many other VCs. As a result, branding in the VC world really means something these days, although it is extremely hard-earned and applies only to a handful of market participants.

Because of this, it is an industry truism that VCs worry constantly about fund-raising: no sooner have they completed the worry-fuelled, arduous fund-raising process to create a freshly-minted investment fund, than they start to worry about whether they can create the kind of track-record that will enable them to raise their next fund some three years on! Parents will recognise the same characteristics that apply to their children's schooling: no sooner have you succeeded in placing the little treasure into a good school, than you start to worry about the move to the next school just a few years away. Truly, VCs can often feel that they are never more than a few years from failing to raise the next fund and being out of business. Please – hold back your tears at the stressful environment that VCs inhabit!

3
The Limited Partnership

3.1 INTRODUCTION

Having established the fact that VCs are playing with other people's money, it is then important to understand the way in which this money is typically made available to VCs for investment into entrepreneurial new ventures. There are three key features to the structuring of the capital flows to a VC's business which dramatically influence the way in which the VC will behave toward entrepreneurs: the characteristics of the VC fund; the nature of the funding commitment from LPs; and the remuneration structure for the VC firm (at this point it is very important to realise that the VC *firm* is distinct from the VC *fund*, as we will discuss in detail below).

3.2 THE PRIMACY OF A LIMITED PARTNERSHIP

A VC investment fund (a "VC fund") may take many forms, particularly where the VC fund only has a local or regional investment focus (as many countries offer big tax and other advantages to attract inward investment), but by far the most prevalent form employed in the marketplace is an entity known as a "limited partnership". There are many countries that possess, and indeed market their own version of this particular fund structure to the investment community, with the most common being those of the United States (particularly the products created by the States of Delaware, New York and California), England, Jersey, Guernsey, Bermuda, Scotland and the Cayman Islands. The features of each system of law are slightly different – and evolve in fits and starts as each jurisdiction strives to offer investment fund products which are high quality, competitive with the offerings of other jurisdictions and address the sophisticated and changing needs of, *inter alia*, investors, managers and regulators.

The reason why limited partnerships have become so popular for VC funds worldwide is largely due to a combination of the vagaries of history and certain very real advantages of flexibility and transparency. The modern VC industry was born in the United States in 1946 and developed apace throughout the next 60 years. At some time during those years, the model of VC investment was exported to Europe and subsequently the rest of the world, but it remains the case that the US is the largest, most developed and most sophisticated market for venture capital, with its structures, concepts, solutions and innovations largely adopted by the rest of the world on an ongoing basis. For cultural and legal reasons that today are no longer as relevant as long historical precedent, the US adopted the limited partnership as the preferred structure for establishing VC funds and this approach has also been largely followed outside the United States.

Of course, not all VC firms manage funds that are structured via limited partnership agreements, The UK private equity firm 3i, one of the largest investors of venture capital in Europe is an investment company – investing cash from its own balance sheet without raising funds from external investors at all. Similarly many large investment banks and even large corporations have private equity divisions some of which are supplied with all their cash from the balance sheet of the bank or institution. These "tied VCs" are entirely dependent on their parent organisation and do not function with the same dynamics as the majority of independent VC firms.

Text Box 3.1:   A brief history of venture capital

Investors have been backing entrepreneurs to undertake risky commercial ventures since Marco Polo sailed in search of riches. Indeed the investors who backed successive waves of commerce in Europe – from canal and railway companies to colonial trading companies – all aimed to reap the financial rewards of entrepreneurial success. In the broad sense of the term, they were the venture capitalists of their day, but the modern venture capital industry has its origins in the US shortly after World War Two.

The first true venture capital organisation is generally recognised as American Research and Development (ARD), created in Boston in 1946 by George Doriot (a retired Army General and Professor at Harvard) and other New England luminaries. ARD is regarded as the first "true VC firm" as, in contrast to the investment firms created by wealthy families such as the Rockefellers and Whitneys, ARD had to raise finance from external backers. It also had a specific remit to both invest in and help the young companies it backed – very much the philosophy of VCs today. Although the groundwork for the creation of ARD had been going on since the 1930s, one of the triggers for its birth may well have been the commercial exploitation of technologies developed during World War Two at MIT and other research establishments in the Massachusetts area. Similarly, J.H. Whitney and Co, an investment firm formed around the same time based on the Whitney family fortune, is well known for backing Minute Maid – also a World War Two innovation, having been developed as a juice drink for American servicemen.

Hence the VC industry was born in the United States, catalysed in part by a wealth of innovation emerging from World War Two, and it is here that the industry grew and evolved through peaks and troughs for the next 60 years. During the 1950s the number of venture capital firms grew steadily as the US government realised the importance of backing innovative new companies. In the early 1970s the US VC industry entered a period of decline triggered in part by changes in US pension laws that prevented fund managers from allocating funds into venture capital (an unintended effect that was later rectified). The industry grew rapidly again throughout the 1980s triggered largely by the boom in computing and biotechnology innovation in Silicon Valley and subsequently in the Massachusetts area. In the US, the industry continued to grow through the 1990s in peaks and troughs as the dot.com boom and bust occurred and biotechnology, software and communications sectors experienced a volatile ride.

In Europe, the venture capital industry has developed at a slower pace, with the UK and Germany leading a significant growth spurt since the early 1990s. The key point is that the rules and business culture of the venture capital industry are US-derived and have persisted over time with a twist of local influence in each particular country where it operates. Even though legal and cultural aspects of VC have been adapted to local European norms the terms and conditions behind the vast majority of venture capital deals remain remarkably similar, whether you are in Germany, Italy, the US or a host of other countries. As we shall see throughout this book, the structure of VC deals is driven by the business fundamentals behind the VC funds themselves, and these fundamentals have their roots firmly within a US-derived business framework.

Notwithstanding historical precedent, limited partnerships continue to offer two key technical advantages for investors – advantages that have been mimicked but not surpassed by other legal forms. Firstly, partnerships offer a high degree of sophistication and flexibility under their constitution, with none of the limitations and restrictions that typically apply to corporations under their applicable laws of establishment, but nonetheless also offering guaranteed limited liability for the passive investors, the LPs, in the same way as for a shareholder in a corporation. For example, the laws that apply to corporations (even those established under the laws of Delaware, a famously commercially-focused system of law) tend to contain a raft of restrictions and prohibitions inherent in maintaining the integrity of an entity that is separate and distinct from its shareholders, whereas by and large the partners in a limited partnership are governed simply by what they choose to write down in the partnership agreement. Over time, given the tendency of the legal profession towards wordiness, the attraction of flexibility has become something of a double-edged sword – flexibility and sophistication yes, but partnership agreements have now become so complex and so long (often several hundred pages) that they now need to be read by a whole series of specialists for the protection of investors.

Secondly, the limited partnership manages in many jurisdictions to combine tax "transparency" (meaning that the entity does not exist for tax purposes and the LP is treated as investing directly in the underlying portfolio assets) with robust limited liability for investors, meaning that even though the investment has many of the same qualities as the purchase of a share in a corporation for the investor (e.g. liability limited to the amount of the LP's investment commitment) nonetheless national tax authorities will ignore the fund for tax purposes, "looking through" to the investor itself and treating it as holding a proportionate interest directly in the underlying portfolio investment. There are many attractions to this in practice, but fundamentally fiscal transparency generally assures the LPs of a "no worse" position than if they themselves had made an investment, with the potential for the VC firm to improve matters further either by careful downstream tax planning and structuring between the fund and the investment, on a case-by-case basis, or by creating separate investment vehicles (either feeding into the fund or investing in parallel with the fund) for particular constituencies of investors, which do not prejudice the positions of the other LPs. In this way, a limited partnership has proven itself to be a robust, sophisticated and highly flexible investment structure.

3.3   FACETS OF A LIMITED PARTNERSHIP

Limited partnerships are, as the name suggests, partnerships. There are two categories of partner: limited partners and general partners.

Limited partners are like shareholders in a corporation, in that their liability for the debts and obligations of the entity is limited to the amount of capital that they have agreed to commit to the entity, but (unlike a shareholder in a corporation) this limited liability is conditioned on limited partners remaining "passive" and having no involvement in the day to day management of the business of the partnership (e.g. investment). In the sophisticated world of a VC fund, safe harbour practices have evolved that permit LPs to participate to a certain extent in specific limited management or strategic decisions (e.g. through the advisory committee structure we discussed earlier) and some legal systems also allow quite significant levels of involvement in the business of the fund without prejudicing limited liability status (e.g. Delaware law, Jersey law, etc).

General partners (or "GPs") manage the day to day business of the entity and their liability for the debts and obligations of the entity is unlimited. Entrepreneurs may hear the senior partners of VC firms referred to as GPs – this is a misnomer, as by and large VC firms are extremely careful to ensure that the unlimited liability of the GP of a VC fund is ring-fenced both from the VC firm and from its senior executives, usually by using a special purpose limited company as the GP of the VC. Therefore, the term "GP" when used in relation to individuals in the VC firm merely connotes "senior partner" (who is usually a LP, directly or indirectly, in the VC fund, as described below).

Confusingly, the GP in fact rarely manages the business of the VC fund. This is partly because of unlimited liability, international tax and regulatory issues, but mainly due to the practical conflict that a single VC fund is of a limited duration and yet the VC firm will wish to maintain its investment operations across the lifetime of several funds. Because of this, it is prudent to maintain the operational infrastructure relating to investment activity in a separate structure to the VC funds themselves. As such, it is very common for the formal GP of a VC fund to be a special-purpose vehicle that will be wound up when the fund comes to an end, and for the ongoing investment management activities (sourcing, evaluating, structuring, implementing and exiting investments) to be located in a *separate* entity or group, which is the entity that will own the VC brand name, employ staff and lease offices, etc (the "VC firm"). The VC firm will be paid by the GP for its investment management activities, enabling the fund management fee (see below) to be streamed to the right place.

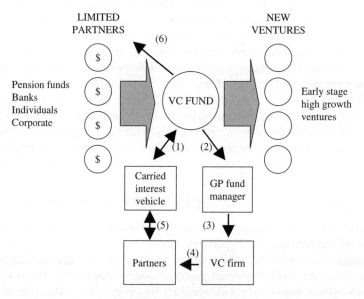

Figure 3.1   The structure of the limited partnership relationship

Expanding on the simplified diagram in Figure 2.1 in Chapter 2, we can see that a number of legal entities are involved in managing the flow of cash between the VC firm, VC fund and LPs.

(1) The Carried Interest Vehicle contributes capital from the partners of the VC firm into the VC fund and receives carried interest allocable to the partners when the fund begins to return profits. Of the profits received by the VC fund, 20% goes to the partners of the VC firm (through the Carried Interest Vehicle) and 80% goes to the LPs (direct from the VC fund).

(2) The VC Fund pays a management fee to the GP Fund Manager (normally 2% of the total fund size on an annual basis although this can vary). The GP Fund Manager is a special purpose vehicle kept separate from the VC firm.

(3) The GP Fund Manager pays advisory fees to the VC Firm out of the management fee received (often the advisory fee will be equal to substantially all of the management fees received).

(4) The VC firm pays the salaries and bonuses of the partners, associates and other employees of the VC firm.

(5) The VC firm's partners contribute capital into the VC fund via the Carried Interest Vehicle & receive returns of their invested capital, together with their 20% share of profits, through the Carried Interest Vehicle.

(6) The VC fund returns LPs' invested capital, together with 80% of its profits, direct to the LPs.

3.4 PARTNERSHIP TERMS

The core document that describes the relationship between the GP and the LPs is the partnership agreement. As mentioned above, none of the formalities and proscriptions of corporate law (for example rules on maintenance of capital that many countries have evolved and which have been promulgated across the European Union by EC Directive) will apply to limited partnerships, and partnership agreements instead simply operate as general contracts, containing whatever provisions that the parties may choose to negotiate and agree. As such, limited partnerships are capable of supporting extremely sophisticated and flexible investment arrangements that can be tailored snugly to the characteristics of any particular VC firm, VC fund and investor base. Modern limited partnership agreements relating to the world's leading VC funds can run to several hundred pages, encompassing not only every detail of the core relationship between the investor and the VC firm, but also a myriad of possible extraordinary events.

Over the last 30 years, the terms of these partnership agreements have also become increasingly standardised in almost all areas, with a certain degree of "flex" in the key commercial terms – the degree of achievable flex depending on numerous negotiation factors, including the state of the fund-raising marketplace and/or the investment marketplace, the reputation of the VC, etc. Indeed research has shown that in difficult financial climates, when VCs are finding it tough to raise a fund, the number of clauses in limited partnership agreements increases as the potential LPs flex their muscles by exerting increased control over the partnership terms! The opposite is true in bull markets, where VCs find it relatively easier to raise a fund and can therefore demand greater freedom under the terms of the LP agreement. Notwithstanding this flex, it is possible to describe certain fundamental building blocks in the core relationship between GP (and therefore the VC firm) and LPs, as described below. It should be appreciated that the description below merely scratches the surface of an extremely complex area, and also does not include any reference to a raft of international tax, partnership law, accounting, informational and regulatory provisions that routinely appear in partnership agreements by necessity, but which have little day to day commercial significance.

3.4.1 Life

A VC fund will have a limited life (usually of ten years), with the potential to extend the life of the partnership for short additional periods (usually of up to a further two years in aggregate).

3.4.2 Capital commitments

Typically, LPs will commit their capital to the fund up front, but only contribute that capital gradually over several years, against draw down requests by the GP. A VC fund will usually have an initial period of five years for draw down of commitments into new investment opportunities (the "investment period"), with draw downs thereafter (the remaining five years of its life) being limited to follow-on investments into those initial opportunities (the "follow-on period"). Sometimes (e.g. see 3.4.3 below) the terms of a VC fund will allow limited "recycling" of the proceeds of a realised investment into new investment(s). Therefore, after five years, typically there will be no investments made by the VC fund into *new* opportunities (mandating the raising of a new fund by the VC firm at that time, in order for the VC firm to remain active in the market). Sometimes LP agreements allow for an extension of the life of the LP when the partners agree that value can be created by incubating remaining investments for one–two years beyond the normal life of the fund. In these cases where a "safety net" is employed, this period usually requires the LPs to pay a reduced management fee to the VCs to account for the fact that the VCs are only managing out a few remaining investments.

Senior executives of the VC firm are often required to commit meaningful amounts of capital to the fund alongside other LPs, to create an enhanced community of interest (typically in the range of 1% of aggregate committed capital).

3.4.3 GP management

The GP will manage the fund investments through the life of the VC fund, and may be ejected only for specified and material adverse events (e.g. insolvency), although increasingly "no fault divorce" provisions are becoming prevalent, allowing a super-majority of LPs to replace the GP (and therefore the VC firm) in their absolute discretion.

For the duration of its management of the assets, the GP will be paid a management fee of some 1.5–2.5% per annum on *committed* capital (whether drawn down or not), although during the follow-on period the fee may fall to some 1.5–2.5% per annum (not necessarily matched to the initial management fee level) on *contributed* capital, as reduced by the return of capital on investment realisations. Some funds allow the GP to "recycle" funds drawn as management fees, by re-investing from investment realisations an amount equal to

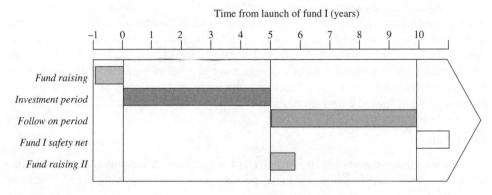

Figure 3.2 The lifecycle of a VC fund

the management fees paid – to ensure that all of an investor's committed capital is eventually put to work in investments.

Fund raising may take up to a year followed by five years of investing and five years of "following on" and harvesting when the focus is on exits and returning profits to the LPs. There is sometimes an extension of the life of the fund when one or two investments remain unexited.

3.4.4   Profit share

To the extent that the fund realises any investment, the LPs will generally recover their invested capital first. Some funds then allocate a minimum return on investment exclusively to the LPs (known as a "hurdle rate", e.g. 8–10% per annum), before the GP (or more usually a dedicated entity owned by the VC firm partners) participates in profits, although hurdle rates are more prevalent in the private equity sector than the venture capital sector. Thereafter, any profits generated on investments will typically be shared 20% by the GP and 80% between the LPs (some "premier league" VC firms are able to command profit shares of up to 35%). The GP's profit share is known as the "carried interest", because it is an interest in the fund "carried" on the back of the LPs' capital commitments. These profit share calculations can be made on a deal by deal basis (known as "deal carry") or on a total fund basis (known as "fund carry") or on a hybrid basis (known as "modified deal carry"), with committed capital, contributed capital, prior realised losses, unrealised write-downs, etc forming part of an extremely complex matrix designed to provide overall fairness to each interested constituency in the calculation and allocation of VC fund "profits". Figure 3.3 summarises the cash flow cycle during the venture capital investment process.

The GP may be required to repay over-allocations of profit share that may emerge for any reason towards the end of the life of the fund (known as a "clawback") and individual VC firm executives may be required to provide personal guarantees in respect of any such obligation. As an alternative, some proportion of the GP's profit share allocation may be placed in escrow and not distributed for an agreed period, to be used for clawback adjustments, as required.

3.4.5   Investment restrictions

The partnership agreement will contain certain broad parameters and restrictions on investment and to ensure basic levels of diversification, often subject to variation with the approval of the advisory committee or the LPs. There will usually be restrictions on the use of leverage in investment (for US tax reasons) and a commitment from the GP to make all investments in as tax efficient a manner as possible.

3.4.6   Transaction costs and fees

Usually, the partnership agreement will provide that costs incurred by the VC firm in implementing an investment (e.g. legal fees, due diligence costs, etc) will be reimbursed by the VC fund (and capitalised as part of the cost of investment), but the costs of new investments that are not completed ("broken deals") may well be for the account of the VC firm. Follow-on investments, whether they complete or become broken deals, will generally be reimbursable by the VC fund because they relate to an existing VC fund asset.

Any fees generated by the VC firm regarding fund investments (e.g. transaction fees, advisory fees, board fees, syndication fees, etc) will usually be for the account of the fund, not the VC firm, and therefore will operate as a deduction to management fee. In some cases, a proportion of these fees may be retained by the VC firm and in such cases there will often be a complex inter-relationship between transactions costs, particularly broken deal costs, and the allocation of such fees.

3.4.7   Further funds

There will often be a restriction on the VC firm raising a new fund until the existing fund is substantially invested. This may be a complex test, given that a substantial part of a VC fund's capital commitments may be allocated to follow-on investments after a few years and therefore a fund may become closed to investment in new opportunities when only a relatively small amount of the committed capital has been contributed (e.g. 60%). Indeed, if assumptions made at the time of the fund-raising as to attrition rates (i.e. company failures) or follow-on requirements (the thirst for further equity investment by existing portfolio companies) prove to be over-optimistic, it may be necessary to provide for a re-opening of the investment period for that fund even after a subsequent fund has been raised and is investing.

A limited degree of co-investment with prior or subsequent funds may be permitted, but in practice VC firms don't like to make "cross-over" investments of this type, principally for reasons of conflict of interest between different groups of LPs in different funds.

3.4.8   Transfer of LP interests

The partnership interests in the VC fund held by LPs ("LPIs") are usually not transferable except with the consent of the GP, so the GP and the LPs are in theory bound together for the duration of the fund. However, in recent years a healthy secondary market has developed for LPIs and nowadays a VC firm will expect there to be modest turnover of LPs in its fund during its life.

3.5   CONCLUSION: THE VENTURE CAPITAL BUSINESS IN A NUTSHELL

In a nutshell, VC investing is all about identifying the best early stage companies to invest in and backing them through successive rounds of finance (summarised in Figure 3.3 below). The ability to follow-on is crucial in building these fledgling businesses towards a successful exit, when the VC fund can divest its stake and distribute the capital gains back to the LPs and the VCs. This is essential in establishing a track record and raising the next VC fund to invest – in other words ensuring the VC remains in business. The VC therefore exists in a highly competitive environment in which other VCs are also attempting to invest in the best companies and raise their next funds from the best LPs.

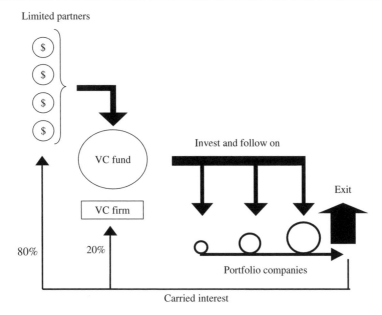

Figure 3.3   Venture capital cash flow

Thus, VCs are under pressure to perform, and in the next chapter we will discuss the competitive VC environment in more detail.

Cash is drawn down to invest in successive rounds of venture financing for portfolio companies. It is essential that the fund reserves sufficient cash to "follow" its investments, prior to exit and redistribution of proceeds.

The Competitive Environment

4.1 INTRODUCTION

VC firms compete in two key respects: they compete for the finite amount of investment capital allocated to the venture capital asset class ("capital competition"), and they compete for available investment opportunities ("deal competition"), in each case in their area of expertise and geographical coverage. Until the early twenty-first century, it was commonly assumed that VCs did not operate in a truly competitive marketplace, either for capital or for deals, and that it was relatively straightforward for a VC to remain in business for many years, irrespective of performance. In many respects, this was a misconception, even through the years of a surfeit of available investment capital and investment opportunities. However, the advent of the prolonged worldwide recession in the VC marketplace in 2000 threw into relief the highly competitive nature of the marketplace, as access to capital shrank, attractive deal opportunities became few and far between, and a marked "flight to quality" by the market occurred in respect of both capital and deals.

4.2 CAPITAL COMPETITION

There is now much greater awareness by the general public of the need for a VC firm to be competitive in performance terms with its peers in order to retain its ability to raise new investment funds in the future (and therefore stay in business). This is largely due to the public debate over access to private equity comparative performance data generated by the United States' Freedom of Information Act (where large public pension funds have recently been required to publish the performance data, normally kept private, of the VC funds in which they invest). This is a debate that has proven unpopular with VCs who would much rather their relatively poor recent performances not be broadcast. This is, however, a debate that is likely to be replicated in Europe as similar legislation is enacted there.

Regardless of public access to performance data, within the narrow confines of the private equity industry itself, there has always been a focus on relative performance, with the assumption that only those in the top quartile of overall performers can be guaranteed sufficient investor appetite for a new fund and only those in the top decile of performers can guarantee a fund-raising on attractive terms (i.e. that they'll broadly be buyers and not sellers in such a transaction). Of course, like so many areas of financial services, you may find it hard to find a VC that does not claim to be top quartile! Investing institutions know better.

4.2.1 Vintage years

So, what are the competitive benchmarks against which a VC firm expects to be judged? Wine analogies proliferate in this area, maybe because the industry was born so close to the Napa Valley, one of the world's leading wine-making regions. A VC fund is judged against other funds that were launched in the same year, referred to as a "vintage year". This is because market conditions, and hence investment conditions, may differ markedly year on year, creating an entirely different set of achievable performance benchmarks in one "vintage year", compared with other "vintage years". This is exactly like the wine business: one year the weather pattern may be conducive to a great vintage, another year may be the opposite.

For example, in the mid-1990s the US economic and market conditions were excellent for VC investment propelled in particular by a wave of technological change engendered by the adoption of the internet as an enabling architecture for business and innovation. Funds in these vintage years not only invested at realistic entry prices, but were able to grow their companies and exit during a long bull market run in which private and public buyers were plentiful. As a consequence, the current mean net return for LPs investing in US VC funds in the 1996 vintage year (after fees, expenses and carried interest) is currently an eye-popping annual internal rate of return ("IRR" – explained in more detail at 4.2.3 below) greater than 90%. By contrast, those US VC funds raised in the 1999 vintage year invested near the top of a bull market at prices that, with hindsight, were too high – and worse then experienced the subsequent market corrections of 2000–2004 which took a terrible toll on businesses and their valuations. As a consequence the current mean net return for LPs investing in US VC funds in the 1999 vintage year is currently a rather more sobering double digit negative IRR.

The vintage year concept ensures that comparisons are made like-for-like as funds go through their peculiar performance cycle. It is very common, for example, for VC funds to show negative performance in their early years of investment, as it naturally takes time to grow successful investments to a point where they can be realised at full value (the industry expectation is five to seven years) and, in the meantime, in the absence of the realisation of gains "pregnant" within the VC fund, performance is artificially skewed to the downside in the form of realised losses on failed investments (that don't get early business traction or which are no longer supported) and the drain of early year deal costs and management fees. For example, the current mean net IRRs for LPs investing in US VC funds in the 2002 and 2003 vintage years are single digit negative and double digit negative respectively. It is for this reason that vintage year performance will evolve markedly through the life of a fund – the game is not yet over for the 1999 vintage, for example.

4.2.2   Sector and geography

Performance benchmarks are also broken down into specific investment sectors. Venture capital tends to be a specialised business with many firms focused on industry niches. The marketplace therefore produces comparative performance data on a diverse range of sectors – for example differentiating between communications, hardware/systems, software/services, healthcare/biotech, consumer/retail, financial, electronics, industrial, energy, environmental, chemical/materials, manufacturing, etc. When combined with vintage year data, they produce even more carefully calibrated performance data, demonstrating how different sectors move in different cycles internationally.

Equally, not all firms operate in all geographies – indeed VC firms are still in general very much regionally-focused businesses (e.g. Northern California, Cambridge MA, Cambridge UK, Saxony, etc). Therefore VCs will also seek to compare themselves with their regional competitors.

4.2.3   IRRs and cash-on-cash metrics

The market's performance benchmarks focus primarily on cash returns to the LPs, either in the form of a net IRR or a cash-on-cash multiple ("cash multiple"). An IRR is a percentage figure comprising the blended rate at which the combined cash flows from/to LPs into/out of the VC fund over time can be discounted back to zero at the current time – essentially the average work-rate of money invested. A cash multiple simply looks at cash distributed by the fund to LPs as a function of cash committed by LPs to the fund. For example, a fund that draws down all $100 M of its capital on day 1 and returns $500 M of gains five years later, would generate an IRR of 100% (ignoring compounding, etc for the sake of simplicity) and a 5× cash multiple. Thus, the VC's competitive focus is entirely on cash.

The performance bar is high. Looking at the data for mature US VC funds in the last 20 years, mean IRRs range between a low of 8.75% per annum, and a high of 95.5% per annum. Over the 1990s, mean IRRs are nearly 46% per annum, even allowing for the debacle for the 1999 vintage and cash-on-cash multiples are nearly 9% per annum, and a high of more than 90% per annum. Over the 1990s, mean IRRs are more than 40% per annum, even allowing for the debacle for the 1999 vintage.

At the same time, it is clear from the market performance data of recent years that the difference in performance between the mean and the top quartile is growing, as is the difference between the top quartile and the top decile. In other words, the performance bar is very high, and it's getting tougher and tougher to keep up with the best performers, who are stretching away into the distance compared to the average performer. By way of example, we can look at the performance of one of the world's most famous VC firms Kleiner Perkins Caulfield & Byers. KPCB has backed many of the companies that have become household names today – including Amazon, Compaq, Sun Microsystems, Google and Genentech, broadly recognised as one of the very first biotechnology companies. According to data made public by one of their leading investors, KPCB's 1996 vintage fund posted a 17× cash multiple on its fund of that vintage (its 1994 fund posted a 32.5× multiple). This is not an environment in which VCs can be complacent.

These benchmarks mean that, to remain competitive, not only do VCs have to focus on the absolute return of their investments (cash multiple) but they also have to focus on the speed of return of that cash (IRR). It's an environment in which a VC which wishes to be a top performer and have the chance to raise another fund has to take significant risks – which of

Fund	Vintage	Multiple
KP II	1980	4.30×
KP III	1982	1.74×
KP IV	1986	1.83×
KP V	1989	4.01×
KP VI	1992	3.33×
KP VII	1994	32.51×
KP VIII	1996	17.00×
KP IX	1999	0.40×
KPX	2000	0.59×

* As published by University of California as at 31 March 2005.

Figure 4.1   Kleiner Perkins Caulfield & Byers fund performance*

itself causes a cascade of issues which determine to a high degree the required VC business model. The focus on IRRs also provides a clue as to why VCs like business models with low, or at least rapidly reducing, capital intensity.

4.3   DEAL COMPETITION

To some extent it is true that in many parts of the world competition for investment opportunities is not as acute as would be expected of a fully mature marketplace. This is because in many geographies, including many of the European VC marketplaces, there is not yet sufficient VC industry critical mass for a natural competitive tension to have evolved. It is still uncommon, for example, for European VCs to compete for an investment opportunity (for example by means of a tender process or by a "battle of the term sheets") or, if they do, it is likely that the "loser" will be invited onto the winner's syndicate in any event (in other words to share in the deal). In Europe, this can be clearly contrasted with the private equity marketplace (e.g. for larger leveraged buy-outs) where real competitive tension exists and transactions are widely marketed and closely fought over. It means that European VCs tend to be "buyers" much more than "sellers" and are not as honed as their US counterparts when it comes to convincing entrepreneurs to take *their* cash, as opposed to the VC on the next block. However, this situation is changing rapidly, and the smarter European VC firm now has to conclude that its environment will rapidly become much more like that for US VCs described below.

By contrast, the more mature and sophisticated US marketplace has evolved towards a more competitive and stratified environment, at least within certain VC hot-spots (for example the San Francisco Bay and Boston/Cambridge areas). In these areas, there is plenty of competition for attractive investment opportunities, albeit that these opportunities seem to be increasingly stratified and matched to the calibre of the VC firms themselves – such that the best deals appear to be initially offered to and competed over by the top tier VCs, the next best by the second tier, etc, so that it seems that a VC's brand has become something of a self-perpetuating phenomenon – a strong brand attracts the best opportunities, which in turn should generate the best investment returns, which in turn should attract the next generation of best opportunities to the firm. This "virtuous cycle" should not be underestimated by an entrepreneur seeking funding. Indeed research carried out in the US has shown that entrepreneurs will accept "worse" investment terms from highly reputable VCs (i.e. allow the VC to invest at lower share prices) just to be associated with the firm. Entrepreneurs do this because they hope to inherit the VC's reputation via a halo effect, and hence attract top quality investors, employees and customers. By definition, they assume that this "added value" is worth the penalty of selling shares cheaply to a top VC when they might otherwise raise the finance on more favourable terms with a less well known VC. However, it should also be noted that, in the US, there is a much greater cult of the individual VC partner than is the case in Europe such that "top tier VC" referred to above could refer equally to a top tier firm or a particular storied individual within one of those firms or even in another firm.

4.4   CONCLUSIONS

Notwithstanding the vagaries of vintage year and developing fund performance through its life, as well as the differing levels of competition for investment opportunities in different geographies, it is possible to draw some broad conclusions about the competitive environment faced by VC firms.

It is clear that the marketplace for VC funds is highly competitive, based upon a plethora of objective data, measuring VC fund performance across a diverse set of criteria and setting the bar very high for a VC fund to be top quartile. Except in periods when there is a surfeit of capital available for VC firms, VCs therefore have to fight hard to be a top performer against the prevailing applicable performance benchmarks. Once they have won their investment capital on the back of their performance data, they then find themselves operating within an increasingly stratified and competitive marketplace for investment opportunities.

In summary, it is clear that the competitive nature of the VC business, both in raising capital and investing it, and the nature of the complex partnership agreements VCs sign with their LPs, drives the behaviour of VCs toward the entrepreneurs they back. VCs must maximise the returns to LPs to stay in business, and must therefore take action to prevent losses when required to – even to the point of forcing the liquidation of a business they have invested in rather than sink more cash into it. This has sometimes given VCs a negative image for "kicking entrepreneurs when they are down" but the reality is that VCs are forced to behave in this way to fulfil the terms of their agreement with the LPs. As we shall see in the following chapters these principles translate into the deals that VCs construct to maximise gains and minimise risk.

5
The VC's Investment Model

5.1 INTRODUCTION

In the previous chapters in Part I, we have examined the fundamentals of the VC's business environment, in terms of where the VC firm gets its investment capital from, the structure under which that capital is provided to the VC, including the VC's remuneration arrangements, and the competitive landscape against which a VC's performance is judged.

These factors, taken together, create the environment in which a VC firm will develop its business model, addressing the challenges of the marketplace and respecting the limitations imposed on it by its own investors. As each VC firm faces near identical issues and challenges, it is not surprising that the marketplace overall demonstrates a high degree of affinity in the solutions and mind-sets adopted to carry on the business of venture capital investment.

Fundamental to a VC firm's approach to doing business is its acceptance of the necessity of taking on risk. From that fundamental proposition flow five core philosophies that dominate a VC's thinking and actions and permeate the classic investment terms that we will examine more closely in Part III:

(1) extreme caution over the act of investment;
(2) obsession with exit potential;
(3) an insistence on an uncapped "upside" potential;
(4) equal insistence on "downside" risk management;
(5) the constant theme of dynamic capital allocation.

Each of these is examined below, but we begin with an explanation of the general need to embrace risk and its consequences.

5.2 FUNDAMENTALS OF VC RISK

Not surprisingly, when faced with a performance benchmark in the region of a 40%+ IRR, or a 3.5× cash-on-cash multiple (in each case after fees and expenses) to LPs over the life of its fund, a VC won't be looking for low risk investments. In order to achieve these high absolute levels of growth within relatively short time periods, the VC must focus on investment opportunities that have the prospect of beating those performance benchmarks in growth and value terms. But by adopting that focus, the VC will inevitably take on high levels of investment risk and as such an equally inevitable level of "attrition" (investment failure) will creep into its investment portfolio – in other words, the VC won't be able to assume risk without the strong probability that the "chickens will come home to roost" in the form of occasional failed investments. Of course, once attrition rates are built into portfolio performance, it requires those investments that are successful to be materially more successful than the benchmark performance target, so that the overall fund performance can hit or even surpass that benchmark – in other words the successful investments have to be sufficiently successful to be able to carry the failures. So, the "stretch goal" of the fund has to be significantly higher than the performance benchmark itself.

Indeed, over time it has been shown that no VC firm, however clever, can "beat the odds" inherent in a high growth, high risk investment strategy. However, within that environment, different appetites for risk co-exist in the marketplace. Some VC firms have a reputation for making extremely risky investments which will provide extraordinary returns if they come off, but this investment strategy generates correspondingly large attrition rates as a percentage of opportunities backed. Other VCs don't have the appetite for that kind of risk and back lower-risk opportunities with correspondingly lower attrition rates. In a market that is receptive to new technology waves, the former strategy can drive extraordinary overall portfolio returns; conversely, in a less bullish market the latter strategy may be the way to go. Both strategies can make sense and can happily co-exist in the marketplace (indeed for an LP they may be complementary and he or she may wish to invest in both types of investment strategy) – indeed it is possible to some extent to switch between these strategies depending on market dynamics – but each strategy demands highly professional, consistent and coherent management of risk by the VC firm.

What should an entrepreneur assume the attrition metrics are, when approaching a VC? The metrics are in fact different for each sector, state of investment and even geography. For example, as a very rough rule of thumb, some 20–30% of an early-stage VC fund's investments (being start-ups) are likely to be failures, some 20–30% are likely to be big winners, and the remaining 40–60% are likely to fall into the category of "also-rans", with modest investment performance. The figures would be very different for a VC fund investing in later stage, lower risk opportunities. Obviously, a VC firm which is able successfully to move to the more attractive end of these metrics will find itself an out-performer. One of the keys to understanding VC behaviour is to realise, firstly, that a VC has relatively little chance of shifting these metrics – unless it's extraordinarily lucky or skilled – and, secondly, that these metrics ensure that the out-performance of a small minority of investments in a VC fund portfolio will usually disproportionately drive the overall investment performance of the VC fund. Indeed, it is not uncommon for two or three investments alone to generate almost the entirety of the profitability of a VC fund, with the remainder of the investments (the failures and the also-rans), taken together, covering their aggregate cost or at best generating a modest overall positive return.

Experiential learning of the nature and consequences of risk and the necessity of its professional management lies behind much of a VC's behaviour towards investment opportunities. Facing these likely attrition dynamics, the VC recognises that each company he or she backs statistically only has a 20–30% chance of being successful (in fact, it has been demonstrated by academics that even the most successful companies in high growth sectors statistically have a less than 12% chance of success – neatly demonstrating how allying with a VC can improve an entrepreneur's chances of success). Therefore, risk mitigation strategies move to the very heart of the VC's activities. It becomes absolutely essential that the VC:

(1) minimises the potential for mistakes on the way in to an investment;
(2) maximises the opportunities for success once invested;
(3) maximises the availability of downside protection tools; and
(4) maximises the opportunity to participate in the upside of successful investments.

These basic risk management themes are the foundation upon which all VC investment terms are constructed and are at the heart of what a VC is trying to achieve in structuring a deal.

Having discussed risk management in general, let us turn now to the five core investment philosophies mentioned earlier and which embody the themes described above.

5.3   EXTREME CAUTION OVER THE ACT OF INVESTMENT

Anyone who has been involved in the investment process with a VC firm will be struck by the extreme caution shown by the VC in examining the investment opportunity from all angles prior to committing to an investment. It can often seem to an entrepreneur that, in a business where risk is axiomatic (indeed essential for out-performance), a VC firm wishes to drive out or re-allocate any and all risks prior to investment. Sometimes, this natural caution can become counter-productive – there is always at least one reason *not* to do a venture deal and if the investment process is drawn out long enough then, sooner or later, just such a reason will present itself and the deal will fail unless a sense of perspective and proportion can be retained by all parties involved in the financing. In any event, it is inevitable that drop-out rates are extremely high through this process, with maybe only 5% of deals that hit the VC's radar screen passing all the way through the investment process to completion.

Of course, to some extent this mindset is counter-intuitive, because one of the most funda-mental risk management tools available to a VC fund is portfolio diversity. Put simply, if a VC concludes only five investments, then the volatility of the risk in that portfolio will be very great, whereas if it concludes 50 investments, then it is ten times more likely that the performance of this sample group of companies will approach the "norm" in performance terms referred to at 5.2 above. To some degree, the business of venture capital investing is all about generating a fund portfolio of companies of optimal size and diversity to allow the odds to play out in a meaningful way – and this requires an appetite to do deals and to take well-understood and measurable risks. Interestingly, the latter is a key characteristic of entrepreneurial behaviour – not some-thing that entrepreneurs normally associate with VC firms. So the entrepreneur actually has a much closer cultural affinity with a partner at a top VC firm than he or she may have realised!

Despite this "portfolio fundamental", a high degree of caution through the investment process continues to be the watchword of many VC firms, manifesting itself in the diverse ways described below.

5.3.1   Focus on proprietary deal flow

One of the ways that a VC firm can lower its investment risk is to ensure that the investment opportunities it considers come from a suitably qualified source that can be trusted and that may have pre-vetted the opportunity. The best qualified source is one that it well-known to the VC and is regarded by the VC as understanding the relevant marketplace well. Because of this, VCs spend a lot of their time developing a proprietary network, composed principally of people deep within the industry sector that the VC firm focuses on – for example, entrepreneurs, senior executives, scientists, engineers, thought-leaders, head-hunters and academics.

Two absolutely optimal places for VCs to get their deal flow from, within this proprietary channel, are, of course, from senior executives in its current investment portfolio or from ex-executives or entrepreneurs who have been successfully backed by the VC in the past ("serial entrepreneurs"). These constituencies are composed of individuals whom the VC has been confident enough to back previously, demonstrating a high degree of confidence in the individuals' judgment and capabilities. In addition, these are generally people who can be expected to be at the "bleeding edge" of the relevant market's ongoing development, with an ear to the ground for exciting next-generation business opportunities and technological devel-opments. But even more importantly, they are above all people who fully understand the key dynamics and criteria for a successful collaboration of entrepreneur and VC and who therefore should be able to pre-calibrate any potential investment opportunity against those dynamics and criteria, ensuring that an opportunity they pass on to the VC is likely to be relevant and "backable". Finally, not only are opportunities coming through this channel highly likely to be both superior and pre-vetted, but they are also likely (at least initially) to be exclusive to the VC, giving the VC a first run at the opportunity without competition.

It is therefore a no-brainer for VCs to focus their efforts on this kind of proprietary deal-flow, reducing the risk in an investment opportunity at the earliest stage of involvement and improving their overall business efficiencies in terms of the opportunity cost of time spent analysing the merits of an investment opportunity, through the early triage of the proprietary channel filter. Of course, just because an entrepreneur initially makes contact with a VC firm outside this proprietary channel does not mean that he or she has no chance of a successful encounter, but for dramatically enhanced prospects, the name of the game for the entrepreneur is to see if he or she can engineer access to the VC through this kind of proprietary channel.

5.3.2   Early exclusivity

Another way in which VCs protect themselves from risk – in particular opportunity cost and deal competition risk – is to require exclusivity to be granted to them early on in the process, often for protracted periods. Under the protection of exclusivity, VCs can then take their time properly to evaluate an investment opportunity, without the risk of their efforts being prejudiced by a competitive event (another VC arriving on the scene, or a different strategic opportunity presenting itself to the relevant company).

The entrepreneur must ensure that his or her own legitimate interests are protected, within the framework of such exclusivity arrangements. This is discussed in greater detail in Part III below.

5.3.3   Due diligence

Not surprisingly, the key focus for a VC, once into an exclusivity period, is on due diligence, being the process of investigating all aspects of the investment opportunity. This process will invariably take several weeks, and may take several months, and will certainly include a deep evaluation of the management team, the core technology (both application and ownership), the marketplace dynamics, actual and potential competitors, every aspect of the business model and long term (three–five year) business plan (particularly cash flows and plan B strategies), as well as the more traditional financial and legal due diligence that is seen on any corporate finance transaction. This diligence exercise will involve not only the VC, but also a raft of contacts, experts, consultants, lawyers and accountants employed by the VC.

From the entrepreneur's perspective, there may be little that can be done to sharpen or accelerate this process – it will be over when the VC says it's over and not before. Obviously, the better the management team is prepared for the process, the more likely it is that they will be able to take command of the process and indeed impress the VC and its team, in terms of being well organised and ahead of the game. Equally, like any corporate finance or M&A transaction, the due diligence process can be extremely disruptive to the core business because of the amount of senior management time required, so it is very important that the entrepreneur pre-plans the interim management of the business through this period, to avoid any adverse impact on the core business objectives and performance metrics: it is not unusual for a company to pay the price, via a lower valuation, for an operational stumble caused by the enormous disruption of a VC's in-depth due diligence.

Equally, the entrepreneur will often find him or herself being asked to pay for the expenses of the VC incurred in progressing due diligence. This issue is discussed in greater depth at Part III below. In any event, whether the due diligence process leads, or does not lead, to an investment by the VC, it is highly advisable that the entrepreneur obtains the agreement of the VC to pass across all due diligence reports, so that at the very least the entrepreneur has the opportunity to learn from these reports and maybe use them in a subsequent financing exercise.

5.3.4   Drip-feed approach to investment

One of the core risk management tools employed by VCs on investment is to drip-feed cash into an investment opportunity. There are two classic approaches to this, both of which are routinely used by VCs. The first is to provide only just enough cash to a company to enable it to reach the next valuation inflexion point, plus a bit of margin for error. Typically, VCs like to fund a business for between a year and two years only, partly because they don't fully trust a management team which is too flush with cash and partly because it enables the VC to allocate its capital dynamically to the investment opportunity. This technique becomes less relevant as a business matures and the pattern of historic success becomes more predictive of likely future success.

Secondly, even within this relatively short-term framework, VCs like to divide their investment commitments into pieces (known as "tranches", as in "tranching an investment") and spread them across certain value-confirming or value-enhancing events (for example, completion of a prototype, entry into a new phase of clinical trials, recruitment of a key executive, first customer, first revenues, etc). Clearly, this technique enables a VC's capital allocation to be allocated in an even more granular, dynamic way.

Both of these techniques enable the VC firm to manage carefully downside exposure on an investment, "dripping" cash in only against significant milestones being passed, and, better still (because almost invariably a tranching structure is committed by the VC at a fixed price up front) the VC will retain the ability to continue to participate in a successful venture at the original price agreed on first investment, so that the overall investment gets cheaper and cheaper as operational risk reduces, but the investment price remains the same. This technique is so fundamental as a risk management tool that many VC firms will not contemplate an early stage investment which is not tranched.

Whilst this may at first sight look like a classic example of VCs wanting to "have their cake and eat it", in fact the position is more subtle. This is discussed in more detail at Part III below. The key issue, of course, is whether short-term, hand-to-mouth funding of a business can be a good thing, except for a very limited period in its early development. There are some signs that the US VC market understands this issue and is more adept at releasing its hold on the purse strings at the right moment, to avoid fettering development, than the European VC market.

5.3.5   Syndication

VCs dream of being able to leverage their investments, in the manner that their later-stage private equity compatriots do routinely. Of course, it is impossible for VCs to be able to do this, in a conventional sense, when for many years their investments typically have few assets (or at least only intangible ones) and strongly negative cash flows, except in narrow areas such as equipment financing, venture leasing and perhaps some types of receivables or working capital financing at a later stage of an investment's development. Across an entire portfolio of course, leverage would provide a highly attractive tweak to overall returns, as well as dramatically lowering the overall portfolio risk volatility profile for the VC by enabling the VC to do more deals across a single fund (on the basis that the more deals that are done, the more likely it is that the portfolio will, overall, match the expected success and attrition rates). It is surprising that, given the consistency of VC fund returns from the top VC firms over many years, financial institutions have not addressed this opportunity.

However, the only way in which a VC firm can consistently "leverage" its investment in this way today is by "equity syndication". Equity syndication is simply the technique of sharing an investment opportunity with others, although in a follow-on financing it is perfectly possible for an incumbent shareholder to generate "leverage" by sitting out of a follow-on opportunity and letting itself be modestly diluted by incoming equity funding from third parties. Either technique spreads the risk on that single investment between a larger group of people and in theory frees up additional capital for the VC fund to invest into other opportunities, deriving additional portfolio risk spreading. There is also the significant comfort factor for a VC that comes from other respected market participants agreeing with its view that the opportunity is worth supporting.

This is the reason why VCs tend to hunt in packs, although there is also a subtle stratification in activity in the marketplace, in that only a subset of VCs appear to have the capability to construct and lead equity syndicates (which involves settling the investment terms with the company, making a cornerstone financial commitment and then bringing in other players around their initial commitment) and the rest are content to follow the lead of these dominant "lead" VCs. Furthermore, a "lead" VC in one geography or sector may be a "follower" in another geography or sector.

There are other reasons for VCs to syndicate deals beyond the notion of simple risk sharing and leverage. VCs often use syndication as a benchmarking exercise for the investment decision, in other words getting a second opinion from another trusted investor as to whether the deal is really worth doing. In the challenging environment of assessing very high risk early stage ventures, a second opinion is worth a lot and may push the decision to invest one way or another. An additional reason for syndication is that VCs live in the hope that showing a good deal to a "competitor VC", will result in the favour being returned with an introduction to an equally high quality deal they would not otherwise have seen. The VCs know that acting in this way with VCs they regards as their peer group in terms of quality, will help them optimise their portfolio and maximise their chances of remaining in the top quartile of performers. VCs feel safe hunting in a pack – as long as they regard the other group members as making the same quality of investment decisions as themselves.

From the entrepreneur's perspective, syndication is usually advantageous, because it lessens the likelihood of shareholder dominance through a single ownership block and lessens reliance on a single shareholder for follow-on financing capability, as well as increasing the options available in using the shareholders' own skills and networks, including at board level. However, care must be taken to ensure that all syndicate members are of high quality, have the potential to add value, and that there are not too many of them to make the administration of the shareholder roster unwieldy.

5.3.6   Internal investment process

Finally, many VC firms operate a formal internal "investment process", designed to ensure that as a matter of good internal corporate governance, certain minimum steps are taken in order for a deal to have the approval of the VC firm and be concluded. Typically, these procedures will operate through the medium of an "investment committee", usually composed of the senior executives in the firm.

There are a wide range of approaches taken by VC firms to manage their risk through defined investment processes. The way in which VCs choose investments has been heavily researched by business school academics and the fundamentals of a typical investment process are described in detail in Chapter 10 in this book. In terms of *who* exactly makes the decision to invest, some firms (typically the smaller or more entrepreneurial firms) significantly empower their partners with deal autonomy and investment committee meetings can happen at the drop of a hat in a very informal way, with the individual deal sponsor largely staking his or her personal reputation to sell a particular deal and the investment committee process being an informal "rubber stamping exercise". At the other end of the spectrum is a more institutionalised approach where investment committee meetings are only held at specified intervals (e.g. monthly), those meetings are highly formal and the decision of the VC firm whether or not to support any investment opportunity proposed to the investment committee genuinely hangs in the balance until the final decision by that body, whether or not it enjoys the full support of the particular deal team. The degree of ex post facto involvement in the investment process by LPs, as part of their own new-fund investment due diligence, and the impact this has on GP processes, should not be underestimated.

Most VC firms employ a halfway house between these twin approaches – they operate a sophisticated system designed to ensure that due process is carried out, but they retain the ability to move quickly and flexibly outside that process, if the circumstances warrant. A typical investment process would start at the sector team level, including preliminary due diligence, a company presentation and a draft investment recommendation to investment committee (putting the deal "on the radar") to elicit an in-principle decision to incur costs and move ahead – and it is as this stage that a term sheet would be signed. The second stage would see the sector team go back to the opportunity to complete due diligence, negotiate the investment documentation and complete a final investment recommendation to the investment committee and at this stage there would often then be a further presentation by the company to a wider group of VC firm executives. Finally, just before planned signing of the investment documentation, the investment committee would give final approval to the transaction.

Obviously, it is critically important that an entrepreneur understands in detail the relevant VC firm's investment procedures before embarking on a transaction, so that he or she can understand how long he remains on substantial risk of a transaction not receiving the support of the VC firm, as well as any way in which he can accelerate the process or enhance the prospects of success.

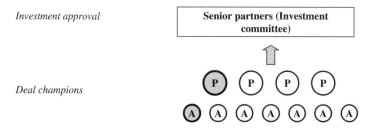

Figure 5.1   The Organisational framework for VC decision making

All investment opportunities under consideration by a VC firm need a "deal champion". This is usually a partner (**P** in Figure 5.1) (assisted by a number of more junior associates (**A** in Figure 5.1)) within the firm, who may or may not have been the entrepreneur's first point of contact at the firm and who has decided this is an opportunity worth moving to the next stage in the process. The deal champion will often work with the entrepreneur to shape and position the business to be presented to a group of colleagues – usually the more senior partners – to gain a consensus decision on whether to spend more time investigating the deal, or to drop it. Investment approval within a VC firm is rarely in the hands of an individual and is usually the result of a group decision. The exact process is described in Chapter 10 in this book.

5.4   EXIT OBSESSION

The only good investment is an exited investment. That's really all that needs to be said, but it is extraordinary how often investment opportunities proposed to VC firms fail on that score alone – they may be very interesting businesses, but there is simply no exit from them. It's very simple – as Chapter 3 made clear, VCs get their money for a maximum of ten years, whereupon they have to give it back with interest. In addition, as a VC fund moves into its follow-on period (the latter part of its life), the fund's follow-on capability will become more rigid (difficult to re-allocate) and may start to dissipate rapidly after six or seven years, meaning potentially unacceptable dilution of a VC's ownership interest in an investment that lingers too long on the books. It's not just a function of the life of the VC fund either – the competitive environment in which VC firms operate, based as it is on IRRs, means that the exit "sweet spot" for an investment is in fact nearer five to seven years from investment, and if they can achieve a viable exit within five years, so much the better – beyond that seven year timeframe even an excellent exit in cash terms can look profoundly ordinary in IRR terms.

Accordingly, in the investment process a VC will obsess about the nature and timing of a likely exit at a value that will meet or exceed the firm's minimum investment performance criteria. The VC will therefore focus on the ability of the business model to effect a rapid and sustained ramp-up of operations, as well as the likely buyers for the business three to five years out and the potential for the company to go public by flotation (although, in recent years, the IPO route to exit has become of secondary importance, as major exchanges have underperformed, stocks in early stage high growth companies have shown excessive volatility and lack of liquidity, and IPO windows to the market have opened and closed rapidly). Sometimes, an unusual exit route will present itself, but usually trade sale or IPO are the end points. There are many situations where a terrific business can be built, but the dynamics are such that a viable exit at full value is not likely: VCs simply cannot invest in such businesses.

Having obsessed about an exit, VCs will then set about identifying the critical path to that exit and roping all of the major constituencies into supporting this critical path, come what may, by a combination of carrots (e.g. incentives to management and other key value-drivers) and sticks (e.g. financing milestones, value ratchets, etc). As such, the mindset of the VC firm will switch immediately upon completion of its investment, from an obsession with the minutiae of a long-term investment to an obsession with the earliest possible exit at full value! Long experience tells VCs that investment is easy by contrast with exit, which is often very hard work indeed.

In addition, the VC will ensure that, if and when an exit is identified (whether it occurs generally or is only available for a particular constituency of owners) the VC fund has the ability to crystallise that exit and participate to the fullest degree possible in that exit. This is the philosophy that underpins investment terms such as sale and liquidation preferences, drag-along rights and tag-along rights.

How should an entrepreneur respond to this mindset? In terms of producing a truly compelling investment opportunity, an entrepreneur must conclude that unless and until there exists an obvious exit route for his business, it will be pointless seeking venture funding and he or she should continue to boot-strap the company's development or finance the company by other means. Once the entrepreneur is confident that a viable exit is available within a reasonable period for the company's business model and market positioning, he or she should spend time in validating the assumptions that underpin that belief and developing realistic exit valuation scenarios, based ideally on prevailing market valuation criteria, to be able to demonstrate the exit potential of the opportunity to the VC. Once a VC has invested in the opportunity, the entrepreneur must simply prepare him or herself for the mindset shift that will immediately occur in his or her VC partner.

5.5   HIGH REWARD FOR HIGH RISK

It is immediately apparent from the dynamics of the VC's business model and the competitive environment it inhabits, that the VC is forced into a high risk, high reward approach to doing business. It is forced to assume material risk in its business, which mandates a portfolio approach and introduces attrition into its business model. Any attrition in the portfolio requires that those investments which perform well must perform well enough both to cover off under-performers and yet still enable the VC fund to reach the necessary performance benchmarks.

But the possibility of higher performance inevitably comes with higher performance risk attached – potentially raising attrition rates further and creating a vicious cycle. In fact, the level of attrition rates generally accepted in VC funds has settled at a level (20–30%) which is offset by what is achievable as an investment return from those high-growth, highly successful companies that are statistically likely to succeed (20–30%). In the minds of VCs, that investment return lies somewhere north of a 10× cash-on-cash return, depending upon the VC's appetite for risk and attrition and consequently its portfolio mix.

As such, it is highly unlikely that an early stage VC will wish to invest in a business which is unlikely to generate a return on investment of less than 10× within the optimal investment period of five–seven years, as to do so would simply wreck the portfolio business model, because (in the absence of pleasant surprises) even if the particular investment beats the odds (e.g. 100/30 against) and became one of the successes in the portfolio, the likely return on the investment would not be sufficient to generate top quartile performance in the fund overall. In other words, it would have been a pointless bet. That is not to say that there is no room for more moderate performers in a VC's portfolio: some VCs (particularly those with less of a "bet the farm" portfolio strategy and consequently much lower attrition rates) will pack the "middle ground" of their portfolio with lower risk, moderate performers where the exit expectation is nearer 4–5×, but the odds of success are more like evens than 100/30 against (for example, later stage investments or accretive business models where technological and market risk are lower).

This means that an entrepreneur has to understand exactly where his or her investment opportunity is likely to fit into the VC's portfolio in risk and return terms. Any opportunity with a demonstrable 10× return capability within the conventional investment period should have no worries – lower than that will require a careful reassessment of the risk/reward curve for the opportunity and the identity and match of investment strategy of the VC fund from which funding is sought. We have already discussed above why lengthening the investment period may not be possible as a solution.

But the potential for high performance is only half of the story for a VC. Because it is equally true that it is the small minority of a VC fund's out-performers that substantially drive overall fund performance, it is absolutely vital to a VC firm that they have full upside participation in all investments they make (to take full advantage of successful investments) and retain the ability to continue to advance capital into those successful investments (to be able to allocate their fund capital dynamically towards the successful investments, as a core risk management tool). This is the core philosophy lurking behind investment terms such as participating shares, convertible rights and pre-emption rights.

While we are on the subject of the VC's high risk/high reward mindset, it is worth recognising one of the fundamental and (slightly) unfair consequences of this approach. It is an unwelcome but inevitable feature of the VC's business model that moderately successful performance by portfolio companies will go largely unrewarded. This is because the combination of an insistence on aggressive stretch goals for portfolio companies, uncapped VC fund participation in the upside and vigorous management of downside risk (see 5.6 below) effectively strips the "middle ground" from under the feet of management, who will not be rewarded for a safety-first, measured growth approach. To some extent, taking VC money goes hand in hand with a "reach the stars or die in the attempt" mentality.

5.6 DOWNSIDE RISK MANAGEMENT

Every investment a VC makes is, like a second marriage, a triumph of hope over experience. A VC will only make an investment if it firmly believes that the opportunity has an excellent chance of out-performance against the market benchmarks. However, VCs also know that, statistically, it is highly likely that some 20–30% of the investments they make will fail and that a further 40% will just barely do OK in terms of performance. VCs also realise that, at the outset of a fund, they are wholly unable to predict which of the totality of their investments will come to fall into those two categories, as opposed to the 20–30% out-performance category . . . if they could they wouldn't make those investments that fell into the former categories, of course! Because of these facts, the logic in risk management terms is that they must assume that *each one* of their investments will perform poorly.

Downside risk management therefore lies at the heart of a VC's business model, for obvious reasons – to the extent that a VC firm can either abandon a declining situation or improve its overall financial recovery from an under-performing investment, it can reduce the drag on overall investment performance of the 60–70% of its investment portfolio that, statistically, will fall into the "bust" or "also-ran" categories. A VC will employ any tool available with which to gain a measure of downside protection – just so long as it doesn't adversely affect or limit its upside participation in success, which in the final analysis will always be the single most important component of its investment strategy.

This inexorable logic, that a VC firm must insist for every investment that it is granted all downside protection levers it can lay its hands on, runs contrary to the deeply-felt belief of every entrepreneur looking for VC finance – that in the case of his or her company, "this time it's different", that success is virtually assured and that there is no need for the plethora of "unfair" and potentially divisive downside protections initially proposed by the VC firm. This represents the inevitable dislocation of viewpoint between an individual investment opportunity and a portfolio investment approach.

In order to make the business model work, a VC simply cannot afford to take unnecessary risks by treating any individual opportunity as "different" or "special" – it has to crank the model out and apply the risk management tools at hand. If it doesn't (and this will be a recurring refrain) not only will it be at risk of overall portfolio under-performance against market benchmarks, but it will also be at risk of a law suit or other claim from its LPs, as it is playing with their money, not its own. Because its LPs will often hold investments in a number of investment funds, they will have an excellent view of the marketplace and in particular a pretty acute understanding of what the "mainstream" is in investment terms...if a VC steps outside that mainstream, therefore, it had better be pretty sure that it can explain to the LPs why it did so (particularly as it's likely to be doing the explaining after "the chickens have come home to roost" and it's lost the LPs' money, and when the LPs will be applying the usual wisdom of hindsight).

So, what are a VC's typical downside protection tools? There are five broad themes:

5.6.1   Tranching of investments

We have discussed earlier the risk management effect of tranching investments. It is a key tool of downside risk management: a VC contributes a relatively modest tranche of capital, together with the right to contribute further capital in the event that certain business or financial milestones are passed. This is a structure that enables the VC to step back from an investment at regular intervals should its development not meet expectations, without limiting the VC's ability to continue to participate (usually by then at a highly attractive price) should the business meet or even exceed those expectations.

We have discussed how damaging this drip-feed approach can be for the long-term prospects of a business and to the management team's ability to get on with growing the business in as creative a way as possible. Ideally, tranching should only be a feature of the very early days of a company's development – sadly, it is such a powerful downside management tool for VCs that this is often not the case.

5.6.2   Price protection

One of the key areas of risk that a VC faces in its investment strategy is the potential for price erosion, or dilution (a concept explained below), on subsequent financings. As we have already discussed, one of the features of venture capital financing, particularly of early-stage businesses (by far the bulk of the market) is that the business which is financed at the outset will almost certainly need to go back to the capital markets for additional equity capital, sometimes on multiple occasions and often in ever-increasing amounts. This tendency, of course, is exacerbated by a VC's propensity to tranche investments and to provide companies with just enough capital to make it to the next value inflection point. It's not wholly the VC's fault, of course – most entrepreneurs also have a natural desire to limit their own dilution by not raising too much capital too early in the company's development (and therefore at a low valuation).

For example, a traditional model for a technology-based company might be for the company to raise $5 M to develop the initial product for a customer trial; then a further $10 M to secure and conclude reference customer trials; then a further $20 M to build a sales force to take the product to market and generate revenues; and finally perhaps a further $40 M to internationalise the business and take the company to cash-flow break-even and profitability.

Each slug of capital is enough to take the company though a defining moment in its evolution (an "inflection point"), at which the value of the business increases substantially (lowering the cost to the incumbent shareholders of raising the new finance): eventually the company becomes sufficiently self-funded to be able to maintain its momentum out of internal resources.

When a company progresses serenely along this path, everything works well for the VC (although most VCs, even then, will fret about not having put more money into the company earlier at a lower price – hence the reason, once again, why tranched financings are attractive, as they effectively enable this to occur). The VC will generally maintain the option to follow-on into a successful investment, at least pro rata (see above) and will additionally have the option of deciding whether and the extent to which it will allow its early investment to be "leveraged" by the incoming higher-priced equity of third parties (see above).

However, it's not always plain sailing and that's where price protection mechanisms come in. It is highly likely that a high-growth, innovative business developing against a background of a dynamic marketplace and economic environment will not perform exactly as predicted. It is perfectly possible that such a business will experience bumps in the road to success, will suffer delays, disappointments, knock-backs and even possibly the need to go for plan B, plan C or even a re-start. In any of these situations, the hoped-for, gradually steepening "J-curve" spread sheet profile of success will begin to have major dents knocked into it. That's the obvious possibility. A VC firm will use price protection mechanisms to guard against this risk.

But entrepreneurs often fail to recognise that there is a second, more insidious possibility that may also trigger price protection for a VC. It is perfectly possible for the business to perform to expectation, even to surpass expectations, and yet to find that, in corporate finance terms, it has remained stationary or even gone backwards. This is because the prevailing climate for raising money in the capital markets will not necessarily remain the same throughout, or be affected by the same factors influencing a company's development. The cyclical nature of the world's capital markets have never been more apparent than over the last decade – at the beginning of the decade the capital markets moved into a boom phase as "irrational exuberance" took hold, leading to a massive bubble in both private and public markets at the end of the 1990s: conversely, at the beginning of the new millennium markets tumbled – first the public markets, followed by the private equity markets. After the tumble, equity markets stayed mired in recession for several years, carving out a bathtub-shaped recovery, with measured improvement in the marketplace in from 2004 onwards, but even this recovery period was characterised by significant levels of volatility and "false dawns". During this highly volatile decade, venture capital underwent a huge "me too" phenomenon, as hundreds of new VC firms were founded and competition for new investment opportunities became absurdly competitive, followed by an even more painful shake-out in the industry, with many VC firms going out of business or retiring wounded to the sidelines.

Imagine being a business seeking to raise capital through this period. A young, exciting technology business starting out in the late 1990s would have been able to raise seed capital at extraordinarily high valuations (often at great speed), with a raft of different VC firms fighting to invest. In a sense a financial time-bomb was acquired. Only three years later the same business (which by now could have made real strides in developing its technology and might legitimately have expected to command a substantial premium to its previous financing valuation) would re-enter the capital markets for development finance to find a highly attritional market, with very few venture firms willing even to consider an investment, transactions being long drawn-out (often placing enormous demands on management and severely disrupting the core business) and above all business valuations at a fraction of where they had been only a few months previously. Such a company might have been able to raise money at best at the same valuation as before (known as a "flat round"), but would be much more likely to suffer the ignominy of a substantial reduction in valuation (known as a "down round") and in fact many businesses in this period were abandoned by the financial community and went into liquidation. To add insult to injury, where a down round was secured by a successful business in such prevailing capital markets, an existing shareholder's price protection rights would apply.

So, a VC firm can use price protection mechanisms to protect itself both from unexpected dips in business performance, and also to hedge against the vagaries of the underlying capital markets. To this extent, therefore, entrepreneurs need to be aware that a very high valuation for their business for a financing transaction may be something of a mixed blessing – undeniably attractive for the owners of the business at the time, but if that high valuation is driven by a bull market, short-term fashions, etc, then the entrepreneur needs to be aware that the investors in his business are likely to pre-wire a subsequent "re-connection with reality" through price protection mechanisms.

The principal price protection mechanism used by VCs is very simple: they ask that if there is a subsequent capital-raising exercise by the company at a lower price, then their shares acquired earlier should be "re-priced" to the same lower value. This is known as "anti-dilution protection" and there are many and various ways in which the concepts of lower price and re-pricing can be calculated and implemented, respectively (see Part III below).

Intellectually and morally, anti-dilution protection is somewhat bankrupt: a VC firm engages in due diligence of an opportunity, forms a view on the value of the opportunity and makes an offer to the owners of the business; that offer is accepted and the parties join together in collaboration to build the business together ... except that if anything goes wrong down the line, the VC has retained the ability (uniquely among the ownership constituencies) to re-price its investment and escape the risk he or she had previously assumed willingly in an arm's length transaction. VCs will tell you that without anti-dilution protection the price they could offer on transactions would be much lower – the rather more prosaic truth is that anti-dilution protection has become a silent, background feature of VC deal terms and there is no longer any material connection between such terms and price. Even if there is, at least entrepreneurs should be made aware of the quantum, so that they can evaluate whether to pay the upfront cost or wear the risk.

In fact, for the reasons described at Part III below, anti-dilution mechanisms generally don't provide the VC in practice with the measure of protection that they appear to do in theory.

5.6.3 Follow-on capability

The ability for a VC firm to follow-on into an investment (in other words a preferential subscription right applicable to future equity financings) is also a crucial component in its downside protection armoury. This may at first blush sound perverse – why would a VC firm wish to use an investment right in a company which, presumably, is struggling? Most people assume that follow-on rights will only be used by a VC firm to ensure continued upside participation in a successful company. However, such a technique also provides the VC with the opportunity to "average down" the cost of its investment, which may be very attractive to the VC where an investment is either struggling temporarily at an operational level (a "bump in the road" scenario), is suffering unfairly at the hands of attritional capital markets when it needs to raise finance (an opportunistic scenario), or is about to undergo a reorganisation of some kind to reinvigorate the business (a restart scenario). Each of these situations is ripe for the VC to use its right to follow-on into a new financing opportunity to provide a similar overall economic impact on its investment as anti-dilution protection – and indeed these two features are often used in parallel.

Imagine that a VC firm invests \$10 M in an opportunity on day one at \$2 a share. Two years later, after much excellent progress, the company has the misfortune to experience an operational knock-back which requires a re-engineering of the business model. The \$10 M capital required to effect this re-engineering and get the company to break-even will go in at a much lower valuation, say \$1 a share. Provided that the VC believes that the prize of a successful re-engineering is sufficiently attractive, it is absolutely crucial that he or she has the right to participate in the follow-on opportunity at the lower price, which will lower his or her average cost of investment from \$2 a share to \$1.33 a share (indeed, if anti-dilution rights are utilised as well, the cost of investment could fall to \$1 a share across the entire investment).

In fact, the laws of many countries provide shareholders with a pre-emption right over new equity share issues for cash, but notably the United States does not and in addition there are many circumstances in which pre-emption rights will not apply, or will apply in a sub-optimal manner for the VC firm. Accordingly, a VC will invariably look for specific follow-on rights.

5.6.4   Information and veto rights

Unlike the private equity industry, where taking control of an investment is the norm, VC firms usually find themselves taking a significant minority position in their investments. To some extent, this can prove to be the worst of both worlds – economic significance without the levers of positive control under prevailing laws. Clearly this is an area of significant risk, which is mitigated by a VC in two key ways – by ensuring timely access to key business information and by veto rights. These rights may operate at the board and/or shareholder levels.

It is obviously vital, as a risk management tool, that a VC firm has timely access to important information about the business in which it has invested, whether that information relates to regular key performance indicators regarding the business, or to extraordinary events that may impact its investment. So the existence of high quality data gathering, reporting and analysis processes within an investment are a focus for a VC firm. It is also vital that a VC is able to use the information freely once data is delivered to it. Perhaps surprisingly, the laws of most countries do not provide a shareholder with many information rights.

In practice, a VC will manage its risk in this area in three ways: by careful due diligence of financial and operational controls and procedures, by seeking appointment to the board of the company and by demanding certain core contractual information rights as an investor.

It is one thing to be aware of a problem or issue, quite another to be able to do something about it. For all sorts of reasons, VCs tend to fight shy of taking positive control of an investment (the ability to force the company to do something), unless it is absolutely necessary, and so their focus will tend to be upon negative control (the ability to prevent the company from doing something) – expressed in the form of a long list of "veto rights", providing that the company cannot effect any of the listed items (e.g. issue new shares, incur expenses above a certain threshold, etc) without the prior consent of an agreed constituency. That constituency will often vary – the board, the VC director(s), the VC fund, or a defined super-majority of shareholders (of which the VC group will usually be a blocking minority), or even different such options for different issues and events.

5.6.5 Special exit rights

One of the most basic of downside protection rights is the ability to "cut and run" if things go badly. Accordingly, a VC will usually wish to create such an ability in relation to each investment it makes. That mentality manifests itself in two different approaches: "piggy back" rights on any exit opportunity engineered by other shareholders (known as "tag-along rights") and a drop-dead right to be bought out, should the VC still be stuck in an investment after a defined period, typically by a redemption of the VC fund's shares.

But this is not usually enough for a VC firm. A VC firm may well seek a preferred position on the division of the spoils if things do turn ugly on an investment, ensuring in the most dramatic way possible that under-performing investments are improved artificially. In other words, if a VC wants to do as well as everyone else in the case of a successful investment, he or she also wants to do better than anyone else in the case of a failed investment. There's no subtlety here, just tightly focused portfolio investment management, in the form of enhanced or preferred exit treatment in the event that certain performance thresholds are not met (typically through the medium of a "liquidation preference").

5.7   DYNAMIC CAPITAL ALLOCATION

It can be seen immediately from this chapter that a VC firm responds to the challenges in its business model in a very sophisticated and diverse way. Fundamentally, however, the game of venture capital is about dynamic capital allocation within an over-arching portfolio approach. Many of the risk management tools employed by VCs simply facilitate this dynamic capital allocation process.

Pursuant to a dynamic capital allocation strategy, a VC will:

(1) back a large number of high-risk investments opportunities which demonstrate exceptional performance potential (the "investment portfolio");
(2) allocate a large amount of follow-on capacity (the "follow-on pool") across the totality of the investment portfolio;
(3) secure the right to use the follow-on pool to invest further capital into the investment portfolio in priority to anyone else;
(4) set the bar high for continued access by the investment portfolio to the VC's follow-on pool;
(5) allocate the follow-on pool dynamically towards the winners in the investment portfolio and those companies with exceptional turn-around potential (with a much smaller allocation to moderate performers and early abandonment of the failures); and
(6) recover as much as possible from the wreckage of the failures (and the more modest moderate performers).

A determined focus on this kind of dynamic capital allocation can transform the prospects of an average portfolio, when compared to a simple, company by company approach (where each company is funded on its merits and evaluated in isolation to the rest of the portfolio). Once one realises that a VC firm should, if it is properly managed, be allocating the time of its senior partners in a similar dynamic way, one starts to appreciate the leveraging effect of this dynamic, portfolio-focused approach and the increasing disparity of treatment between those portfolio businesses which get business traction quickly and those who do not.

Let's look at a simplified example – assuming a VC firm has a $200 M fund to spend and backs ten companies, and using the core statistical assumption that 30% of deals will fail, 30% will succeed (assumed to be at a 6× blended performance multiple on all money invested) and 40% will do OK (assumed to be at a 2–2.5× blended performance multiple on all money invested).

(1) Step 1 – the VC backs the ten businesses with $10 M each, but puts the money into each company in two tranches, the second conditioned on a business milestone a year later.
(2) Step 2 – a year later, two of the companies fail the milestone and are written off. Liquidation preferences in these two failed investments enable the VC to recover 20% of its money, no one else gets anything. The remaining eight receive a further $5 M each in the second tranche.
(3) Step 3 – a year later, the eight remaining companies are coming up to a new funding round, each needing a further $10 M to fund their original ambitious business plans. One further company is now experiencing difficulties and is put into liquidation: the VC recovers 80% of its cost of investment through the liquidation preference. Of the remaining seven companies, two have become lower-growth and therefore are funded on a reduced basis ($5 M each) and sold, with only five receiving the full $10 M each. The VC uses the liquidation preference feature to ensure that it recovers 2× on the sold investments overall.
(4) Step 4 – a year later, the five companies need a further $10 M for a final development round. By now, two further companies have fallen off the growth curve and are funded on a reduced basis to break even ($2.5 M each) and sold, with only the final three high performers receiving a further $10 M apiece. The VC uses the liquidation preference feature to ensure that it recovers 2.5× on the sold investments.
(5) Step 5 – some time later, the three final investments are realised at a blended performance multiple on all monies invested of 6× each.

Obviously, this model is wholly unrealistic and over-simplified. But it does demonstrate powerfully the basic impact of dynamic capital allocation techniques. Simply through that mechanism, the above fund will return more than $720 M on an investment of $185 M – a near 4× multiple, cash on cash, despite only 30% of the investments performing well. This, in essence, is the business of venture capital.

5.8   THE HUMAN ELEMENT

To conclude an analysis of the business of venture capital that makes the model appear purely driven by dynamic capital allocation tools is misleading. The human capital dimension is equally vital and VC firms recognise that, both in terms of downside risk management and upside performance enhancement, the "people factor" is absolutely vital. In small, high-growth organisations such as venture-backed companies, one individual can have a huge impact. Accordingly, VCs are as focused on intellectual and human capital, as they are on pure financial capital.

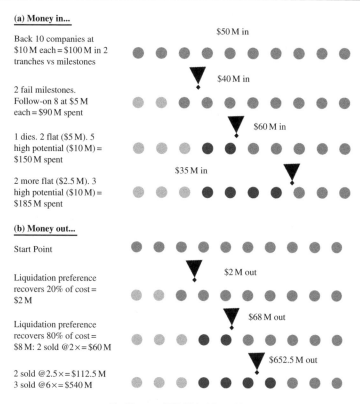

(a) Money in...

Back 10 companies at
$10 M each = $100 M in 2
tranches vs milestones

$50 M in

$40 M in

2 fail milestones.
Follow-on 8 at $5 M
each = $90 M spent

$60 M in

1 dies. 2 flat ($5 M). 5
high potential ($10 M) =
$150 M spent

$35 M in

2 more flat ($2.5 M). 3
high potential ($10 M) =
$185 M spent

(b) Money out...

Start Point

$2 M out

Liquidation preference
recovers 20% of cost =
$2 M

$68 M out

Liquidation preference
recovers 80% of cost =
$8 M: 2 sold @2× = $60 M

$652.5 M out

2 sold @2.5× = $112.5 M
3 sold @6× = $540 M

Total Return = $722.5 M = [4] × multiple

Figure 5.2   Dynamic capital allocation

In particular, VC firms will:

(1) carefully evaluate the management teams they are backing and seek to implement continual strengthening of that team as the business develops and the challenges and skills requirements change;

(2) make sure that their own organisations have a rich, diverse range of skills and experience on which their portfolio companies can draw – in particular that the key relationships between the VC firm and the portfolio company are highly experienced and able to add value commercially and strategically to the management team. It is no accident that many successful VCs have either been in the investment business for many years, or have themselves been serial successful entrepreneurs in the sectors in which they now invest.

(3) draw on a professionally managed and constantly increasing network of contacts, which is also capable of delivering added value to the VC fund portfolio – entrepreneurs, scientists, engineers, management talent, head hunters, customer and supplier relationships, lawyers, bankers, accountants, consultants and other professional advisers.

These influences can clearly on occasion make a material difference to the performance of a portfolio company. They can assist a company to develop the right business model, avoid classic pitfalls, get commercial traction at key moments, develop workaround strategies and, above all, maintain the ambition, nerve and momentum necessary to ensure that the business opportunity reaches its true potential. There are many $1 B opportunities that become $100 M "successes" because the organisation lacked the resources and the vision to break out of its early stage incarnation.

5.9   CONCLUSIONS

Having examined the fundamentals that drive a VC firm's investment model in some detail, its attitude to risk and the portfolio management tools it employs to manage such risk, the next question is what does this all mean for an entrepreneur seeking to raise capital from the VC community. The picture we have painted is one of a VC obsessed with risk management, exits and returns to impatient LPs – hardly the hands-off easy going investor that many entrepreneurs dream of. Doing business with VCs is a full-on, high maintenance task and is not for the faint hearted. Part II of this book guides entrepreneurs through the VC investment process and highlights the pitfalls and solutions to managing a difficult and occasionally fraught process. Part III addresses the specific terms usually present in a VC term sheet, with suggested approaches to reaching a win-win deal for both entrepreneur and VC, thus ensuring that the newly formed business relationship gets off on the right foot and moves in the direction everyone expected it to.

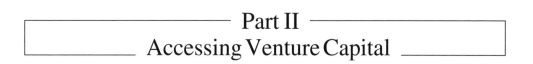

Part II
Accessing Venture Capital

6
Introduction to Part II

Having examined in outline the fundamentals of venture capital investing, Part II of this book turns to look at the process of accessing venture capital finance and differentiating between venture capital firms.

In terms of accessing venture capital finance, it is very important for an entrepreneur to identify at the outset why it is that he or she believes that venture capital is the right source of equity capital for his or her business. This book does not seek to offer alternatives to venture capital funding, but it does try to make sure that an entrepreneur identifies the peculiar characteristics of venture capital and matches those characteristics against his or her own ambitions and circumstances, to ensure as far as possible that an entrepreneur approaches a fund-raising process with a VC firm with his or her eyes open and fully apprised of the somewhat "faustian bargain" that is about to be struck. The conclusion to be drawn is that venture capital finance is highly attractive, but suitable only for a small minority of developing businesses, and the remainder are either wasting their time (they won't be funded) or sowing the seeds of eventual disaster (or at least damaging discord) when the interests and needs of the founding team start materially and inevitably to diverge from the interests and needs of the VC fund shareholder brought about by the demands of the VC business model.

When there is a natural fit between a particular business opportunity and the aims, ambitions and business dynamics of the venture capital industry, then it can be a match made in heaven. As we discussed in Part I, although the jury is most certainly out in some sectors, studies in others have shown that venture-backed companies on average out-perform other companies materially. Studies by DRI-WEFA, for example, demonstrated that not only are US venture-backed companies on average significantly more productive than other companies in good times (for example, >60% more sales per $ of assets), but they are also materially more robust in hard times. Similar studies by the BVCA in the UK have concluded that private equity-backed companies create jobs more than 30 times faster than the national private sector average, and grow sales at more than twice the rate of the FTSE 100 average. More than three quarters of UK private equity-backed companies believed that their backers had made a major contribution to the business outside money.

Nonetheless, entrepreneurs should be aware that there are a variety of alternative sources available for seed and development funding of high growth businesses and that some of these options may be more attractive to an entrepreneur, either because they offer a tighter match with the entrepreneur's aims and ambitions, or because they are more appropriate in light of the nature, position or prospects of the business for which funding is being sought. These options may include funding from any of the following: own resources (re-mortgaging the house), friends and family, angel or angel network finance, asset-based finance, bank finance, government grant or other national, regional, local or institutional (e.g. university) programme funding. Indeed, depending on location there is an increasing number of government-backed schemes aimed at helping entrepreneurial businesses find their feet.

Once it has been determined that venture capital is the right option, then the hard work begins, in terms of identifying the optimal way to access the venture capital community, including differentiating between the members of that community, successfully managing the process of securing a financial commitment from one or more VC funds, and ensuring that maximum value is derived from the relationship with those funds into the future. Part II examines the process of accessing and choosing a VC and managing the capital-raising process and Part III below examines the terms on which a financing will typically be made.

7
Is Venture Capital the Right Option?

7.1 INTRODUCTION

Before an entrepreneur commences the process of soliciting venture capital funding, it is highly important that he or she first asks a very basic question – "is venture capital the right kind of equity funding for me?" As mentioned above, there may be many other types of equity or quasi-equity funding available in the particular circumstances, and it is vitally important that the entrepreneur matches the needs and dynamics of the business he or she wishes to develop to the fundamentals inherent in the venture capital business model and in particular to the behavioural idiosyncrasies of VC firms brought about by the particular features of their business model and the prevailing competitive environment.

Even if venture capital is the right choice to make for the business, the entrepreneur also needs to be sure that venture capital will also fit with his or her own values and aims in important areas such as lifestyle, control, ambition, etc. If the personal price of a business that is successful (in venture capital terms) is ultimately likely to be unacceptable to the individual entrepreneur, then it is very important that this is identified in advance of an arrangement that may force the entrepreneur to work closely with a VC firm for many years.

To decide whether venture capital is indeed the right choice, the entrepreneur must both examine the alternatives as well as the nature of the "trade-off" in raising venture capital investment. The key questions that an entrepreneur must ask include the following:

7.2 WHAT DO I WANT MY BUSINESS TO BECOME?

Venture capital is ideal for highly ambitious entrepreneurs who want the acorn of their idea to grow not only into a mighty oak tree, but an entire forest of mighty oak trees. As we have discussed in Part I, VCs will only look at businesses that have exceptional upside investment potential, which as a rough rule of thumb we can take to be a minimum of ten times value growth in five to seven years. Quite how high this drives the exit valuation of an opportunity will often depend materially on the amount of money that the opportunity requires, but these kind of growth dynamics mean inevitably that it is essential that the management team of a VC-backed business has the drive, ambition and goal of delivering extraordinary business growth within an exceptionally short time-frame. Cautious, measured growth is not an option.

Venture capital fits well with entrepreneurs for whom the most important thing is to change the accepted order of things in the world (the wave of creative destruction that we discussed in Chapter 1) and who are prepared to accept the inevitable risks that will be attendant to such an approach. It's a "succeed gloriously, or die in the attempt" mentality. This is not a mentality with which all entrepreneurs are comfortable.

7.3   CAN MY BUSINESS MATCH THOSE AMBITIONS?

Even if the entrepreneur has this level of ambition, of course, it is perfectly possible that the business opportunity he or she wishes to present to the VC community does not have the characteristics to support that ambition. If that's the case, then it is highly unlikely that a VC firm will wish to invest in the opportunity, and other types of financing will be more suitable. It may be that a period of validation of the opportunity is necessary, before the entrepreneur is able to confirm the match with a VC firm's ambitions, in which event alternative funding may be required to take the business through this validation process.

As will be discussed in more detail subsequently, a business with the upside potential that is required by a VC firm will usually have the following features:

(1) a proprietary and defensible technology which creates a compelling opportunity, or answers an important need in a very large addressable market;
(2) a cogent strategy to access that market and subsequently to retain a significant competitive position in it;
(3) a product or service that can be built and should work;
(4) a business model with manageable capital intensity;
(5) the ability to charge for the product at a level that will ensure early profitability and the maintenance of strong margins over a sustained period;
(6) a strong and balanced management team
(7) a plan B (at least).

7.4   HOW MUCH CAPITAL DOES MY BUSINESS REQUIRE?

This may seem an odd question, but it is increasingly relevant as far as the VC industry is concerned. While at first glance, there should be no reason why a VC firm would turn down a business that only needs a relatively modest capital infusion, in fact as the VC market matures, it is becoming increasingly difficult to gain the interest of the VC community in such circumstances.

Over the last 20 years, VC funds have generally become much larger, in terms of the amount of their committed capital. By contrast, the organisations managing this money – the VC firms – have not grown at the same pace. For example, a five partner firm which ten years ago would have been managing a new \$100 M fund every three years may now be managing a \$500 M fund, but the organisation may only have grown by 60% to eight partners. Whereas the five partners had each been responsible for putting to work \$20 M each, which could comfortably be put to work in (e.g.) five deals of \$4 M, suddenly the current organisation faces putting to work \$62.5 M per partner – which can only be achieved either by doing more deals of the historic \$4 M size (e.g. nearly 16 deals per partner) or maintaining the deal numbers and increasing the capital put into each deal (e.g. \$12.5 M per deal in five deals). Because the time commitment from partners in working on an investment are pretty much the same whatever its size, "partner bandwidth" tends to be the most influential factor, driving the firm "upmarket" into investment opportunities that require more capital and causing the firm to turn down perfectly valid investment opportunities that cannot put enough capital to work for the firm's requirements.

In addition, with larger VC funds, it is also inevitably the case that investments that require lower levels of investment will, even if they return quite startling exit multiples, not return in absolute terms a figure that will be capable of making a significant contribution to the overall investment performance of the fund. This is important, because a VC firm will know that only some 20–30% of its investments are likely to be highly successful and that this sub-group in the portfolio absolutely need to be capable – on their own – of substantially driving the performance of the fund. A $2 million investment that delivers 50× (a $100 M return) is clearly capable of doing this for a $100 M fund – but that's no longer the case for a $500 M fund, even at that phenomenal investment return rate. Accordingly, the larger VC firms may be forced to decline this kind of smaller investment opportunity, despite its seemingly alluring qualities.

Unfortunately, this move "upmarket" by the incumbent VC firms has not led to the entry of sufficient new, smaller VC firms to fill the "equity gap" that has inevitably emerged, nor have alternative financing options (e.g. angel financing) been entirely successful in doing so either. This can leave an entrepreneur who needs the "classic" $1 M to develop his or her business in something of a quandary. Dealing with the equity gap created by this migration to larger deals has become a key aspect of government policy around the world, and in Europe has led to the creation of various government-backed funds with a remit to invest small.

The converse is also true – a business proposition with a really chunky capital requirement may only be able to raise such capital from the deep-pocketed VC community, making it even more vital that the business can match the expectations of the VC community in every other way (including the evolution and/or manageability of the capital intensity of the business model over time, to ensure that the chunky capital requirement is not front-end loaded). If a start-up business needs $30–50 M to take its product to market (e.g. a biotechnology opportunity), the entrepreneur probably doesn't have many other options than to knock on the door of the larger VC firms.

7.5 DO I WANT TO CONTROL MY BUSINESS FOR A LONG TIME?

Control of his or her business through the longer term may be important to the entrepreneur: owner-management may be the cornerstone of what he or she set out to achieve by entrepreneurial activity. This is unlikely to be achievable alongside venture capital investment in the business, for two reasons.

Firstly, the growth dynamics that are demanded by a VC investor will give rise to enormous development and change in the underlying organisation, making huge demands of the key management and almost certainly mandating regular change in the senior management appointees, as the nature of the skills and experience demanded of each role changes in line with the internal and external challenges facing the business over time. Put simply, if the entrepreneur is CEO of the business at the time he or she seeks venture funding, it is highly unlikely that he or she will still be CEO of that business three years later. If entrepreneurs are fortunate, they will be able to migrate into a position that reflects their ongoing high value to the organisation (CTO, CMO, CSO, VP BusDev, etc) and offers them real challenges and excitement: if entrepreneurs are not so fortunate, they may find that their only interest in the company going forward is as a shareholder.

Secondly, the influx of venture capital, combined with an aggressive development profile is likely to mean a series of subsequent capital-raising exercises, management incentive programmes and other strategic opportunities which leverage the equity capital base of the company. If the entrepreneur holds the majority of the equity in the business at the time venture funding is sought, it is highly unlikely that he or she will still control that business three years later. It's the natural price the entrepreneur has to pay to have a substantial piece of what will become a very large opportunity.

By contrast, a more measured approach to growth (for example constrained organic growth funded out of free cash flow) could allow the entrepreneur to build a business gradually while retaining full control of the business and remaining CEO. It's the difference between owning substantially all of a \$10 M business and 5% of a \$1 B business. The old cliché about a small piece of a big pie is no more apt than in this situation. It is simply a choice that entrepreneurs must make.

7.6 WHAT KIND OF LIFE DO I WANT TO LEAD?

It will have become immediately apparent from the above and from the description of the venture capital business model in Part I, that those who take money from a venture capitalist cannot expect an easy ride thereafter. The relentless emphasis following a venture capital funding round is on high growth, rapid progress and a seemingly endless succession of "stretch goals". This is unlikely to be an environment in which quality of life will feature highly for a senior executive. If the entrepreneur values a sensible work-life balance – if he or she doesn't find compelling the idea of subjugating the next five to seven years to the demands of the business and its shareholders – then venture capital is not the right choice. If venture capital is the only option for the business, then the entrepreneur is going to have to actively consider succession planning, and take more of a back seat in the development process: but at the same time recognising that this may not be attractive to the VC community and may lower the value at which they are prepared to invest, or even render the opportunity uninvestable.

7.7 AM I COMFORTABLE WITH AN EXIT?

As we have seen in Part I, a clear path to a demonstrable exit in the medium term is an essential feature of the venture capital business model. Upon investment, the VC firm's mentality will switch focus from investment to exit. There are really only four ways in which such an exit can be achieved for a VC fund – the sale of the business to a third party, the flotation of the business on a stock exchange (known as an "IPO" or initial public offering), a recapitalisation of the business (under which existing or new shareholders will buy-out the VC firm) or the redemption or buy-back of the VC firm's shares out of free cash flow generated by the business. By far the most common exits, however, are a trade sale or IPO.

We have discussed above the fact that, in seeking VC funding, an entrepreneur must be able to identify a realistic medium-term exit opportunity and the critical path to that exit. But, much more fundamentally, the entrepreneur should ask whether he or she is comfortable at all with the concept of such an exit – selling the business to a third party (probably a large company) or taking his or her business public and submitting to the ownership of institutional investors. For many entrepreneurs, these concepts are an anathema. If that's the case, venture capital is almost certainly not the right choice. If venture capital is the only option for the business, the best option may be to come clean and identify an alternative exit scenario that demonstrably can deliver an attractive exit premium for the VC investor: it will be an uphill struggle to convince the VC community to invest on this basis, however.

So, from the above it can be seen that the act of taking development capital from a VC fund is a critical moment, not only for the business concerned but for the entrepreneur who has founded the business and built it to its prevailing position. From that decision will inevitably flow a number of consequences – engendered by the significant ownership interest of the VC fund: the participation of its senior representatives on the board of the company, the terms and conditions in the investment documentation and the realpolitik of the VC fund's lock on future funding into the business. These consequences will include the assumption of big risks commensurate with big rewards, a compulsion with the need to exit, a 24/7 "full-on" working environment, and constant demands and change for the business and its staff: but they will equally include the creation of an environment of limitless ambition capable of taking the business and its core technology to the absolute apogee of its potential, and even beyond – indeed to change the world order of things.

If the entrepreneur enters into a business relationship with a VC firm, but doesn't share the values and needs of the venture capital business model, then sooner or later the entrepreneur and the VC are going to get into a serious argument about the future direction of the business. It's an argument the VC usually wins and, whoever wins, the argument itself is usually enough to seriously disrupt, damage or even kill the business itself.

The choice of where to seek and secure capital for his or her business is up to the entrepreneur. What's important is to understand the nature of the choices available and the consequences that will inevitably flow from any particular choice.

8
Choosing a VC Firm

8.1 INTRODUCTION

Once the entrepreneur has decided that venture capital is the right option, the next key decision to make is about *which* VC firm is the right one. To make this decision, the entrepreneur clearly has to find out as much as possible about the VC community and the differentiators between the members of this community. It is absolutely vital to do so, as there are massive differences between different firms. Picking a VC firm that matches the aims, ambitions, ethos and values of the entrepreneur will not only improve the chances of successfully raising finance, but also the prospects of eventual commercial success for the business.

There are many ways in which an entrepreneur can conduct research about a VC firm – ranging from the firm's own website, to taking references from companies previously backed by the VC firm. Remember, "due diligence" is a two way street – VCs will spend countless hours assuring themselves that they are making the right decision in backing an entrepreneur; likewise entrepreneurs should assure themselves they are accepting investment from the right VC. Allowing the wrong investors to buy substantial equity stakes in a business can be disastrous and there are a few simple factors for entrepreneurs to look at to make sure they are talking to the right VCs. The entrepreneur may not be able to gain sufficient knowledge on every front in advance of meeting the VC firm, but will be able to narrow the field of attractive VCs by focusing on issues of real importance in the planned-for relationship. The following are some of the key issues for an entrepreneur to consider prior to approaching VCs:

8.2 SUBSTANTIAL LONG-TERM RESOURCES

It is perhaps surprising that this should be considered as an issue at all, as it is very common for an entrepreneur to take for granted the long term viability of the VC firm and its associated fund. But it should not be taken for granted – and a failure by a significant investor may be of great importance to the entrepreneur and the fledgling business.

When an entrepreneur raises venture capital from a VC fund, it is highly unlikely that this will be a one-off event but rather the beginning of a relationship with an equity funding partner that will last for many years. There are many reasons why this is the case – as we have discussed in Part I, the venture capital model is founded on the principles of tranched investment and dynamic capital allocation through follow-on investment, as well as leveraging an investment through the participation of other equity investors. In addition, as discussed more fully in Part III, an entrepreneur will also want to raise just enough external equity capital as is necessary to get the business through the next major value inflection point, so that he or she does not suffer undue dilution to his or her economic interest in the business.

So, just as a practical matter, it is going to be highly attractive if the VC firm which funds the business has sufficient follow-on capability to be able to contribute fully to the needs of the developing business over the medium term. This will ensure that the business will continue to be able to access capital from an existing shareholder who knows the company intimately, hopefully ensuring that the capital-raising process will be speedy, flexible, pragmatic and efficient – causing minimum disruption to the business.

The alternative (a VC fund that does not have the resources to follow-on) can be disastrous. Clearly, in such circumstances the entrepreneur will have to search again for a new equity finance partner prepared to fund the business through the next stage of its development. Apart from the additional time that this will involve (bringing a new investor up to speed on the investment opportunity), the lack of active participation by an incumbent VC can cause real difficulty even where new investors can be found, for the following reasons:

(1) Even if the reason why the VC is passive in the new financing is lack of follow-on capability, there will still be a negative connotation to the VC's passivity and incoming investors will worry that there's something the incumbent VC knows that they have missed, which may cause them to drop out or to reduce the price at which they are prepared to fund the company.

(2) Follow-on rounds which are led by an incumbent VC, or in which an incumbent has made a substantial commitment, are primed for success – in particular the incumbent VC is able to play a leading role in price formation for the round, as well as the development of the term sheet detailing the key terms and conditions that will apply, and will often be able to drive those terms through quickly on the back of the momentum caused by its insider knowledge about the company and its significant new financial commitment. To this extent, the incumbent VC forms the corner-stone of the financing round and will be highly influential in convincing new investors to join its syndicate and come on board as investors in the company.

(3) An incumbent VC will possess a significant chunk of the company's capital (the rough rule of thumb is that a company will sell some one third of its post financing share capital in each financing round), as well as a wide range of rights (including board nomination rights and board and shareholder veto rights). The combination of these factors may well mean that the incumbent VC has the ability to block any new fund-raising it doesn't like – and this means that it can play "dog in the manger". The very best VCs recognise that if they are in a position where they are out of follow-on capacity, or they have decided not to follow their investment, the "game is over" for them and they are usually prepared to step aside and allow themselves to be washed out by an incoming investment syndicate. Many other VCs, by contrast, do not behave so honourably and can be expected to be extremely difficult about any dilution to their position caused by the incoming finance, perhaps focusing on strategic alternatives that are sub-optimal for the business but which preserve the incumbent's position. Obviously, this can be very damaging for the company's prospects of raising new finance and sometimes can even threaten its very survival.

(4) Even if an incumbent VC allows a financing to go ahead, often its residual interest in the business (shareholding, shareholder and contractual rights, board nomination, etc) can be very distracting for management, with the potential for conflict with shareholders and other key constituencies in the future as the interests of the passive shareholder may diverge from those of the other constituencies – for example when it comes to strategic opportunities for the business, further financing rounds, management incentive programmes, and above all the timing and nature of an eventual exit.

As described in Part I, VC firms raise ten year funds, and for various complex reasons they generally don't like to make "crossover" investments – investments by one fund into the portfolio of an earlier fund managed by the same VC firm. It is therefore very important that a VC firm allocates sufficient follow-on capacity against each investment it makes, at the time of initial investment, to ensure that it is able to participate fully in future funding opportunities in its portfolio out of the internal resources of the fund. An entrepreneur should have no qualms in asking his or her VC firm what level of follow-on reserve has been allocated to the business – and then taking a view as to whether this is enough to see the business through a reasonable period of development (ideally to a point where it will have reached the promised land of positive cash flow that we referred to in Part I).

So, an entrepreneur must be comfortable that the chosen VC fund not only has sufficient funds committed over the medium term to make the initial investment and to continue to support the business as its leading investor going forward, but also has thought through its follow-on allocation and has reserved sufficient capital to invest over the longer term.

8.3   LONG AND RELEVANT EXPERIENCE

It is obvious that a VC firm with strong relevant domain expertise will be a better partner for an entrepreneur than one that is coming to the sector for the first time, or is a generalist investor without real depth and breadth of experience in the relevant sector. Relevant "domain expertise" (as it is frequently termed by VCs) and investment focus will both smooth the investment evaluation process and provide the entrepreneur with a value-added partner going forward, as the business meets challenges and opportunities in the future.

In addition to domain expertise, it is also highly valuable that the individuals in the VC firm have extensive operational experience within the relevant sector, as well as long experience of venture capital investment in that sector. Broadly, the partners of VC firms can be broken into two types: those with a non-operational, professional background (e.g. corporate finance, banking, consultancy, accountancy, law, etc) and those with extensive operational experience within the sector on which they focus their investment activities. As far as an entrepreneur is concerned, the latter category is more likely to provide a proactive, value-added investor at a *commercial* level for a business in the early stages of investment.

However, an equally important influence on the value of that relationship will be long experience as an *investor*, which will inform crucial areas such as corporate finance cycles, what long-term investing really means, turn-around experience and the fundamental dynamics of the venture capital business model, so the technical background of the individual is not always the over-riding criteria. Only an experienced venture capital investor will truly have an appetite for risk – indeed will understand the necessity of embracing that risk in his or her investment strategy – and will be able to handle wisely and maturely the inevitable twists and turns of fate lying ahead for the businesses in which they invest. It's also true that an experienced investor will have seen many different business models at work over the years, as well as many different problems and opportunities – and this type of experience can be highly valuable and is not common among those with narrow industry experience. Such an investor is a worthwhile business partner for an entrepreneur.

8.4   A LEADER, NOT A FOLLOWER

Strategically, it is highly advantageous to select a VC firm that is noted as a "leader", not a "follower". This concept of leadership touches on three areas:

(1) leadership in innovation in the relevant domain – meaning that there is evidence that the firm is either a thought-leader in the sector or demonstrates its willingness to back others who are;

(2) the firm has a track record of leading investment rounds, both initial rounds and follow-on opportunities, as opposed to picking up spare investment capacity as a syndicate follower; and

(3) the firm has a track record of building and leading investment syndicates.

8.5   SCALING THE BUSINESS

As we discussed earlier, there are a number of ways in which a VC can assist a venture-backed business, and whether or not that proves to be the case in practice, an entrepreneur should pick a VC firm to work with that appears to have the capability and willingness to do so. There are four key areas of potential value-add that should be considered:

8.5.1   Powerful proprietary networks

The more successful VCs have built up extensive proprietary networks over the years, based on the aggregation of the individual partners' own contact databases, as well as the networks that have evolved from years of portfolio investment, deal flow generation and sector involvement. These networks – essentially composed of contact points with a diverse range of institutions (academic, technical, industrial and governmental) – can be extremely useful for a young business and the VC firm should be used shamelessly by its portfolio companies to open doors for them, to effect introductions and to generate value-added contacts that would otherwise be difficult or impossible to achieve for the portfolio companies alone.

8.5.2   Portfolio community

The larger and more established VC firms will also be managing a large portfolio composed of those companies in which their managed VC funds have invested but not yet exited. This can typically be some 50+ companies. These will often be companies in the same sector or geography as the entrepreneur's business and many of these companies will have experienced exactly the same problems and issues as lie ahead of the entrepreneur – for example in important strategic or operational areas such as business model, share incentive programmes, government grants and rebates, hiring strategies, internationalisation of R&D and sales and marketing, etc. Better still, it is unlikely that any of these companies will be directly competitive with the entrepreneur (presuming that a VC firm will not want to have mutually competitive companies in its portfolio). As such, the VC firm's portfolio will offer a ready-made community for the incoming entrepreneur, with the potential to provide guidance, support and experience, as well as more direct value-add such as customer, supplier or collaboration relationships.

8.5.3 International capability

One of the biggest challenges that any business faces in its evolution will be the internationalisation of its business model, when fundamental issues such as the evolving group structure; tax and regulation; hiring, employment and incentive issues; and of course local business culture and contacts loom large and can easily derail a company's business plan or at least suck in vast amounts of senior management time. If an entrepreneur is partnered with an international VC firm – for example one with offices in several jurisdictions key to the development of the business (particularly a transatlantic presence) – then the entrepreneur can expect to gain the benefit of hands-on assistance from the VC firm in opening up new markets and establishing local operations quickly and effectively. This can have a material beneficial impact in terms of management focus, time and costs.

This is less of a concern for a US-based business, with the vast US market to attack, but much more relevant to a European or Asian business, for which international expansion may be vital.

8.5.4 Additional skills leverage

Some VC firms have an extensive range of skills within their organisations and these skills may be drawn on from time to time by smart portfolio companies, often without charge. For example, most VCs will have extensive corporate finance and M&A experience and can be expected to play a leading role in assisting a portfolio company on it's strategy and execution of such transactions. Some VC firms even have specialists performing such roles internally.

For example, an increasing number of VC firms have international legal and tax capabilities and clearly from time to time this resource can be valuable to a portfolio company, as well as generally being in a position to leverage and distribute widely among the portfolio know-how on developing issues and generally applicable solutions. A smaller subset of firms have established "human capital" capabilities, which seek to professionalise the firm's contacts, as well as the process of building and developing top class management teams in portfolio companies and attempting to recycle senior management talent within the firm's own portfolio: such resource can be very useful in terms of executing new hires, planning and implementing compensation and incentive programmes, and implementing reorganisations.

8.6 SUCCESSFUL REPUTATION

It obviously helps if the VC firm backing your business has a reputation for successful investment. As described in Part I, the US marketplace has evolved in a stratified fashion such that the best opportunities tend to go to a super-group of top tier VCs, creating a virtuous cycle of investment success. As we discussed earlier, and as research has proven, having a top tier VC on one's shareholder register can create a "halo effect" and entrepreneurs in general are prepared to sell equity at lower prices just to have these investors on board.

8.7 PERSONAL CHEMISTRY

Clearly personal chemistry is not something that will leap off the page as the entrepreneur investigates the VC firm's website, but it is nonetheless of exceptional importance. The partner who sponsors the investment opportunity within the VC firm will come to play a very important role in the development of the entrepreneur's business over the years. This individual will be on the board in a non-executive capacity, will be the focal point for all communication with and assistance from the firm, and will be the ongoing internal advocate for the business within the VC firm as new financing or other strategic opportunities emerge, including eventual exit. Above all, he or she will work alongside the entrepreneur through every twist and turn in the road, as the business develops and matures, and it is inevitable that at some stage in that journey trust, maturity, wisdom, morality and patience will be required from both entrepreneur and VC in difficult and trying times. It is therefore absolutely essential not only that the entrepreneur likes the VC partner on a personal level, but that the entrepreneur is confident that the VC shares his or her vision for the business and, equally importantly the entrepreneur's values and approach to doing business. As a VC colleague once commented "if you don't want to have dinner with them, then don't bother". That is probably good advice for entrepreneurs too.

9
The Entry Point

9.1   INTRODUCTION

Most entrepreneurs approach the VC community for money in a way which makes failure inevitable.

VCs are busy people. They are busy because the business makes multiple demands on their time – generating deal flow and networking, managing the investment process for selected opportunities, monitoring and managing investments that have been made, and generating and managing exits. They are also busy because most VC firms remain small and boutique-like, with little hierarchy or leverage for the partners themselves. Accordingly, partners usually over-trade aggressively and are pulled in many different directions at the same time. Given that a single partner who has been in the industry a while will probably be serving on eight to ten boards of portfolio companies, up to half that individual's time may well be spent on existing investments, with the remaining time spent on generating new deals, enlarging their personal network and evaluating and executing investment opportunities.

The more established VC firms will receive thousands of business plans and pitches a year. For such organisations (which remain small in absolute terms), triaging these opportunities is almost impossible and only the most prominent or lucky will gain the focus of the firm. This is an environment in which *qualified access* to the VC firm is crucial – both from the perspective of the entrepreneur (to take serendipity out of the equation) and the partner in the VC firm (to be efficient in an already overloaded environment). Indeed, we have already discussed the many benefits to the VC firm of proprietary deal flow in Chapter 5. The best (indeed arguably the only) kind of access for an entrepreneur who wishes to be taken seriously by a VC firm is qualified access through the VC firm's proprietary network.

Research carried out at Tanaka Business School on how entrepreneurs in the biotechnology field identify and contact potential investors has identified three clear groups of entrepreneurs: (1) "Hopeful Achievers" – who have absolutely no idea how to contact a VC and subsequently run in all directions; (2) "Potential Achievers" – business savvy individuals who have some corporate experience and compile a rational hit list of VCs and (3) "Repeat Performers" – those who have done it before and simply open their address books and call the VCs they know directly. Those in group (3) tend to raise more money, faster and on better terms than those in group (2) and (1) respectively. The conclusion is that experience and contacts count in the business of raising capital.

9.2   WHICH QUALIFIED ACCESS ROUTE?

Knowing a senior partner in a VC firm is about as good as it gets in terms of access routes. For the majority of entrepreneurs this is usually not the case, and there are a variety of alternative access routes worth considering.

The starting point is first to identify the sub-set of VC firms that are attractive to the entrepreneur. This is discussed in some detail in Chapter 8 above. Assuming that the entrepreneur has an investor short-list, the next step is to identify the right access point for each

VC on the list. There is no right answer here, but an entrepreneur could do worse than consider the following order of priority:

9.2.1   A personal contact

As mentioned above, a professional or personal relationship with a senior partner in a target VC firm is likely to be the optimal access point, for obvious reasons.

9.2.2   A portfolio company contact

A professional or personal relationship with a member of the senior management team (ideally the CEO) of a company in the target VC's portfolio, in other words an entrepreneur the firm has already backed, and therefore trusts. A VC will usually assume that the CEO of an existing portfolio company will understand what the firm is looking for and will only suggest deals that meet certain quality thresholds. This is an important point, because the CEO's own credibility is on the line in this process. He or she will know that forwarding a poor deal to a VC, perhaps as a favour to a friend, is going to alter the VC's perception of their own judgement, and may damage the relationship in subtle ways.

9.2.3   Industry gurus

A professional or personal relationship with a "heavy-hitter" or "thought leader" in the business sector in which the entrepreneur is active (including business angels), although somewhat less attractive than the above access points, nonetheless will constitute a qualified, endorsed access that will carry weight for a VC (particularly if the VC would like to gain additional "quality time" with the introducer).

9.2.4   Professional advisors

One of the entrepreneur's professional services providers who knows someone at the VC firm may be able to provide the entrepreneur with access. Although of much lesser influence to the VC firm than the above access points, introductions from lawyers, accountants or other advisors count for something and will often be sufficient for the VC firm to have a look at a business opportunity that would otherwise not get any attention.

9.2.5   Professional intermediaries

There are many professional intermediaries in the marketplace (such as corporate finance boutiques and consultancies) touting their skills in helping entrepreneurs raise VC funding, and although their influence can be exaggerated, an introduction managed by an intermediary is still better than a cold call. But only just! Most of their value will be in helping the entrepreneur choose the right VC and making the introduction if the intermediary knows a particular firm or individual well. This is the key point – many intermediaries don't know the VC well and effectively make a cold call on the entrepreneur's behalf. The worse case scenario for an entrepreneur is to use an intermediary who has a poor reputation in the VC industry. If an intermediary has a history of introducing poor deals they immediately lose their shine, and any future introductions they make are branded with the same stamp of poor quality. Such intermediaries do more harm than good for a hopeful entrepreneur and it is extremely important to choose carefully in selecting an intermediary to work with. In fact there are only a small number of professional intermediaries whose introductions cut any ice with VCs (and these probably fall into the lower priority category anyway). Most VCs will strongly prefer early engagement directly with the entrepreneur and management team leading us back to the access routes described at the top of our list.

9.2.6 Cold calling

If all else fails, the entrepreneur can send in a business plan direct to the VC firm. This route demands a good deal of luck, because the plan will have just joined the morass of other plans that hit the desks of VC firms every day. It is largely down to extreme good fortune whether the entrepreneur's plan will get the attention it deserves, or moves directly to the waste paper bin. (In fact there is a story that goes around the industry – most likely a myth – about the VC who automatically tossed 50% of all business plans straight into the waste paper bin, on the basis that business success is partly about luck, and the entrepreneurs who did not go straight into the bin were, by definition, lucky. Those were the people he wanted to back!).

The better approach is for the entrepreneur to ignore the last three options in our list and to focus 100% on generating qualified access points through personal contacts, CEOs and industry gurus.

9.3 GENERATING A QUALIFIED ACCESS POINT

Clearly, the first step in generating a qualified access point is for the entrepreneur to map out his or her own contacts and networks and see where they intersect with the target VC firms. Many people find that identifying qualified access routes into a VC firm is actually easier than first imagined – it just takes a little creativity and persistence. If the initial contact comes easily, or is already in place, it is worth taking the time to upgrade these contact points or perhaps add to them. A VC will often be impressed by an entrepreneur's resourcefulness in creating or upgrading links and it may even improve the prospects of success if the entrepreneur is able to create a number of access points into the target VC firm, which may be operated to complement each other. It is axiomatic that the development of these opportunities will take time and careful planning – and therefore action will have to be undertaken well in advance of the planned contact with the target VC firm.

There are three classic ways in which an access point can either be generated, or upgraded:

9.3.1 Portfolio company access

The entrepreneur should find out which companies in the same or contiguous business sector have been backed in the past by the target VC firms. Ideally, the entrepreneur should focus on those which are already commercially successful, or are particularly highly regarded in their sector. Their details are easy to find, as virtually every VC firm advertises the members of their investment portfolio on their websites.

Once a shortlist has been identified, the entrepreneur can then construct a plan to meet up with the CEOs or other appropriate members of senior management of the businesses on the shortlist. The entry point into these companies could be anything from commercial opportunities, the swapping of information about market developments, or the entrepreneur could even ask about their experience of being backed by a particular VC firm. The senior management of a VC backed company will often make time for a meeting and may well be happy to talk about the development of the marketplace and the relative merits of the entrepreneur's new business. After all, they were in the same position once (probably not so long ago) and will remember what it felt like. They may also see the meeting as an opportunity to expand their own networks, gather information, and increase their standing among their own investors should they recommend a deal that eventually is backed. They should be able to provide the entrepreneur with valuable input about the dynamics of the marketplace, the optimum future direction of the business and the likelihood of whether that business will be attractive as an investment opportunity for the target VC firm: they may even be able to strengthen these attractions with some form or business collaboration. The entrepreneur will also learn a lot more about the target VC firm too – hopefully a "warts and all" viewpoint that will help them to understand whether that firm is the right one or not.

If the entrepreneur can use these meetings to enthuse the individuals present and even turn them into collaborators and promoters of the business, there is no reason why those individuals would not pick up the phone, when the entrepreneur is ready, to effect an introduction to the target VC firm. If it doesn't work out, then it nonetheless should have been a valuable experience for the entrepreneur.

9.3.2   The great and the good

Exactly the same approach can be undertaken with identified movers and shakers in the industry in which the entrepreneur intends to participate. By talking to respected figures in the industry, it is possible to learn a great deal about the strengths and weaknesses of the business plan, and gain a raft of other advantages, including potential angel finance, as well as being better positioned to access the target VC firm.

9.3.3   Personal contacts

The entrepreneur should not underestimate the potential to develop personal contacts with specific partners in the target VC firms. For example, these individuals regularly expose themselves to the "hoi polloi" at conferences and industry events. The entrepreneur could simply pick the most likely events in the industry sector and attend them – ideally speaking at those conferences or participating on panels, to ensure he or she is seen as a thought-leader and innovator: in other words, making sure the VC will feel this is someone they really ought to know. The entrepreneur should make an effort to establish contact with senior members of the VC community at those events – that doesn't mean button-holing them and earnestly pressing a business plan into their hands, it means stimulating them and providing value to them, for example with insights on and understanding of the developing marketplace and new opportunities that may emerge. From that small beginning, the entrepreneur may be able to let the professional relationship develop naturally towards a point when an introduction to the VC is a next step.

It is a subtle psychological point, but if the entrepreneur can get the VC to appear to give chase, rather than the other way around, then he or she stands a much higher chance of success in raising finance. It's like the old adage about men, women and marriage: "he chased her and chased her until at last she caught him".

9.4   COMMUNICATING THE INITIAL MESSAGE

It's certainly true that eventually a VC firm will expect the entrepreneur to develop and deliver a detailed business plan and budget for the investment opportunity. However, it's absolutely the last thing that a VC will want landing on his or her desk at the initiation of contact!

The key to making first contact with a VC is to provide concise and relevant information in the form of a "teaser document" – something halfway between an extended executive summary and a short business plan. This document should be brief and to the point, focusing on the key attributes of the business – the "who, where, why and how". This does not require pages and pages of market analysis, or a descent into arcane technological verbiage. It is a sales pitch – the aim of which is to obtain a first meeting with VC. This requires a very clear idea of the over-arching "big idea" (this will essentially be the entrepreneur's "elevator pitch") and the core strategy of how to take the grand vision and translate it into a real business, with real customers, revenues and ultimately profits. Underpinning those ambitions will be a description of the management team, demonstrating their skills and experience. Structurally, this plan should start with an executive summary that should ideally be less than a page in length (this will be the page copied to other members of the VC's team, if the idea has sufficient promise), built upon a clear, concise and cogent positioning of the company which should not run to more than ten pages. Anything that can't be said within these ten pages isn't worth saying at all at this stage. There is no need to bother with detailed financial projections (especially spread sheets). At this stage, it is important for the entrepreneur to stipulate how much money he or she is looking for and to spell out briefly what this will be used for and how it builds value in the business – in other words how the VC's investment will become more valuable! Remember also that at this stage it is highly unlikely that the teaser document is confidential in the hands of the VC firm, so the entrepreneur shouldn't say too much about his or her idea that is commercially sensitive either.

VCs are extremely busy people, with a large number of business plans crossing their desks every day – so the teaser document has to be concise, well presented and reasonable, allowing the top level information to be extracted very quickly (via the executive summary) and with a sufficient level of follow-up information (via the back-end) that is coherent and well-structured, enabling it to be digested quickly. If the plan is weak in an important area – it should be addressed head-on to show that the entrepreneur is aware of key deficiencies and has thought of how to deal with those issues. This kind of honesty and foresight is very refreshing for VCs to read and indicates to them that the remainder of the plan is more likely to be believable.

9.5   WHAT IS THE VC FIRM LOOKING FOR?

Every VC firm's website will tell an entrepreneur what the firm is looking for, and Part I has already developed some of these themes. Broadly, a VC firm will be looking for at least a majority of the following elements in any investment proposition:

(1) a grade A++ management team – ideally this should be a team which includes individuals who have both demonstrable experience of successfully growing a business in the same sector as the investment proposition and also of being venture-backed previously – in practice this is by far the single most important area of any investment proposition (an old adage attributed to George Doriot, the founding father of the modern VC industry goes something like "better an A grade management team with a B grade technology than a B grade management team with an A grade technology");

(2) a large addressable market which demonstrates either a need or an opportunity that can be met with the relevant business proposition – there are many and various market access strategies and business models, but at the core of any investable proposition must be a market that is sufficiently large to drive meaningful exit valuations based on sensible market share assumptions;

(3) a cogent strategy to attack that market – it is one thing to identify a large market and a need or opportunity, and quite another to solve the problem of how to access that market, engender change, convince customers to buy and defeat the defensive strategies of the market incumbents;

(4) a competitive position in that market that is defensible over the medium term – this requires that the business model is capable of sustained competitive advantage, for example because of a step-change in the market, an ability to lock others out of the market (e.g. by ownership of core intellectual property), by constant innovation, or by embedding the technology into the new market paradigm (e.g. a "hub" licensing strategy);

(5) a product that can be developed quickly, which is likely to work. A VC firm will accept substantial risk in a product (one of the VC industry mantras is that "technology risk is in inverse proportion to market risk" – a VC will inevitably need to swallow one or the other), but will need to understand in real detail the developmental pathway ("forks in the road") and the opportunities for work-arounds at each such fork in the road;

(6) A product for which people will pay a sum sufficient for the company to be profitable – this is often a key area: will customers pay for the product and if so will they pay enough to generate acceptable levels of return on the capital investment required to generate the opportunity?

(7) a business model with low, or manageable (i.e. stepped or gradual) capital intensity, enabling the costs of the business (and hence third party investment) to be increased gradually and in line with declining business or execution risk – VCs tend to be very wary of "if you build it, customers will come" propositions which involve very large up-front development costs, as it lowers IRRs and minimises the ability to manage risk through dynamic capital allocation;

(8) a "plan B" – it is absolutely vital that the management team are able to demonstrate their creativity around "what if?" scenarios, should things not turn out as planned at each key juncture (as is almost certainly going to be the case); and

(9) the potential to exit at full value – as mentioned at many places in this book, it is absolutely vital that the entrepreneur can demonstrate a deliverable medium term exit for investors at full value (and, ideally, one that does not depend exclusively on IPO markets being open), and the pathway and key milestones to that exit.

9.6   CONCLUSION

Gaining access to a VC via a qualified route, and providing the right information in the right way should maximise an entrepreneur's chances of reaching the first true milestone in the process of raising finance – securing that all important first meeting and the opportunity to sell the vision for the business face-to-face. At this point the entrepreneur enters the investment process proper and as we shall see in the next chapter, an entrepreneur's ability to navigate this process is fundamental to a successful outcome.

10
The Investment Process

10.1 INTRODUCTION

From the moment that an entrepreneur engages with a VC firm, he or she is entering an investment process which is significantly, if not exclusively, driven by the VC firm. Understanding the nature of the investment process – what is required by the VC firm from that process, how long it will take and, in particular, any way in which the investment process may be managed and optimised – is essential if the entrepreneur aims to increase the odds of a successful outcome.

The exact steps in the VC investment process have been studied by numerous business school researchers, and although different firms undoubtedly employ a variety of approaches, there is general consensus over the sequence of stages in the process. Following an initial introduction into the investment process, preferably via one of the qualified access routes we

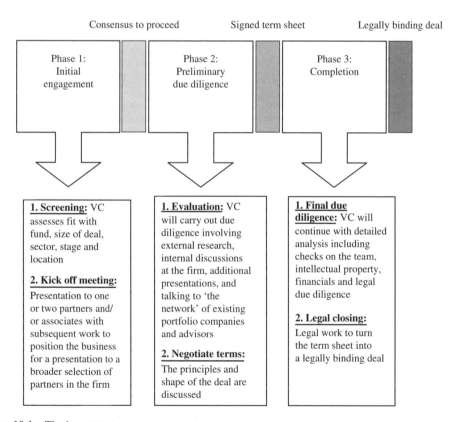

Figure 10.1 The investment process

described above, the first step for the VC is usually a screening stage in which the VC will very quickly assess whether the investment fits with the general strategy of the fund – is it in the right sector, at the right stage of development, in the right geography and importantly is the investment of the right size? At this stage a VC may also consider whether this type of deal fits with the existing fund portfolio and whether there is the potential for a timely exit. Screening can often amount to a quick skim through the business plan, and a "no" decision can be reached in a matter of minutes. If the entrepreneur has entered the investment process via a qualified access route the answers to these questions will hopefully be "yes" (otherwise one would have to question whether the access route was indeed qualified) and the VC will pick up the phone and invite the entrepreneur in for an initial meeting. After the first meeting the investment will pass into a more detailed evaluation or due diligence stage in which it is analysed in more detail. It is important for entrepreneurs to appreciate the difference between the activities of "screening" and "evaluation" because they may find their business plan rejected very quickly simply because it does not fit the VC's fund, and not as a result of a detailed evaluation of the plan. This is important as it means that a rejection from one VC does not mean all VCs will reject it or that it is a poor business idea – it simply does not fit.

Although the investment process will differ slightly from VC firm to VC firm, every investment process may be broken down into three broad phases: initial engagement with the VC firm; due diligence by the VC firm leading to term sheet proposal; and final due diligence leading to a conclusive investment agreement. Within each of these phases are detailed processes, both external (between the VC firm, the entrepreneur and the market-place) and internal (within the VC firm). This chapter seeks to describe the key elements and drivers of each phase of the investment process.

10.2   PHASE ONE – INITIAL ENGAGEMENT WITH THE VC FIRM

Having engineered the right kind of qualified access point into the VC firm, and having provided the right kind of teaser document the first real milestone is the kick-off meeting at which the entrepreneur has a first (and sometimes last) chance to sell the vision for the business to the VC. Everything so far has been focused on getting the entrepreneur to this first meeting and its importance cannot be overstated.

10.2.1   The kick-off meeting

If the access to the VC firm is qualified (see Chapter 9 above), the entrepreneur should be able to follow up relatively quickly with their contact person at the firm, to see if the idea has merit (indeed it may even have been possible to leap-frog the teaser document and move straight to a presentation). If not, then the entrepreneur will have to give the VC a couple of weeks to sit on the document before following up by telephone to gauge the VC's level of interest in the investment opportunity.

From this point on, the VC firm will drive the investment process. This process will be driven at the outset by a single individual (the "deal champion" we referred to in Part I who may or may not be the entrepreneur's contact). The deal champion will be a partner or other senior person in the organisation who will "sponsor" the investment opportunity through the investment process. The entrepreneur may not necessarily meet this individual at the initial meeting, as sometimes these kick-off meetings are farmed out to more junior members of the team, but a senior partner will arrive on the scene pretty quickly thereafter.

Almost certainly, the kick-off meeting will involve the entrepreneur giving a presentation to the sponsoring partner, an associate or even a small group explaining the business and discussing the opportunity in some detail. The presentation should address the key aspects of a business that VCs focus on and, as we described in the previous chapter, should have appeared in the teaser document. This requires that the entrepreneur has taken the teaser document and developed it into a power point or similar electronic presentation, at the same time developing the information to a slightly deeper level (for example, it is at this point that the entrepreneur should drop in high-level financial projections and preliminary conclusions as to capital requirements). The entrepreneur should also have to hand a detailed business plan and initial budget – it may not be needed at this stage but it should be available in case it is requested or if the entrepreneur believes it's the right thing to provide it to the VC.

10.2.2   The initial presentation

The power point (or similar) presentation will be the cornerstone of the first and subsequent meetings with the VCs – it will be the visible manifestation of the entrepreneur, and the business, and it will frame and drive the debate about the business and the investment opportunity at that meeting. The entrepreneur will therefore find that committing a significant amount of time and investment to professionalise that first presentation will pay enormous dividends. In particular:

(1) the structure and coherence of the presentation should be rock solid and there should be a natural flow and logic, creating the impression of an opportunity that "makes sense";
(2) the lay-out of the presentation should be interesting and engaging – using pictures, diagrams and colours (and above all a strong brand for the business) to stimulate the recipients of the presentation: avoid page after page of bog-standard bullet points;
(3) the team which will make the presentation should consider carefully (i) who speaks, (ii) when the hand-over points occur through the presentation and (iii) at which point to break for questions;
(4) the team should practice assiduously their key messages and script and their delivery (and if necessary leave at home team members who find presentations difficult, or even invest in presentation training to hone skills), identify all likely questions from the VCs and pre-agree the answers that will be given.

It is commonly assumed that this level of preparation is a nonsense and of course in an ideal world it would be. However, it remains the case in the real world that the ability of a management team to present their case optimally is a hugely important attribute because VCs are subjected to all manner of presentations in their business activities and therefore "ordinary" presentations risk not standing out, however alluring their underlying premise – why run that risk? Even more critically, the sponsoring partner will also know that the presentation will be the first of many more – not only to raise further capital (perhaps even by IPO) but also on eventual exit. Therefore the management team's ability to present well has long term implications. Worse, the sponsoring partner knows that he or she will shortly (see below) have to introduce the management team more widely to the other partners in the VC firm, again usually by means of a presentation, so even if he or she takes the time and trouble to dig deeper beyond a boring/poor initial presentation, sooner or later the other partners (many of whom will not know much about the sector or technology and so will judge on more superficial issues) will have to form their judgement too, primarily on the back of another company presentation. At this point the entrepreneurial management team will be representing the sponsoring partner as much as themselves, and the VC partner is staking his or her reputation on the presentation. Many VC firms will, however, make the effort to help a management team develop their presentations and presentational skills, if the investment opportunity warrants it.

The second (or perhaps third) presentation to a VC firm will be to a broader selection of partners at the VC firm, and this is the key gating issue for the early part of the VC investment process. It is at this point that the sponsoring partner can obtain the consensus to continue working on the deal or to drop it if there is insufficient "traction" amongst the partners. If the presentation and subsequent discussion does indeed go well, the VC team will swiftly decide to invest the time to progress the investment process to the next stage. If the meeting does not go well, it may be extremely difficult to recover any kind of momentum – there are seldom second chances in the VC world and the VC firm will move swiftly on to the next opportunity.

10.3   PHASE TWO – PRELIMINARY DUE DILIGENCE TO TERM SHEET

10.3.1   Preliminary due diligence

Once the VC firm has decided to progress to the next stage of the investment process, three separate streams of preliminary due diligence work will begin – two external to the VC firm and one internal. During this process, which typically lasts for four to six weeks, the VC will:

(1) continue a dialogue with the management team regarding the business opportunity, including additional meetings, site visits, further presentations and Q&A, collaborative technical due diligence and mutual development of the business plan and budgets. This process will in part be influenced by the work streams emerging out of the activities described below, but in principle will comprise the testing out of the potential working relationship of VC firm and management team, and the recapitulation and development of the business model underlying the investment opportunity;

(2) conduct an external desk top review of some of the key assumptions underlying the investment opportunity. This will largely comprise a market (customer, competitor and opportunity) and top-level technical review, which the VC will carry out by means of interrogation of the firm's proprietary network (which can be carried out swiftly and free of charge) by calling up management teams in the VC firm's portfolio, contacts, thought-leaders, sector consultants, etc and chatting through the key dynamics of the investment opportunity (on a no-names basis where necessary), garnering the maximum sector and market intelligence possible to determine whether the idea could fly, identifying risk factors and potential flaws and/or improvements and then taking such issues back to the management team for further discussion and evolution of the opportunity.

(3) develop internal team discussions within the firm. This will involve extending an evaluation of the investment opportunity to a larger group of people, which may include a wider, or even international sector team, or an evaluation committee of the partners (often termed "investment committee"), or even (particularly if the firm is small) all partners in the firm. Usually the involvement will come about by means of a series of internal meetings for discussion, the circulation of core investment proposition materials (usually the sponsoring partner will bring the issues together in a summary document – the

investment memorandum), and widening the scope of people who have met the management team by conducting one or more additional presentations from the management team to a larger audience of VC firm partners. Once again, ideas, concerns, risk factors and potential flaws and/or improvements regarding the investment opportunity raised in this internal review process are taken back to the management team for further discussion and evolution of the opportunity.

10.3.2   Term sheet negotiations

If the investment opportunity is progressing nicely on these three fronts, the sponsoring partner will start to develop an outline investment term sheet, detailing the terms on which the VC fund would in principle be prepared to invest in the business opportunity. This is a document, fully discussed in Part III below, which is more of a statement of principle than a legally binding agreement but nonetheless serves an extremely valuable purpose in concluding the second phase of the investment process and setting the parameters for the third and final phase. Provided that the sponsoring partner has obtained the required preliminary approval from the other partners in the firm (and the investment committee if there is one), a first draft term sheet will be delivered to the entrepreneur for further discussion.

It is at this point that the entrepreneur will appoint legal advisors, to support the negotiation process and agree an acceptable form of the term sheet. Three distinct areas will usually be covered in a term sheet:

(1) the terms on which funds will be committed or contributed to the investment opportunity, and the arrangements under which the VC fund will hold its investment thereafter;
(2) the work that will needed to be carried out to bring the transaction to a conclusion, invariably comprising the completion of due diligence and preparation of legal documentation, but may include many other conditions precedent specific to the transaction; and
(3) the terms on which the VC firm will have exclusivity in putting the transaction together, and cost-sharing arrangements regarding the transaction – usually, the VC firm will both be granted exclusivity and a significant measure of protection in relation to the expenses it may thereafter incur on progressing the investment opportunity.

Once a term sheet is in agreed form, it will be signed by all parties. The VC firm's investment committee, or other executive body or group, will approve the execution of a term sheet by its VC fund, but that approval will not be the final approval of the deal, which will await the completion of the third phase of the transaction. The process of negotiating a term sheet typically takes some two to three weeks, usually in parallel with the initial due diligence.

A signed term sheet is the apogee of an investment transaction for an entrepreneur and the business – it is the point at which the best possible terms have been secured from the VC firm following what has hopefully been a professional and wise negotiation process. For the entrepreneur, the third phase of the investment transaction will be all about preserving this value through the attritional processes of final due diligence and legal documentation: it is very likely that the terms agreed in principle with the VC firm will not be susceptible to significant improvement during this process (even if additional good news emerges), but it is virtually guaranteed that an adverse event emerging during this process will have the potential to upset the applecart.

10.4   PHASE THREE – FROM TERM SHEET TO COMPLETED INVESTMENT

The third phase of an investment transaction is the most frenetic, most costly, and in some ways also the most risky from the perspective of the entrepreneur. Two streams of work will be undertaken in all circumstances – completion of due diligence and negotiation and finalisation of the legal documentation implementing the term sheet proposals. In addition, where the investment is to be syndicated, the third phase of the investment transaction will see the VC firm conclude the syndication process. Finally, there will invariably be an internal process within the VC firm, leading up to final approval of the transaction, following which the VC fund will be prepared to commit itself unconditionally to the transaction.

10.4.1   Final due diligence

At this point, the VC firm will usually have secured significant protection from the business, or its owners, against costs and expenses incurred by the VC firm on completing its due diligence exercise. This gives the VC firm a relatively free rein to engage consultants and other advisers to assist it in further investigating and eliminating risk in the transaction. The VC firm's due diligence will focus on the following areas:

(1) *the management team* – the VC firm will complete their due diligence on the backgrounds and qualities of the management team, including seeking third party references and feedback;

(2) *marketplace* – all of the work carried out during the preliminary review of the marketplace (product, customers, competition, market access, etc) will be taken to a deeper level, including where necessary by appointing specialised consultants and by conducting detailed interviews with thought-leaders in the marketplace;

(3) *intellectual property* – specialist consultants (e.g. patent lawyers) will be appointed to review the ownership of the underlying intellectual property of the business, which may include an assessment of the robustness of the patents (where the business already has patents or patent applications), or an assessment of the patentability or other appropriate protection mechanism for the intellectual property, and views on the likelihood of actual or future infringements and/or potential work-arounds by third parties – clearly this is an absolutely crucial review for any investment opportunity which is reliant on technological innovation for the competitive advantage;

(4) *financial controls and procedures* – it is clearly vital to a VC firm that a business is properly managed internally and that information generated by the business, particularly financial information, is both produced in a timely fashion and is highly accurate and so the VC firm will appoint accountants to conduct a review of these compliance aspects, as well as to confirm the appropriateness of the business's accounting standards, policies, practices and procedures;

(5) *business model* – the VC firm will progress the business model to a high degree of detail, testing every assumption carefully and seeking to understand every key inflection point in the development of the business and the plan B and C scenarios that could be adopted if the optimal outcome is not achieved;

(6) *investment structure* – the VC firm will spend some time, usually with its international tax advisors, analysing the optimal investment and corporate structure for the investment opportunity, in the light of the five year projected business model which may mandate

preparatory steps to permit the business's group structure to evolve optimally (e.g. internationally) for the development of the business;

(7) *"special situations"* – some business models will require additional, specialised due diligence to be carried out by consultants – for example a life sciences business with products in, or about to enter the clinic might require a Good Clinical Practices analysis, a Good Manufacturing Practices analysis and a general regulatory review of the clinical development strategy in light of the European and US regulatory environments; and

(8) *legal due diligence* – legal due diligence sweeps up all those items of risk not covered by the above specialist or commercial reviews and will be carried out by the VC firm's legal counsel – a typical exercise will cover real property, employment and benefits, tax, intellectual property (focusing on the contracts – e.g. licenses – not the patent strategy), environmental, contracts (customers, suppliers, collaborators, etc), litigation, compliance and anti-trust issues.

As can immediately be seen from the above shopping list, the due diligence process is lengthy – typically four to eight weeks – and can impose greatly on the business itself. It is also potentially very costly unless the exercise is run extremely tightly. It is therefore incumbent on the entrepreneur to identify in detail the exact ambit of the VC firm's due diligence plan, to make sure that the plan itself is reasonable and to ensure that the roll out of this plan is accomplished in a cost and time-efficient manner. This will require extensive planning with the VC firm in advance of the roll-out of the plan, and regular monitoring of and involvement with the various teams involved in the due diligence exercise as it rolls forward.

10.4.2 Legal documentation

As soon as the term sheet is signed, the parties' respective legal counsel will commence the process of drafting, negotiating and finalising the legal documentation that will implement the investment transaction. It is usual for the VC firm's legal counsel to take the lead on drafting and to retain responsibility for the administration of all documentation and the signing and closing process. This is seen as highly attractive for the VC firm because it ensures that, as far as possible, the documentation is in the standard form well-known and trusted by the VC firm – mitigating another obvious area of risk – and it is also the case that a small advantage is gained in negotiation by the side whose counsel controls the documentation process, in terms of making amendments and circulating new drafts.

For this very reason, an entrepreneur may want to take the initial position that his or her counsel will lead the drafting and control the documentation process. This position has real credibility, as the company's counsel may be expected to understand the company's legal position best, there will be a significant amount of corporate compliance work required to implement the proposals (changes to the company's constitutive documents, board meetings, shareholders meetings, etc) and using the same firm for both pieces of work is probably more efficient. It may even be the case that the investment transaction is not the first round of equity funding, but builds on prior angel rounds or even a prior institutional round of funding – if so, then company counsel can be expected to have a major advantage in terms of their knowledge of what's gone before and the way in which the new investment terms can be efficiently integrated into the *status quo*. It will only wash with the VC firm, however, if the legal firm concerned has real credibility in the VC financing marketplace.

On the other hand, unless company counsel is clearly in an advantageous position as described above, using the VC firm's counsel may be expected to reduce the overall costs of the transaction, because the first draft documents are likely to reflect the VC firm's preferred position and drafting style on every point (for example on warranties) – a position and style which will have become very sophisticated and political, because investment transactions are, after all, the core of the VC's business (unlike the company itself). This may not be materially disadvantageous to the entrepreneur, either, if the term sheet is sufficiently detailed to describe adequately each important aspect of the investment transaction – because the drafting style will then be one of nuance, not substance, as it will not be possible for the substance of the documentation to deviate significantly from the term sheet. By contrast, company counsel's inevitably different style is likely to cause the VC firm's counsel to engage in a "battle of the forms" and to seek to make significant cosmetic and semi-cosmetic changes: inevitably leading to materially higher legal costs that are to the benefit of neither the VC firm nor the entrepreneur. In such circumstances, it's usually better to be pragmatic and accept that the VC firm's counsel will lead . . . and retain cash for the benefit of the business, rather than pay it across to law firms for legal costs that have no material benefit to the entrepreneur.

Indeed, there's one situation where it might actually suit the entrepreneur to have the VC firm's counsel running the deal. Towards the end of an investment transaction, the VC firm may be potentially exposed to significant legal fees, either because it is uncovered if it withdraws from the transaction, or because it is taking a significant credit risk on the company (essentially repaying itself out of its own investment), or just simply because it is incredibly unlikely that a VC firm will ever sue a company for recovery of their expenses if a company refuses to pay them. If the entrepreneur has let the VC firm's counsel take the lead and ensured that his or her own legal counsel operate reactively and only seek change where absolutely necessary, the business may find that its exposure to expenses is significantly less (plus it will have developed template documentation for an alternative transaction). This has the beginnings of a small shift in the balance of power which may be reflected in two ways – the VC firm may lose the appetite to fight on certain late amendments to the documentation and they may in addition look favourably on ceding legal work to the company's own counsel at a late stage. Both of these features can be exploited by the entrepreneur for long term benefit.

The key legal documentation will consist of:

(1) *an investment agreement* – detailing the mechanics around the subscription of shares for cash by the VC firm or investment syndicate – this agreement will have a usefulness limited to the longer of the length of the VC firm's capital commitment and the limitation for warranty claims: usually no more than 18 months (for example if the capital contribution is tranched);

(2) *a shareholders agreement* – which will describe all the rights of the different shareholders, both vis à vis the company and amongst each other, which will be expected to last for the duration of the time that the institutions remain shareholders of the company and as such will have many of the characteristics of a joint venture agreement;

(3) *the company by-laws or articles of association* (or similar constitutive document) – which will embed certain core rights and obligations of the shareholders in the very constitution of the company, ensuring maximum enforceability; and

(4) *a registration rights agreement* – under which the company will agree to grant the VC firm or syndicate certain assistance relating to US securities laws.

10.4.3   Syndication

As already discussed in Chapter 5, syndication of investment transactions is an important feature of the VC business model. The advantages and disadvantages for an entrepreneur are discussed in more detail in Chapter 15. If the investment opportunity is to be syndicated, the process will usually begin after, not before, the term sheet is signed. This has significant advantages for all three affected constituencies:

(1) the company does not have the initial phase of the transaction disrupted by the involvement of multiple investing parties (with the attendant cost escalation and delay) but instead settles terms with the lead VC firm around which the syndicate will be formed in an efficient manner thereafter;
(2) the VC firm (essentially, the syndicate lead) gains the opportunity to develop the deal in the way that suits it best, with an eye on eventual syndication for sure, but without having to build consensus on every point, and with maximum ability to extract particular advantage for itself, including in terms of the lion's share of the deal; and
(3) the syndicate members are able to piggy-back on all of the early deal development work carried out by the lead VC firm, saving themselves significant time (and money), receiving notification of an investment opportunity only once the VC firm itself has developed the transaction to the point at which it has received support in principle within the VC firm and agreement on outline terms with the company (and is therefore much more likely to progress to closing).

Accordingly, the VC firm will usually initiate syndication of the equity commitment immediately upon signing the term sheet. Although the initial calls to potential syndicate members will be made by the VC firm and although, as mentioned above, much of the due diligence and legal documentation activity will be led and managed by the VC firm in the capacity of syndicate leader – nonetheless the one certainty is that each syndicate participant, large or small, will want to meet the entrepreneur and his or her management team and ask a few questions... and so the number of business presentations and follow up meetings will proliferate for a short period, while the syndicate takes shape.

10.4.4   Special situations

Many investment transactions will have features which necessitate a parallel stream of activity at this juncture. These parallel streams will invariably be prefigured in the term sheet. Some of the most common include:

(1) a reorganisation of the corporate group structure, so that it is optimised for investment, or business development, or exit – it is not uncommon for the group structure to change at the time of first institutional investment, as the nature of the shareholders and their ambitions change, the growth dynamics of the business may enlarge and the concept of the exit route for the VC firm/syndicate comes to the forefront of the debate;
(2) many investment opportunities involve a business which must first be spun-out from a larger institution and as such as separate work stream will be required to effect the spin-out before the equity financing can occur;
(3) it is not uncommon for the VC firm to require that certain underpinnings to the business model be secured prior to first closing – for example a key customer or supplier contract is achieved; a key collaboration or development agreement is closed; a patent application

is submitted; a first patient is dosed in a clinical trial; working silicon is received back from the fabricator, etc;

(4) sometimes shareholder approvals for the transaction can be sufficiently complex that they require separate planning and organisation in parallel with the investment process (this is particularly true for small public companies); and

(5) investments in certain industries or situations may require regulatory pre-clearance, for example under US national security-based legislation, under US or EU or local anti-competition laws, or in relation to highly regulated industries (e.g. financial services, utilities, telecommunications, transport, gaming, the media, etc).

10.4.5   Internal approvals

While each of the above work streams are continuing, the VC firm (and indeed each separate syndicate member) will continue progressing all required internal approvals within their organisation. Obviously, the final such approval will come only once the work streams are all completed and the final documentation is completed and ready for signature. Only at that point will final approval (or otherwise) be given, enabling the transaction to complete.

10.5   AFTERWARDS

It is not the purpose of this book to describe how to optimise the relationship between the entrepreneur and the VC firm in the many months following completion of the investment process leading up to exit. Suffice to say, however, that by comparison with the task of successfully growing a venture-backed company and creating an exit opportunity for the backers at full value, securing initial equity investment is easy and as such, although receiving VC funding is nonetheless a significant achievement, that process represents not the beginning of the end, not even the end of the beginning, but merely the beginning of the beginning.

11
Preparing for the Investment Process

11.1 INTRODUCTION

Whilst perhaps this chapter ought to have preceded Chapter 10 above, to create chronological accuracy, it is only after an entrepreneur has gained a detailed understanding of the investment process that he or she will be able to gauge how important it is to prepare assiduously for this process well in advance, and to commit sufficient management resource to the process to ensure that it runs smoothly and productively. Such preparation and management is absolutely vital. In fact, most entrepreneurs neither prepare for the onslaught of the investment process, nor manage the process once is has been engaged. Not surprisingly, this all-too-common deficiency often results either in investment transaction failure or, at best, in sub-optimal investment terms – needlessly ratcheting up the risk for the entrepreneur and the business and haemorrhaging value.

This chapter seeks to help the entrepreneur to identify the key areas where preparation and management are important, to enable the entrepreneur to gain the maximum control possible over the investment transaction, to be ahead of the game at every stage and to pre-wire the response at every fork in the road, thereby minimising the potential for transaction failure, or for the VC firm to take unfair advantage of the entrepreneur.

A venture capital financing transaction is similar to a classic sell-side M&A transaction – in other words selling a business. The entrepreneur is selling the business and the VC firm is a buyer – a buyer of a chunk of the equity of the business. Unlike a conventional business sale transaction, however, the "seller" (the entrepreneur) remains in the company and becomes the partner of the "buyer" following completion of the transaction. Nonetheless, many of the techniques and preparation issues that apply in an M&A transaction will in theory apply equally to a venture capital financing transaction.

The fundamentals of effective preparation for any capital-raising exercise include:

(1) an understanding of the optimal timing for the fund-raising transaction;
(2) consideration of the drivers of optimal business valuation;
(3) a review of the likely universe of optimal investors;
(4) effective grooming of the business for entry into the fund-raising transaction;
(5) an early decision as to the right transaction structure to employ; and
(6) detailed logistical planning for the execution phase of the fund-raising transaction.

Each of these issues is discussed below or elsewhere in this book. Suffice to say that preparation is key to a successful outcome.

However, it must of course be recognised that not every aspect of the conventional planning process will be relevant to every venture capital financing – for a seed or very early-stage financing, for example, issues concerning timing of the financing may not be relevant. Above all, in many cases the inevitable dominance of the VC firm in the negotiations may negate the intellectual credibility of an entrepreneur's position on a particular issue and can neuter even the most professional planning! Nonetheless, the entrepreneur will still benefit overall by examining each of the above issues and preparing accordingly. Accordingly, each is considered in greater detail below.

11.2   TIMING

11.2.1   Timing the approach

Timing the approach to VC firms for venture funding is something of an art form. The most common mistake that is made by entrepreneurs is to leave themselves with just enough cash to get though a conventional fund-raising process. This means that if the fund-raising process extends modestly, they deliver themselves up to the VC firm, self-trussed and bound, out of cash and out of options. It's an opportunity the VC firm can't resist. And guess what – even if the business has just enough cash to last through the investment process, it will be extremely clear to the VC that the business is running low on cash towards the end of that process, and so inevitably the bargaining position of the entrepreneur will start to erode markedly as completion of the transaction starts to loom... exactly the worst time for the entrepreneur to become vulnerable.

The best advice for an entrepreneur in this area is to ensure that the business has sufficient cash to last it comfortably through not only an extended fund-raising process but also through a "plan B" scenario as well – for example seeking alternative financing, or a sale of the business, or a reorganisation of the business onto a lower cash-burn model to secure its immediate future outside an external financing. Usually, this means that a business should have at least one year's cash in the bank at the time that the fund-raising is initiated (the take-home message is "the best time to raise money is when you don't need it..."). Of course, not all businesses have this luxury, but it is disappointing to see how often businesses commence the search for venture funding with an out-of-cash date only two quarters away. These businesses will not be masters of their destiny for very long.

11.2.2   Raising enough funds

The other timing issue that is of critical importance in the fund-raising process is to ensure that enough money is raised by the business to carry it through at least its next valuation inflection point (e.g. an event or operational milestone that will effect a step change upwards in the value of the business – markets willing) *and* through a subsequent fund-raising process on the back of that value inflection point being passed. The trick here is to figure out what milestones will increase the value of the business before it is necessary to go out and talk to investors again. Only by answering this question will entrepreneurs be able to raise cash at a higher share price, and hence sell less of the business, than the first time around. Following on the principles of 11.2.1 the take home message here is "better to raise too much money than too little...".

11.3   VALUATION

11.3.1   Introduction to valuation

Apart from timing, the other most significant variable facing the entrepreneur in a fund-raising is the "valuation" (or share price) at which the new money will be raised – in other words how much equity has to be sold to raise the required amount of finance to build the business to the next stage. The key lesson here is that the price of shares in the business, and therefore the total valuation of the business is defined simply when an investor agrees to invest at a certain share price. Investors essentially place a notional value on the company by buying shares at what they believe is the market value for the company. This is very different to the true "value" of the business – perhaps based on calculations of the future profit streams of the business – and is rather a market based valuation based on what people are prepared to pay for shares in the business at that moment in time.

Before we get into further discussions about valuation, it is probably worthwhile mentioning two core (and potentially extremely confusing) concepts routinely used by the VC community in describing valuation of investment opportunities:

Pre-money and post-money valuation – VCs use the term "pre-money valuation" to describe the value of a business before the fund-raising round has completed and "post-money valuation" to describe the value of a business after the fund-raising round has completed. There is no magic in this whatsoever – but an entrepreneur should be conscious of what these two terms actually mean. This is best illustrated by considering the following example:

A VC offers to invest $5 M in return for a 50% stake in the entrepreneurial venture. After some initial wrangling over the percentage, the entrepreneur who currently owns 100% of the equity eventually agrees to the offer.

What is the valuation of the business:

(a) Immediately after the investment?
(b) Immediately before the investment?

The correct answers are the following:

(a) The VC buys 50% of the equity with $5 M in cash, therefore if he or she owns 50% of the shares having spent $5 M, 100% of the shares must (by definition) be worth $10 M. This is the total equity value of the company once the transaction is complete – referred to as the **post-money valuation**.

(b) If 50% of the equity is worth $5 M, the remaining 50% (owned by entrepreneur) must (by definition) be worth $5 M. By investing $5 M, the VC has valued the entrepreneur's stake in the business at $5 M. Prior to the deal, this amounted to 100% of the equity in the business. In other words, the investor has valued the business, immediately prior to the transaction at $5 M. This is referred to as the **pre-money valuation** – the value of the business without the $5 M in cash.

This may seem like an odd notion, and for those with experience in corporate finance this may seem like a very simplistic view. What we have just described is *not* an absolute valuation formula that gives us a true "value" for the business. It is not the net present value (NPV) of the business! It is a *notional value* resulting from a negotiation between founders and investor – it sets the share price at a fixed moment in time.

Entrepreneurs will naturally focus on the pre-money value, which essentially is the valuation at which he or she is selling stock in the company. A VC firm, on the other hand, will focus just as closely on the post-money valuation, as this is the benchmark for any subsequent financing and indeed an exit. If the VC believes that the post-money valuation is too high to generate the minimum required return, then there are only two levers available to get things back on track – reduce the finance required to be injected (i.e. make the business model less capital intensive) or lower the pre-money value (i.e. lower the share price).

Undiluted and fully diluted – The second concept to deal with at this point is the notion of undiluted versus fully diluted valuation. VCs use the concept of "dilution" to describe the existence of an "equity overhang" on the issued share capital. This overhang comprises any rights over unissued share capital, usually in the form of warrants or options over shares (e.g. an all-employee share option programme), but the concept can operate more widely if the circumstances dictate – for example to include equity earn-outs in commercial contracts or any other arrangement under which a person will gain the right to buy, subscribe or receive shares or other securities in the capital of the business. It is absolutely vital that the entrepreneur clarifies the basis on which a valuation is provided, when a VC firm bids to invest in the business – as whether a valuation is "undiluted", "diluted" or "fully diluted" (and what is in or out of the calculation of that concept) can make a material difference to the effective price at which the entrepreneur will be admitting a VC fund to the shareholders' roster. It is an extremely common practice for VCs to quote a fully diluted valuation at entrepreneurs, but to include in that "fully diluted" concept not only all shares and options outstanding at the date of the proposal, but (for example) any increase in the share option programme put in place at the time of the financing (or even planned to be put in place thereafter) – thereby ensuring that the entrepreneur bears the entirety of the dilution created by the enlargement of the option programme (which benefits the VC fund equally), possibly reducing materially the "real" valuation from the entrepreneur's perspective. The only place that this will be evident will be in the capitalisation table which is usually supplied with the term sheet. It is essential that the entrepreneur examines the capitalisation table thoroughly to understand the real effect of the VC's valuation proposals.

Clearly, the above concept of "dilution" is different from the conventional use – which applies to the dilutive impact of a financing upon pre-existing shareholder constituencies, as the issue of new shares reduces the percentage interest of the existing shareholders.

11.3.2   Valuation bases – the entrepreneur's perspective

It is vitally important for an entrepreneur to identify in advance what is the optimal approach to valuation of the business. In some cases, this may be straightforward, with conventional and readily measurable proxies for value being well-established (e.g. multiples of revenues, earnings, EBITDA or free cash flow; asset-based or DCF-based approaches; NPV or addressable market-based approaches, etc), in other cases there may be public company comparables, transaction comparators or intellectually credible proxies for value. It is very important for the entrepreneur to establish a firm basis from which to defend fundamental value.

Once different valuation parameters and bases have been established, the entrepreneur should run the numbers to understand fully which is the optimal way for the business to be valued and where the "flex" and sensitivities lie in determining value under the optimal approach(es). Once this has been determined, the entrepreneur should think carefully through the opportunity to adjust or reprioritise the development of the business in the short-term both to establish and strengthen the credibility of the preferred valuation methodology and to optimise the pre-money valuation that this methodology spits out. This may lead naturally into the kind of strategies discussed in more detail at 11.5 below.

11.3.3   Valuation bases – the VC's perspective

At this stage, the entrepreneur has simply built a beautiful castle in the air. In developing a strategy around valuation methodology, it is vital to remind ourselves that we are talking about a "price" not "value" (whatever the terminology actually used!). In the context of a venture capital financing of an early-stage or developing company, very rarely will the pre-money "price" equate to the actual "value" at which the business could then be sold to a trade buyer in an arm's length transaction, and if a technology start-up ceases trading, it tends to have zero value.

In other words, whatever elaborate construction an entrepreneur may use to develop a valuation approach that looks sane at first blush, the pre-money value of an early-stage business is generally not intrinsic (such that price and value match), but is based on a combination of expectation, assumption and projection (extrapolations of revenue, earnings and net assets models, etc), the amalgamation of a whole series of proxies for value, as well as funding-market dynamics and cycles (which can be extremely volatile) and the potential dilutive impact on the key value-drivers in the business. These are all used by a VC firm to triangulate an offer. Because the process is not about fundamental value or truth, it is absolutely essential that an entrepreneur understands the VC's perspective on valuation, which is based on seeing the pre-money valuation as an "option value" – the price at which the VC is prepared to enter the game. The pricing of that option principally depends on four factors, all of which relate to the fundamental risk profile of the investment opportunity in the business:

(1) The expected exit value for the business, if all goes to plan – this number obviously will vary greatly depending on the underlying business and the nature of its exit potential (we have discussed minimum exit multiples earlier). Exit value assumptions are also fundamentally driven by prevailing market sentiment, which may be very different from market sentiment at the time of the eventual exit, and can also experience enormous volatility over the medium term: one year, exit multiples may be $0.5\times$ earnings, a couple of years later, they may be at $5\times$, influenced by a large number of market, sector, micro- and macro-economic factors.

(2) The amount of capital required to take the company to exit (known as "capital intensity") – the degree of capital intensity in the business model will be a very important factor in developing a valuation for an investment opportunity, because it directly affects the return on investment multiple achievable on the back of the exit assumption (capital out divided by capital in), a core performance metric for VCs in the venture capital marketplace.

(3) Time to exit – once again, this is a function of underlying risk, but also recognises that IRR is another fundamental performance metric for VCs in the venture capital marketplace.

(4) The volatility of the business risk – this is all about pricing the likelihood (or otherwise) that the assumptions taken for exit value, capital intensity and timing turn out to be incorrect.

These four features come together into a sophisticated inter-linked model that seeks to deliver an option value for the investment opportunity. At the same time, the VC firm will be looking at the marketplace (recently completed transactions and deals going on at the time) and benchmarking or validating its approach to what others are doing in the marketplace. That marketplace is extremely dynamic.

Notwithstanding the pseudo nature of much of this "science", it does demonstrate the pain points for VC firms in valuation terms (and hence in terms of the fundamental do'ability of an investment proposition) – high capital intensity in a business model makes it difficult to finance unless the time to exit and exit potential are phenomenal. Equally, long exit horizons are difficult unless the capital intensity is low and the exit potential is extraordinary, etc.

From the entrepreneur's perspective there are also a number of softer issues which determine the eventual valuation of the business. These issues do not form part of a valuation calculation but certainly influence the decision to accept or reject an offer from a VC:

(1) How soon does the entrepreneur need the money? If it is vital to launch the business within six weeks or risk being beaten by the competition then the entrepreneur may well accept a lower valuation and get on with running the venture.

(2) Entrepreneurs may simply draw a line in the sand, for example at 50% and not be prepared to move below this. This figure is usually chosen in the mistaken belief that they will retain control of the business if they hold greater than 50% of the shares, but as we shall see later the classes of shares that VCs purchase usually gives them a great deal of power even as minority shareholders.

(3) The number of VCs competing to invest in the deal. If an entrepreneur is lucky enough to be regarded by VCs as having a "hot deal" to invest in, then the competition to invest is likely to drive the valuation upwards. The converse is that if entrepreneurs have only one interested VC they are in a much weaker negotiating position!

(4) As we have discussed previously, the reputation of VCs may also influence valuation. Entrepreneurs who are particularly keen to have a well known or reputable VC back the business, will accept a valuation that is lower than other offers from less well-known investors. Why would an entrepreneur do this? The answer is that their reputation and experience actually provides value to his or her business.

11.3.4   Why value is important

Given the castles in the air built by entrepreneurs and the pseudo Black/Scholes-type approach of the VC firms, what are the fundamentals that valuation must deliver for both parties? There are five key attributes that valuation *must* deliver in an equity financing:

(1) *Market benchmarks* – the valuation must be benchmarked closely to the marketplace for venture funding in the relevant sector at the relevant time. To a large extent this will be a function of perceptions of exit value and risk volatility at the time, and so may vary materially through corporate finance cycles. We all remember, for example, the extraordinary boom and bust cycles that took us through the late 1990s and into the twenty-first century. The VC operates in this dynamic market and cannot step outside it.

(2) *Meaningful participation* – as discussed in Part I above, much of the game of venture capital depends on the VC fund having a meaningful stake in each investment opportunity in its portfolio, such that it can meaningfully follow its initial commitment by making substantial further investments into success stories and can reap fully the rewards of outperforming investments. Therefore, the pre-money valuation must deliver a meaningful stake to the VC syndicate – which as a rule of thumb should be assumed to be in the 20–33% range (fully diluted) for an early stage investment.

(3) *Reaching the next inflection point* – it is a statement of the obvious that the cash raised by the business must be capable of taking it to the next material value inflection point – through

a milestone of achievement that will give rise to a step change upwards in valuation (market willing). This is where capital intensity comes in, in a very practical way.

(4) *Dilution* – pre-money valuation is the driver of the entrepreneur's ownership interest in the business following the financing and throughout the period when the business has to raise external financing. The dilutive impact of the pre-money valuation to an entrepreneur's percentage ownership is clearly of fundamental importance, as it determines the level of ownership, incentive and reward for him or her. As such, the pre-money valuation must deliver against the expectations of the entrepreneur in these categories, not just immediately, but as projected to the point of exit or, if earlier, financial independence of the business.

(5) *Success reference point* – the pre-money valuation in a single financing transaction is a key reference point along the pathway of the business to independence, which may eventually include the exit of the investment community. In other words, the first financing transaction will provide a key reference point against which to judge future value growth and subsequent follow-on financings will put further markers down, developing a pattern or profile, which will hopefully demonstrate accelerating success in the form of a healthy J-curve. The very existence of a developing J-curve will connote success, and conversely deviations from that J-curve profile will, fairly or unfairly, be taken as evidence of failure or at the best as bumps in the road and may consign a company to a slower development track. It is therefore extremely important that the entrepreneur takes a long term view on valuation, to give the business the best chance of developing this kind of J-curve profile.

11.3.5 Conclusions for an entrepreneur

So, what are the take-aways for an entrepreneur in this highly complex and emotionally charged area? Fundamentally it is that the entrepreneur must hold true to the optimal approach on fundamental value and take the lead in carving out a robust defence of that value, vis à vis external investors. Taking up the mantle of thought leadership in this area will demonstrate practical leadership qualities, as well as drive the development of the underlying business model in a very positive way. At the same time, however, the entrepreneur must remain aware of the unusual perspective of the VC firm, regularly test his or her own valuation assumptions against each element of that perspective and make adjustments (or accept that venture capital will not be available) if too great a disparity emerges between their own perspective and the VC perspective.

Above all the entrepreneur must try to avoid seeing valuation as linked only to a single moment of capital-raising activity, but rather as part of a longer process or continuum that will lead to investment exit or business independence some years down the line, perhaps after three or four financing rounds. In developing the business model for the business, the entrepreneur needs therefore to plan ahead, to understand the entire fund-raising cycle to financial independence as an organic whole, tweaking the different levers of value in the business plan accordingly to try to ensure that venture capital funding will remain available under its self-imposed rules, that the post-money valuation of each round will successively maintain an upward trajectory, and that when the end-game plays out the entrepreneur will have sufficient chips on the table to make all his or her efforts worth the while.

Raising finance in stages is an important aspect of any entrepreneurial financing strategy – for example raising the entire $20 M required to cross the Valley of Death at the outset would be pointless and expensive. Although the business needs $20 M to cross the Valley of Death, it does not need it all up front. Most of the money would sit in the bank for years. That seems fine until you factor in the price of raising that equity finance. Selling 90% of the equity in the business in return for the $20 M is just a waste of the founding equity. Better to raise finance in stages, at increasing share prices to minimise dilution of the founding equity.

In summary, entrepreneurial businesses cross the Valley of Death in stages, not in one great leap. By doing so entrepreneurs are able to secure the finance on better and better terms as they hit milestones and prove they are likely to be a success.

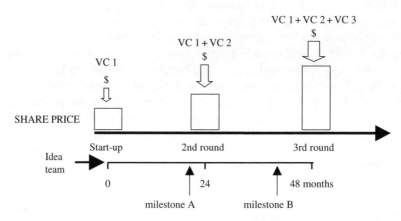

Figure 11.1   Raising finance in stages

The relationship between VC and entrepreneur is a long one. The journey is made more complex by the fact that the relationship usually does not involve just one VC firm. As a venture progresses through several rounds of finance, it usually gathers a growing shareholder base as new investors join. Milestones A and B could, for example, be the production of a first prototype and making a first sale respectively.

11.4   CHOOSING AN INVESTOR

Some tips about how to decide whether venture capital is the right choice, and if so to differentiate between the universe of VC firms, are set out at Chapters 7 and 8.

11.5   GROOMING THE BUSINESS

Grooming the business for a fund-raising transaction is extremely important. "Grooming" is the process of revisiting timing and value assumptions and aligning the business in the short term as closely as possible with those assumptions, to maximise the fund-raising potential inherent in the business. It may involve, in some areas, a decision to prioritise short-term transaction enhancement above longer-term value – and possibly a short-term realignment of the business – which may be a small price to pay in order to lower significantly transaction risk or to increase transaction value.

11.5.1 Revisiting timing and value assumptions

In any event, but particularly where the entrepreneur is engaged in a series of fund-raising events, it will be important as a first step to revisit the preferred valuation philosophy for the business (see 11.3 above) and ask whether the preferred valuation metrics still hold true in the prevailing marketplace and/or whether these metrics still provide the optimal pre-money valuation for the fund-raising.

So, the entrepreneur must ask him or herself what the key value drivers are for the business at the current time – e.g. revenues, earnings, cash flow, customer traction, R&D milestones, etc. Having identified and validated these, he or she must also identify those matters which have to be delivered through the investment transaction and beyond – a period that may run for as long as 12 months (two quarters to close the investment transaction and two quarters of "runway" after closing) and possibly longer if there are investment milestones to be satisfied after the first closing of the investment transaction. For example, these matters might be stable revenue/earnings growth, quarter on quarter, a gradual progression to cash flow break-even status, successful completion of a set of R&D milestones, or a ramp-up of new customer signings.

Once those issues have been revisited, identified and validated, the entrepreneur should give careful consideration to any and all means to optimise achievement of these milestones (and hence the pre-money value for the business in the upcoming venture financing). In particular, he or she should consider prioritising the short-term business strategy around the key valuation metrics, consider any new strategies that are accretive in the short-term and seek to remedy any areas of perceived weakness in value terms. Everything else is of tertiary importance. It is important to realise that this does not involve a wholesale de-railing of the business's ongoing activities, merely a slight re-jigging of priorities and elimination of "hostages to fortune" to clear the path in the short-term to the fund-raising milestone. For example, if the key valuation driver is signing a first customer, then clearly in the short term the assets of the business should be prioritised around that goal, perhaps de-prioritising other "nice to have" add-ons that will not materially drive valuation but certainly focusing efforts on a narrower range of customer traction points to give the company the maximum potential to deliver the value-add in the shorter term. If the valuation drivers are revenues or earnings, then the short-term focus may be on accelerating revenue traction, enhancing operating margins and removing all non essential costs (e.g. R&D, advertising, etc). Above all, the key short-term operational risks should be identified and evaluated and then steps should be taken to prioritise their neutralisation.

Sometimes it may even be best to ensure that the business doesn't "over deliver" in the run-up to a financing opportunity (as opposed to afterwards), for example if it is believed that this will not attract a premium valuation for the business beyond a particular point (for example closing more than one customer ceases to have the same impact as closing the first customer), or if *failure* to deliver on particular initiatives might actually be very harmful to valuation (in other words the risk/reward profile of the strategy, in the context of the fund-raising does not make the failure risk of a more ambitious strategy worth the while). Indeed, there may even be circumstances where it is possible to refine a business's strategic focus in the run-up to an investment transaction (for example, by focusing on a narrower set of short-term objectives) and at the same time increase the potential of the business to deliver future upside outside valuation (e.g. satisfying investment milestones, demonstrating continued business success, etc) by bringing through those strategic priorities that were soft-pedalled in the run-up to the investment transaction (for example switching back on the more ambitious sales and marketing undertaking that had been shrunk back previously). Pacing the business in line with short-term financing objectives may pay long term dividends, potentially facilitating a higher pre-money valuation and a track record going forward of under-promising and over-delivering.

11.5.2   Ensuring management stability

One of the key areas where entrepreneurs fall down in planning for an investment transaction is in the area of day to day management. In essence, it is extremely common for a management team to materially under-estimate (or simply be unable to respond to) the amount of time that will be required of them to initiate and close a round of venture capital financing. By the time that they have all been sucked into the process and discover that it is all but impossible to continue their normal roles in the business, it may be too late to do much about it. This can be hugely damaging to the business, both in terms of its immediate prospects in the investment transaction and also longer term.

For example, a business which is running hard to raise venture funding may find that it ends up being punished severely for missing the very targets that underpin its pre-money valuation (for example a particular step in R&D, or self-imposed revenue targets) just because management either took their eye off the ball or the business simply ran into the sand, while they were bringing the equity finance in. This may severely damage the pre-money valuation of the company at the time of the financing or even derail the financing altogether (there are always many reasons for a VC firm to say no to a deal...). Worse, even if the business doesn't suffer an adverse event that is immediately apparent, it may be that the loss of a significant period of development (e.g. six months out of the market) proves to be materially adverse to the long-term prospects of the business – by reducing the competitiveness of the business or the time to market of the first product, etc, proving to be even more detrimental to the business over the medium term.

It is therefore absolutely vital that the entrepreneur plans conservatively to deal with the disruption to the management of the business caused by the investment process, to minimise any adverse effects. In doing so, the following key issues must be considered:

(1) *Who will be required in the fund-raising process?* The entrepreneur will need to map out the persons who are likely to be drawn into the investment process and the degree to which their participation in that process will be required.

(2) *Who has relevant experience?* It may be very beneficial to the investment process if it is led or guided by someone who has had recent experience of the process, and who can therefore plan efficiently for the commitment of resources, etc and drive the process professionally. This is one reason why the support of an incumbent VC firm in subsequent financing rounds is so crucial. The entrepreneur should consider specialist internal support, where the transaction is extremely complex, but usually this expertise can be acquired through the business's legal counsel or accountants.

(3) *Who will "mind the shop"?* The entrepreneur must confirm the key operational milestones that absolutely need to be achieved (i) to meet the business's short-term objectives, (ii) to meet the assumptions underpinning the pre-money valuation for the investment transaction, and (iii) to maintain the medium-term momentum and strategic fundamentals of the business. Having identified these milestones and the pathway and timing exigencies

to achieve them, the entrepreneur must then identify the minimum resourcing needs of the business. This may lead to a decision to reinforce second-tier management, to ring-fence members of existing senior management from the investment transaction, or to hire interim management – or some other creative solution.

(4) *Is value dependent on an individual?* It is quite common for early-stage companies to be highly dependent operationally on one or two key individuals, the departure of whom could be highly damaging for the business. If this is the case, the entrepreneur (who is likely to be one such individual) must examine ways in which such persons can be "locked in" during the run-up to investment and their interests aligned with the drivers of a high pre-money valuation and indeed the closing of the fund-raising process itself. In other words, it may be time to unlock the equity in the business a little to create an alignment of interests.

The answers to these questions will drive a series of operational imperatives, which will need to be put in place and bedded down well in advance of the commencement of the investment process. The benefits for the business will be enormous.

11.5.3 Spring cleaning

Every business preparing to go through a financing transaction should undergo a thorough "spring clean" operationally, financially, legally and administratively, to ensure that the business is fully prepared for what lies ahead and is "shining like a new pin" when the VC firm and its cohorts enter the building. This spring cleaning should cover the following areas:

(1) *The sales pipeline* – the entrepreneur should review the sales pipeline over the next 12 months, to make sure that the projected pipeline is robust and that promotional literature and PR are closely aligned with the ambitions of the company and above all are fully deliverable in the context of a new and powerful shareholder coming on board.

(2) *Fixed assets and inventory* – in the case of a business with significant assets and a balance sheet that is material to valuation, the entrepreneur should review the valuation and usefulness of the business's assets (among other things, the production of an assets register might be nice) and review the level of provisions and inventory.

(3) *Creditors and debtors* – the entrepreneur should review aging debtors and creditors and generally look at bad debt provisioning, to ensure that the treatment is fully justifiable to an incoming investor, and take active steps to shorten the average debtor days for the business.

(4) *Cash management* – we have already demonstrated how important cash management may be to the business as it works through the investment process, and clearly the entrepreneur must review the level and sufficiency of the business's cash resources.

(5) *Financial controls and procedures* – as this is an area that will be specifically due diligenced by the VC firm, it is absolutely essential that the business prepares in advance by making sure that its budgeting and reporting processes are professionally designed and implemented, that the financial information thrown out by these processes is timely, accurate, consistent and high quality and that the company has in place sensible controls and procedures to guard against fraud and to notify senior management promptly of any issue of concern. In addition, the management team should carefully review the accounting policies and practice of the business – particularly in areas of potential concern (e.g. revenue recognition, capitalisation of costs, etc) – making sure to review these

policies and practices against current industry standards. Because VC firms will often insist on US GAAP reporting (or at least a reconciliation to US GAAP) going forward following investment, it may be valuable to form a view on the potential impact of such approach.

(6) *Taxation* – the entrepreneur should review the compliance pattern of the business as regards tax compliance – particularly in sensitive areas such as VAT, R&D credits, tax reliefs, tax losses and intra-group transfer pricing.

(7) *Legal issues* – the entrepreneur should engage internal or external legal resources to carry out a wide-ranging review of the business's compliance from a legal perspective and to effect all necessary remedial action. This will include a review of (i) all core intellectual property and its ownership and protection, (ii) all employment, service and consultancy agreements, as well as incentive programmes (iii) title deeds and leases, etc to all major assets, (iv) any actual or potential disputes, (v) all material contracts (customers, suppliers, collaborators, etc), and (vi) as relevant, any regulatory, compliance or anti-trust issues, etc. The legal review should at the same time coalesce the business's document management systems into a form that supports a data room for the forthcoming investment process.

It will be immediately obvious that much of the above spring cleaning amounts essentially to prefiguring the VC firm's own commercial, legal and financial due diligence, to ensure that the business has conducted its own mini due diligence in advance of the "main event", giving the management team the chance to identify and ideally fix any problems or areas of weakness, or at least be aware of those issues that can't be fixed and to have a coherent and professional response on them if and when they are spotted by the VC firm. By doing this, the management team will ensure that the VC firm's due diligence process itself will be efficient and well-managed, will hold no fears and that even potential problem areas will burnish the reputation of management, because they will be able to respond to questions about these areas in a well-prepared and capable way.

11.6   TRANSACTION STRUCTURE

We have mentioned at Chapter 10 above that a VC firm will explore in detail during the investment process whether the prevailing structure of the business is optimised for the VC fund's own investment and for the future direction and growth potential of the business. This may mandate a reorganisation of the group structure of the business contemporaneously with the closing of the investment transaction.

This exercise is much less likely to occur in relation to US investments than those outside the US. Within the US, the use of a US corporation (often a Delaware corporation) is very much the norm, although the use of limited liability partnerships ("LLPs") and limited liability companies ("LLCs") is increasing. Outside the US, however, an entrepreneur may find that several issues are driving the thinking of the VC firm in making its evaluation including the following:

(1) *Corporate finance considerations* – the VC firm will recognise that its own investment in the business opportunity will in all likelihood not be the last and that it is vital strategically to maintain a corporate structure that maximises the potential for the business to raise finance in the future – and therefore that a corporate structure that will appeal to the widest possible investor constituency will be the best. Where is the world's largest investor community? The answer is the US and so many VC firms start from the premise that,

sooner rather than later, the corporate structure of their investments should be optimised for investment by US institutions and, for good or ill, this often means a US corporation – the entity best known and trusted by US investors. However, over the last several years, US institutions have become more sanguine about investing in non-US entities and a wider group of corporate entities are now often considered as not unattractive to US corporations, including Bermudian, UK, Irish, Swiss, Dutch, Israeli, French, Scandinavian and German companies. But safety first still demands a US corporation. Of course, if the business proposition appeals to a core investment constituency closer to home – for example a European or "Eurovision" constituency, then a local solution in corporate structure terms may remain attractive.

(2) *M&A considerations* – In a similar vein to the sub-paragraph above, the VC firm will, upon investment, immediately turn its attention to the exit opportunities for its investment. This may focus on IPO (in which event the considerations above will apply in corporate structure terms) but it is at least as probable, if not more so, that the exit route will be by trade sale. Accordingly, the VC firms will want to ensure that the corporate structure will appeal to the widest possible community of buyers. Where is the world's largest buyer community? The US again. Rather like their investor counterparts, it is believed that most US buyers prefer to buy a US corporation, an entity that they know and trust. There is a slight wrinkle here, because there are some circumstances (usually associated with asset-heavy businesses) where a US buyer may benefit materially from purchasing a non-US business. Equally, it may be that the likely buyers come from a more diverse community geographically, or are not prejudiced against non-US corporations, in which event the corporate structure may be very different.

(3) *Legal system considerations* – when a VC comes to implement an investment transaction, it aims to put in place an extremely sophisticated and inter-connected set of terms and conditions (prefigured in the term sheet) which are intended to operate dynamically throughout the lifetime of the VC fund's investment in the business. It is essential that the governing law that applies to and implements these terms and conditions is able to accommodate their philosophy fully and to support the natural process of their evolution and development over the years in a manner which allows change to be accomplished quickly and for the interests of all important constituencies to be properly protected. Once again, the US legal system comes up trumps in this area, largely because the venture capital business model was evolved in the US and therefore it is not unexpected that the legal environment should have grown to support the key terms and conditions inherent in that model (although at this point it is worth recognising the extraordinary achievements of the US legal system in consciously developing a modern, commercially-oriented and high quality system of corporate and commercial laws which has been used to support entrepreneurialism in the US for many years and which is increasingly exported around the world for the same purpose). However, in the face of competition from the US legal system, many other legal systems have developed similarly flexible and high quality legal systems. For example, many common law-based legal systems (e.g. the UK, Ireland, Bermuda, Germany, Jersey and the Cayman Islands) are not dissimilar in many respects to the US system and offer a high quality product for private equity investment that enables the core philosophies of the VC model to be implemented flexibly and robustly. Legislators in other countries (e.g. Switzerland, Holland, the Scandinavian region and France) have also recently made deliberate and high quality strides to bring their offerings up to date in this respect, too.

(4) *Taxation considerations* – One of the primary considerations in the development of any corporate structure is to ensure that taxation levels on corporate earnings are as low as possible. In the case of a venture capital investment, there is an additional concern to ensure that there are no adverse tax consequences to an investor in making its investment into a particular structure. As such, a VC firm will be keen to ensure that the corporate structure minimises corporate taxation in the medium term and takes full advantage of all available credits, grants and rebates that may apply to young, high growth businesses – in each case without prejudicing the position of the investors in the business. This is an extremely complex area and it would take many more pages to go one level deeper into this topic. It is possible to construct clever and elaborate international group structures to benefit from arbitraging international tax rules, although it goes without saying that any such structure must have commercial and strategic legitimacy that goes well beyond their attraction in purely tax terms. Suffice to say also that the wiser VC firms will strongly support simpler corporate structures, even at the cost of paying slightly more corporation taxes in the longer term, because of the cost and disruption to management time (as well as the risk of challenge) that can be created by complex tax-sparing structures. At the end of the day, for an early-stage business that may be expected to generate tax losses for many years, tax optimisation falls into the "nice to have" category and moving into a position where corporation tax is payable can be seen as the type of problem which the business would love to have! Nonetheless, provided a simple solution can be found, the net present value of significant tax savings or efficiencies can greatly increase the value of a business.

(5) *Regulatory considerations* – An additional item in constructing a corporate structure will be regulatory considerations, which may require a presence in a particular jurisdiction. A good example of this is the life sciences sector, where the prospective developer of a drug product through clinical trials must have a presence in the US for FDA IND approval and in the EU for EMEA IND approval.

(6) *Employee incentive considerations* – It will be important that the corporate structure enables the key value-drivers of the business (the staff) to be adequately incentivised in a tax efficient manner. There are several jurisdictions that strongly embrace and encourage employee share ownership programmes (e.g. the US, the UK and France) and the prevailing corporate structure should be examined closely to ensure that it is and will remain competitive in terms of enabling the entrepreneur to offer compelling packages to attract the best talent needed to drive the business on to greater things.

(7) *Practical considerations* – By far the most influential consideration in determining the optimal corporate structure will always be the ambitions of the business, as elucidated in the business plan. This will pre-determine where the weight of operations will be over the next five years or more and where senior management members are likely to be located. This reality is inescapable and although the arrival of a VC firm on the scene will undoubtedly accelerate and catalyse this development process and heighten corporate ambition (particularly in terms of attacking new markets – for example moving from Europe to the US), the fundamental driver to the corporate structure will largely be where management operations are to be located. Around that central plank will be built the tax and corporate finance strategy.

It can be immediately seen that this area is extremely complex, with different considerations pulling in different directions, such that there will seldom be an obvious "best" solution – all will depend on the relative weight given to each consideration in the particular circumstances, which itself will depend largely on the proclivities of the owners of the business. Although the entrepreneur will of course have a vested interest in optimising the corporate structure, it is probably best at this point for him or her to remain tightly focused on growing a successful business operationally, and let the debate on corporate structure be led by the VC firm.

11.7   TRANSACTION LOGISTICS

Having identified timing and valuation issues and optimised the business for the fund-raising process, there are still a number of logistical and administrative issues that will need to be thought about and prepared for. Some of these are discussed below.

11.7.1   Confidentiality

One important logistical matter is confidentiality. When an entrepreneur embarks on a fund-raising transaction, he or she will have to decide when issues of confidentiality begin to loom large and at which point it becomes necessary to seek formal protection. For example, it will be hard to deliver an informative initial presentation to a VC firm and let the Q&A thereafter develop naturally at the kick-off meeting, if the entrepreneur feels that there's a risk that important business secrets are going to be discussed in an environment where those secrets may not be fully protected.

It is at this point that we encounter a potentially unreasonable stance taken by the VC community towards investment opportunities – VC firms generally don't sign confidentiality agreements (known in the trade as "confis" or "NDAs"). Why do they take this stance? Two reasons – firstly, it's because in general (particularly if the industry acts together, as they do on this point) they can get away with it, as entrepreneurs desperate for finance will often take the risk of confidentiality breach as the price of access, and secondly, it's because a tidal wave of confidential information washes over them continuously in the form of raw ideas and concepts – and VC firms are (quite naturally) completely unable to respond to the challenge of "tagging and bagging" this information stream. There are two reasons why most entrepreneurs become sanguine about this state of affairs – firstly, they recognise that in most cases the "confidential information" that they envisage sharing with a VC firm is merely a raw business concept or idea, of itself only of passing value – the real value is in allying the idea with execution. Secondly, they realise that a VC firm has better things to do with its time that to seek to misuse or appropriate confidential information provided to them – they're simply too busy – and even it they had the time, energy and inclination to do so, their market reputations would be destroyed rapidly if they followed that approach.

So, while it is always worth pressing for a signed confidentiality agreement before the kick-off meeting, an entrepreneur should be prepared for this initiative to fail. There are, however, two cases where it is more important to obtain a full confidentiality agreement: where it is envisaged that confidential information will be passed by the VC to third parties for review (e.g. consultants and other due diligence advisers – which will occur in the final due diligence phase of the investment process) and where the particular information being furnished goes beyond mere ideas or concepts, business plans, etc and into the underlying raw proprietary technology, especially if the intellectual property has not been fully protected.

Even if a confidentiality letter is obtained however, great care should be taken, as these agreements are never "bullet-proof" – the main protection is the tool of injunctive relief through the courts (a court order enjoining the addressee from disclosing information), which can only be used where a pending breach of confidentiality is discovered. Once a breach of confidence has occurred, most remedies under a confidentiality letter amount to "shutting the stable door after the horse has bolted". Therefore, it is pragmatic to assume that confidentiality will be breached in any event and to protect oneself as far as possible in a practical matter by:

(1) graduating disclosure as much as possible, keeping back the most confidential or sensitive materials until the last possible moment, so that as far as possible the entrepreneur only provides information that he or she can afford to lose control of, or (at least) where increasing confidentiality risk is offset by decreased transaction risk;

(2) ensuring that all recipients of information, direct and indirect, are covered by formal or informal confidentiality obligations, so that every use of the information throughout the investment process is covered;

(3) making sure that all materials delivered to the VC firm (or any other person in the investment process) are appropriately marked "confidential" (on every page) and are legended with wording that seeks to impose usual confidentiality obligations on the recipient – this alone will probably be enough to dissuade the VC (and third parties) from temptation in borderline cases;

(4) ensuring that not only the confidential information itself, but all materials generated from, using or extracting the confidential information (e.g. notes, presentations, models, reports, etc) are included within the obligation of confidentiality and prohibition on mis-use;

(5) attempting as far as possible to prevent unauthorised copying, amendment or manipulation of the information provided – the most rigorous approach is to locate key materials in a tightly controlled data room at the business site and to refuse to circulate copies to the VC firm or third parties, but a softer approach (perhaps for less confidential materials) might be to number all documents, colour the confidentiality restrictions (to inhibit copying) and record the distribution of all materials; and

(6) requiring recovery or destruction of all materials, should the transaction fail.

11.7.2   Non-solicitation

It is amazing how often solicitation issues are missed by entrepreneurs, even where they are dogged on confidentiality issues. There is clearly a tight relationship between the business's employees and issues of confidentiality – in essence all of the know-how of the business will be located in the employees themselves and all innovation will be derived and developed (and sometimes even owned) by such persons. Stating the obvious, in large part the employees of the business will in many cases *be* the business – the key assets of the business will turn off the lights and go home every night.

It is therefore extremely important that any confidentiality obligations are supported by non-solicitation covenants from the VC firm (covering both itself and its portfolio companies) and any other persons involved in the investment process who might find it attractive to poach employees of the business away.

11.7.3   Preparing for site visits

It is inevitable that during the investment process many people will visit the business premises – ranging from the VC firm and its syndicate partners, to the many and various professional advisers engaged by the VC firm as part of the due diligence process. It is vital that the entrepreneur is prepared for this influx of nosy people and has responded appropriately to a number of prosaic issues that this throws up. For example:

(1) Simply as a matter of people-flow, the business will need to be able to accommodate these visits, which are likely to include a series of on-site meetings which could be disruptive to the business.

(2) It is important either that these meetings can be conducted confidentially (such that staff don't worry about the sudden influx of strangers) or that the staff are fully apprised of what is going on and how they can support the process. In any event, the meetings themselves will have to be capable of being conducted in a private and confidential manner.

(3) Although the VC industry is full of tongue-in-cheek advice to drive twice around the car park to check if the cars are parked neatly, it really does matter that the business premises are clean and well-organised when third parties attend on-site: it gives a reinforcing impression of control and professionalism if the business environment is clean, tidy and well laid-out – conversely a working environment that suffers from clutter, dirt and unprofessional behaviour can be very detrimental to the way that the business is perceived by the VC firm.

11.7.4   Poison pills

Finally, the entrepreneur should consider any "poison pills" that may lurk – being external items that may threaten the completion of the investment transaction, usually being items that will come to have a disproportionate power when it comes to closing the investment transaction. For example:

(1) Is there a vitally important customer, supplier or collaborator of the business? If so, then it may be necessary to engage the customer, supplier or collaborator at an early stage to gauge their support of the investment transaction and to ensure that they are "on message" and fully attuned to what lies ahead and the part they will play in the process.

(2) Are there any issues in the company's material contracts that might be artificially triggered by the investment transaction? This question will form part of the fundamental legal review. For example, an investment transaction may give rise to a technical "change of control" in the business, either because the incoming investment syndicate gains control (as defined) or because an existing shareholder loses control (even though no new shareholder gains control) – and such a change of control may terminate or invalidate supplier, customer, collaborator, financial, regulatory or even real property agreements or arrangements. If that is the case, then the entrepreneur will have to develop work plans to deal with these relationships and circumstances, in order to recover, or even improve the position.

(3) Is a shareholder unwilling to be diluted? One of the features of a venture financing is that the entrepreneur will almost certainly require the consent of at least a majority of each class of shares currently issued in the company, as well as potentially other categories of security holder (such as banks, holders of debt or mezzanine or derivative securities,

holders or options or warrants) depending on the terms on which they hold their securities. Some of these constituencies may not be too pleased at the thought of a VC firm joining the fray – for example because it may spell the end of their effective control of the business, or they may believe that the transaction is overly-dilutive to their own investment in the business. It is absolutely essential that the entrepreneur identifies these constituencies at an early stage in the transaction and develops a strategy to deal with any questions, concerns, or even resistance from any constituency which could disrupt, damage or even derail the fund-raising transaction.

11.8 CONCLUSION

Part II of this book has explored in detail the VC business model, and how the entrepreneur engages with and navigates the investment process in an attempt not only to raise finance but raise it on favourable terms and with the entrepreneur-VC relationship intact. A well structured deal is the solid foundation for a productive ongoing dialogue between the two in the quest to build a successful company.

Creating the right kind of deal, however, presents many challenges and establishing the correct valuation can be the very first sticking point. Ultimately, the only way to deal with this issue, as with many others, is to understand the market. The advice to entrepreneurs must be "talk to lots of VCs, and listen to what they have to say". Consistent messages will start to appear – such as the range of valuations and typical deal terms used in the market at that time. An overview of market sentiment is extremely valuable in this field and the best way to get that is to listen!

Negotiations with investors are not all about extracting the best financial deal at any cost. This is not a purely financial transaction. There is a strong human element involved in VC deals, as equity investors in the new venture become business partners. They are buying a share of the business, and entrepreneurs and VCs are going to have to work together in the interests of the business for a number of years until a suitable exit event enables them to sell their stakes.

This is a key point to remember in conducting negotiations, and in Part III of this book we will explore in detail the nature of the venture capital deal. We will walk through the terms of a typical VC term sheet in a blow by blow account of the clauses: what they mean, why they are there and how entrepreneurs and VCs can use them to their advantage.

Part III
The VC Term Sheet

12
Introduction to Term Sheets

12.1 PURPOSE

Parts I and II of this book introduced the reader to the business of venture capital and to the investment process followed by a VC firm. Part III aims to examine in detail the terms that a VC firm will introduce to an entrepreneur in a term sheet at the end of the first phase of an investment transaction, as these terms represent the embodiment of the venture capital business model – the extrapolation of all of the different features of that business model into a set of dynamics that must be operated consistently, investment by investment, across a portfolio in order to generate the VC fund portfolio dynamics demanded by the competitive VC marketplace.

Although the ability of the entrepreneur to negotiate freely in this environment may in many cases be severely restricted, because of the relative negotiating power of each constituency, nonetheless Part III aims to identify the philosophy lying behind each component of the terms and conditions of an investment proposal, to explore the "flex" in each of these terms and conditions, to suggest compromises, work-arounds and solutions that may accommodate the wishes and needs of both parties in the relevant circumstances, and to put the entrepreneur on his or her guard against common areas where value might be needlessly given away or the seeds of future disaster might be sown.

12.2 WHAT IS A TERM SHEET?

A term sheet is the document which is developed as part of the second phase of an investment transaction (see Part II above), detailing the essential components of the investment transaction proposed by the VC firm. A term sheet may be extremely short, perhaps as little as two pages, or it may be much longer, sometimes running to some 20 pages or more: the example provided below is relatively long-winded, to aid discussion, but represents a reasonable example of a more detailed term sheet. For other examples, see the websites of the National Venture Capital Association (www.nvca.org) and the British Venture Capital Association (www.bvca.co.uk), each of which carry standard term sheets. The term sheet will invariably be drafted initially by the VC firm and delivered to the entrepreneur for comment and discussion (this is the case even if the term sheet is signed when initially delivered to the entrepreneur – appearing to be final and non-negotiable). Whether it is short or long, the term sheet will invariably cover three key areas:

(1) the terms on which funds will be committed or contributed to the investment opportunity by the VC fund, and the arrangements under which the VC fund will hold its interest in the company once it has invested;
(2) the work that will need to be carried out to bring the transaction to conclusion, comprising the completion of due diligence and preparation of legal documentation, but potentially also the satisfaction of other conditions precedent specific to the transaction; and

(3) the terms on which the VC firm will have exclusivity in putting the transaction together and cost-sharing arrangements regarding the transaction. Usually, the VC firm will both be granted exclusivity in the deal for a defined period and a significant measure of protection in relation to the expenses it may thereafter incur on progressing the investment opportunity.

Usually, only certain parts of the term sheet will be expressed to be legally binding (see below) but the whole of the term sheet will be morally binding – in other words the market reputation of the VC firm will be riding on it progressing the investment transaction in accordance with the provisions of the agreed term sheet (in the absence of any material change in circumstances, of course) and the entrepreneur too will be expected to support the "in-principle deal" as the investment transaction moves into its third and final completion phase. Indeed, in some jurisdictions (for example many Continental European jurisdictions) the term sheet will actually create a legally enforceable duty of good faith negotiation on the signatories, requiring them to act reasonably, fairly and expeditiously on the basis of the terms set out in the term sheet in progressing the investment transaction from term sheet to completed transaction and giving rise to legal liability to the injured party should a party breach such duties (for example by seeking changes to the investment terms of an arbitrary or unreasonable nature). Other jurisdictions may in certain circumstances even treat a term sheet as binding, whatever the express intentions of the parties and so great care should be taken by both the VC firm and the entrepreneur to ensure that the term sheet has exactly the legal qualities that they intend to create.

12.3   WHY HAVE TERM SHEETS AT ALL?

The term sheet has become an essential gating item for the investment process. There are three reasons for this:

12.3.1   Risk management

A term sheet enables all parties connected with the investment transaction to manage their risk appropriately, at a time when the continuation of the transaction will involve significant time commitment and cost escalation (particularly the due diligence and legal documentation processes). The term sheet identifies the way forward to a level of detail that enables all parties to be confident that all of the important points concerning the proposed investment transaction are fully understood and agreed. The consequence of this is that the parties should be able to progress from a position of negotiation and potential confrontation in the formation of an agreed term sheet to a more collaborative approach in the final phase of the investment process, which by then should involve only the formalisation and finalisation of an agreed transaction. To this extent, a term sheet both simplifies and accelerates the remaining transaction processes, ensuring lower overall transaction costs.

In the absence of a term sheet, both the VC firm and the entrepreneur would find themselves progressing the investment transaction in an environment of considerable uncertainty, while at the same time incurring significant costs, both in terms of their own time and the considerable fees and expenses of professional advisers. In practice, because of the constrained resources that an entrepreneur will usually be subject to, a less structured approach will usually be greatly to his or her disadvantage.

To this extent, therefore, the term sheet has much less relevance and impact if it does not contain enough detail for all parties to be happy that all material items have been covered adequately. Entrepreneurs should be extremely wary of short-form term sheets which fail to deal with key issues in sufficient detail, because they may be merely a means for the VC firm to seize exclusivity in the investment opportunity without providing an appropriate level of comfort to the entrepreneur on the terms of investment (as the "price" for ceding exclusivity). A multitude of sins can be hidden in such superficial documents, particularly when they refer to "standard market practice" or otherwise leave open issues of relevance to the entrepreneur. It is invariably better to flush out these issues in sufficient detail before agreeing to a term sheet, because they will only be more difficult and more expensive to resolve in the document- ation phase of the transaction. Clearly, it is also possible to veer in the other direction and find oneself effectively pre-negotiating the final, legally binding documentation as opposed to formulating key philosophies in key areas, and if the term sheet becomes too long or too detailed, then some of its purpose may be lost and the transaction may lose momentum. But better too long than too short, from the perspective of the entrepreneur.

12.3.2   VC policy

From the VC's perspective, a term sheet is a very useful tool to drive consistency in deal-making throughout its organisation. A sophisticated VC firm will generally use a standardised term sheet to promote and support an integrated organisation of high standards (particularly if it operates multi-regionally or internationally) and to enable the firm to develop and deliver consistency on "house policy" across the different sectors and geographies in which the firm invests. In addition, the term sheet itself will promote awareness inside the VC firm about the critical issues in any venture financing, in particular the potential "flex" that the VC firm may allow on any point – enabling the VC firm's staff to operate openly, confidently, fairly and flexibly in their engagement with investment opportunities.

12.3.3   Deal syndication

A term sheet also facilitates the deal "syndication" process. "Syndication" describes the process by which the VC firm will bring in other investors into the investment transaction, around its own "cornerstone" investment commitment (see 5.3.5 above and Chapter 15 below). Indeed the completion and signing of the term sheet triggers the process by which the VC firm will seek syndicate partners by making contact with likely investors, pitching the opportunity to them and sending them the signed term sheet, with a view to securing an investment participation from other putative syndicate members around the agreed deal terms. As we have discussed earlier, the process of syndication is valuable both to the VC firm (e.g. in validating its views on the investment, spreading risk and sharing transaction costs) and the entrepreneur (e.g. in diluting the single block of control otherwise held by a single VC firm, extending the network, skills and experience available to the business, and providing for a greater pool for follow-on financings by the business).

In the absence of a term sheet, the process of syndication would have to involve every potential syndicate member being closely involved in the formation of the deal terms, probably at the stage of documentation of the deal. As such, each member of the syndicate, together with the professional advisers, would have to become intimately involved in the transaction, greatly increasing the overall cost of the transaction and the time required to agree, document and close it. In addition, without a template term sheet to focus on, free rein is permitted for each investor to add its own "gloss" to the investment terms from its own particular position, potentially greatly increasing the complexity of the deal terms and the likelihood of an arbitrary or unattractive outcome (particularly for the entrepreneur, as he or she is likely to suffer from a "lowest common denominator" outcome, as each syndicate member takes it in turn to hold out on important points). Armed with a signed term sheet, however, a VC firm can more easily market the deal in a consistent fashion, minimising further change to the deal terms and ensuring that potential syndicate members can both sign up to the transaction very quickly, as well as rely on the VC firm's existing professional advisers in developing the documentation required to close the transaction and, often, "piggy back" on the lead VC firm's due diligence.

12.4   WHAT HAPPENS TO A TERM SHEET?

Once a term sheet has been signed, it operates in large part as a template for the implementation of the investment transaction. Item by item, the term sheet will facilitate the drafting of the core legal documents implementing the investment transaction, which will usually comprise an investment agreement (containing the VC firm's investment commitment and the conditions to investment), a shareholders agreement and the company's articles of association (together containing the arrangements under which the shareholders in the company will interact going forward), and other specialist arrangements such as registration rights agreements, management rights agreements, share option plans, etc (which implement specialist features of the term sheet and which will be explained later).

Once again, the term sheet will serve its purpose well if it enables the legal counsel tasked with documenting the investment transaction to focus exclusively on "writing it down", as opposed to taking negotiating positions on key aspects of the transaction documentation.

12.5   METHODOLOGY OF PART III

Part III of this book will work through an example of a term sheet and describe the key provisions in that term sheet, to enable entrepreneurs to understand in detail each component in a standard term sheet. The discussion is based around common law legal concepts that will resonate generally with, for example, US, UK and Irish law, but may be alien to some civil law (e.g. Continental European) jurisdictions where different tools may be applied to achieve the same end result. From time to time the more unusual of these alternative approaches will be mentioned.

The key terms identified are grouped into the following broad themes, chapter by chapter: Business Valuation; Investment Structure; Syndication; Investment Milestones; Corporate Governance; Equity Participation; Share Incentives; Share Vesting; Pre-emption Rights on Securities Issues; Anti-dilution Rights; Provisions Relating to Share Transfers; and Deal Management Terms.

Each chapter below will commence with example wording of the kind of provisions found in a typical term sheet, explaining the meaning and purpose of the particular clauses and go on to analyse why the VC firm will ask for such provisions, the entrepreneur's negotiating position vis à vis the issues and areas to watch out for. Some chapters will break this wording down into several pieces and a range of choices for ease of discussing individual sub-elements. Part III is therefore designed to be an extremely practical and granular guide to term sheet formation, which an entrepreneur (or VC) can use as a reference guide when negotiating.

Set out below is a template term sheet in full, from which key paragraphs are drawn and discussed in greater detail in each subsequent chapter of Part III. It is not necessary to read Part III "in sequence" and indeed Part III is designed so that the reader can skip between chapters to focus on different aspects of the term sheet, some additional choices of wording in specific areas are provided and explained in Part III below.

PRO FORMA TERM SHEET

Simon Barnes Esq
Chief Executive Officer
SilicoLabs Limited
Greendale Business Park
Greendale

Date: [ ] 20[ ]

STRICTLY PRIVATE & CONFIDENTIAL
SUBJECT TO CONTRACT

Dear Simon

$10 000 000 Series A Equity Financing Round (the "Financing"), led by Trojan Horse Ventures

Following on from the extensive inter-action between the Company and our team at Trojan Horse Ventures ("Trojan Horse") and the completion of our initial due diligence, I am very happy to confirm that we remain very interested in investing in SilicoLabs Limited (the "Company"). Accordingly, we have pleasure in setting out below the principal terms on which we would currently be willing to progress the Financing.

As I am sure you will fully understand, at this stage of the potential transaction, the terms set out below have to remain subject to contract and are also provided to you subject to (i) completion of our due diligence, which may raise issues of concern, (ii) the approval of the Financing by Trojan Horse's investment committee, who may require changes to the investment terms or even fail to approve Trojan Horse's investment and (iii) formation of a satisfactory investment syndicate, to complete the aggregate financing commitments required to complete the Financing around Trojan Horse's cornerstone commitment.

If you have any questions concerning any of the terms set out below, please do not hesitate to contact me or my colleague Randy Avalon.

1   Transaction Size and Valuation[1]

We understand that you are hoping to raise $20 000 000 to fund the next stage of the development of the Company. However, for the reasons we have shared with you during our initial due diligence, we continue to believe that $10 000 000 is a more suitable ambition for the Company, in light of its immediate business objectives and the state of the private equity funding markets and we therefore propose a Financing at this aggregate level.

We have shared valuation information with you during the initial stages of this potential transaction. We confirm that we are willing to implement the Financing on the basis of a fully-diluted pre-money valuation for the Company of $20 000 000, which we believe represents a very attractive valuation for the Company at this time in the prevailing marketplace. This valuation assumes that there is established immediately prior to the Financing an employee stock option programme over 20% of the fully-diluted post-Financing equity share capital, of which not less than one half of the programme remains unallocated on completion of the Financing.

---

[1] Chapter 13 – Business Valuation.

We enclose with this term sheet a detailed capitalisation table spread sheet which illustrates the pre-Financing and post-Financing share capital position of the Company (as well as all intermediate steps), based on the terms set out herein, which we trust clarifies the impact of the above valuation and below investment terms.

2   Group Structure[2]

It is very important that we take the opportunity afforded by this transaction to review the structure of the Company's business and operations in the context of the Financing, future financing requirements and the medium term plans for the development of the business. This review should ensure that the Company's structure is optimised for future financing transactions and the growth and internationalisation of its business activities.

Following a preliminary review, we believe that the current group structure should be reorganised (in as tax-efficient a manner as possible) prior to Initial Completion of the Financing by (i) creating a new Delaware holding company for the business and operations (ii) relocating the group headquarters to the United States, (iii) developing a US sales and marketing activity in the United States and (iv) relocating research and development activities to the Republic of Ireland. The terms set out herein assume that such a reorganisation (the "Reorganisation") is completed prior to the first draw down under the Financing.

We are happy to work with you to test the conclusions of our preliminary review and to agree an optimal group structure as described above, going forward from Initial Completion of the Financing.

3   Investment Commitments and Syndication[3]

Trojan Horse believes that it is optimal for the Company to receive investment commitments from a small number of high quality investors, as opposed to a single large and potentially dominant investor, or a very large number of smaller investors of indeterminate quality and commitment. Trojan Horse believes that it has the networks and track record to deliver the optimal investment commitment arrangements for the Company.

Trojan Horse is therefore willing to lead an investment syndicate (the "Syndicate") which will invest $10 000 000 in aggregate in the Company, subject to the pre-completion group reorganisation specified in paragraph 2 above. Trojan Horse itself is willing to invest up to $5 000 000 in the Company as a cornerstone investment around which the Syndicate will be formed. Trojan Horse will use all reasonable efforts to procure investment commitments from future Syndicate members to provide the balance of the Financing not otherwise provided by Trojan Horse.

Trojan Horse may in its absolute discretion elect to increase or decrease its aggregate investment commitment to the Company, depending on the level of Syndicate demand. Members of the Syndicate proposed by Trojan Horse must be pre-approved by the Company but allocations of investment commitments among the Syndicate members will be made in the absolute discretion of Trojan Horse.

In recognition of Trojan Horse's services as cornerstone investor and Syndicate leader as described above, the Company will grant Trojan Horse warrants to subscribe 200 000 new A Shares (with the rights as described below), exercisable in whole or in part at any time in the five years following the completion of the Financing, at the discretion of Trojan Horse, at a subscription price of $1 per A Share.

All investment contributions by the Syndicate to the Company will be made pro rata to their investment commitments.

[2] Chapter 14 – Investment Structure.
[3] Chapter 15 – Syndication.

4   Completion of the Financing & Investment Milestones[4]

The Financing will take place in two phases, the first phase being unconditional and the second phase being conditioned upon the achievement of certain key business development steps by the Company.

On completion of the Financing, tentatively targeted for a date not later than six weeks following the date of this term sheet, ("Initial Completion") the Syndicate will contribute $5 000 000 in aggregate to the Company by way of the subscription of 5 000 000 new A Ordinary Shares ("A Shares"), at $1 per A Share. This initial investment contribution will be unconditional.

In the event that the Company completes the business development milestones described below (the "Milestones") by the first anniversary of Initial Completion, the Syndicate will contribute a further $5 000 000 in aggregate to the Company by way of the subscription of a further 5 000 000 new A Shares at $1 per A Share. The relevant Milestones are:

- *An agreed level of progress in the development of the product prototype;*
- *Recruitment of an agreed Vice President of Sales and Marketing; and*
- *Enrolment of the Company's first customer for a paid trial.*

Trojan Horse, on behalf of the Syndicate, may agree to defer or delay any Milestone deadline or even to waive any Milestone, in its absolute discretion. Whether or not any or all of the Milestones have been completed at any time, Trojan Horse may, on behalf of the Syndicate, at any time after Initial Completion decide to accelerate the contribution of all or any part of the further $5 000 000 investment commitment described above, in which event the Company will be obliged to issue new A Shares as described above as though the Milestones had been satisfied in full.

5   Corporate Governance Matters[5]

The Company will be expected to adopt a public company-style board structure on Initial Completion and to adopt best practice in all material areas of corporate governance and internal controls and procedures, in an effort to bring significant additional value to management decision-making through the medium of the non-executive directors and to provide the Company with a solid base from which to grow its business and operations and to evolve into a successful international business of substance.

5.1   Composition of the Board

The board of directors (the "Board") will be composed of a maximum of seven persons, of which a majority will always be non-executive directors. On Initial Completion, the Board will be composed of three executive directors (the Chief Executive Officer, the Chief Financial Officer and the Chief Technical Officer) and four non-executive directors (a Trojan Horse representative, a Syndicate representative, an independent non-executive director and an independent non-executive Chairman).

Both Trojan Horse and the Syndicate as a whole will have the right to nominate one non-executive director to the Board, and both Trojan Horse and each other Syndicate member committing more than $1 000 000 in aggregate to the Financing will have the right to send a non-voting observer to Board meetings. The two independent directors will be nominated by Board agreement, by means of a bare majority to include the agreement of the Trojan Horse and the Syndicate board representatives.

If the founder of the Company, Simon Barnes, shall for any reason cease to hold a position conferring automatic representation on the Board (Chief Executive Officer, Chief Financial Officer or Chief Technical Officer), then for so long as he holds at least 10% of the fully diluted equity share capital of the Company, he will have the personal right to nominate one non-executive director to the Board. In such circumstances, Trojan Horse may stipulate in its absolute discretion that either the Chief Financial

---

[4] Chapter 16 – Investment Milestones.
[5] Chapter 17 – Corporate Governance.

Officer or the Chief Technical Officer will cease to serve on the Board. The Company will pay the non-executive directors their reasonable travel and accommodation expenses to attend Board meetings and will provide directors & officers' insurance cover to a level and on terms satisfactory to Trojan Horse in respect of such persons' activities.

5.2   Timing of Board Meetings and Board Governance

Board meetings will be held at least six times a year at intervals of not more than ten weeks and the quorum will be any two directors, to include the representative of either Trojan Horse or the Syndicate. However, in order to ensure that non-attendance by Trojan Horse's or the Syndicate's representatives does not prejudice the deliberation of important Company business, in the event that a quorum is not present at the time that any Board meeting is due to start, the business (and only the business) of that meeting may, in the discretion of the attending Board members, be adjourned to a date not less than a week later and no minimum quorum requirements will apply to the adjourned Board meeting. Board meetings may take place in person, by telephone or by webcast.

On Initial Completion, the Company will establish:

(1) a remuneration committee of the Board, to be composed exclusively of the Trojan Horse and Syndicate representatives and an independent non-executive director, with full delegated authority to determine the remuneration of all directors and senior employees and the creation, amendment and issue of any and all employee incentive programmes;

(2) an audit committee of the Board, to be composed exclusively of the Trojan Horse and Syndicate representatives and an independent non-executive director, with full delegated authority to supervise the Company's budget, financial planning and audit functions and the Company's financial controls, reporting and procedures; and

(3) a nominations committee of the Board, to be composed exclusively of the Trojan Horse and Syndicate representatives and the Chairman, with full delegated authority to nominate members of the Board.

In the event that any director becomes aware of an opportunity for the Company or its business to be sold or floated on a stock exchange, the Board shall forthwith establish an exit committee of the Board, to be composed exclusively of the Trojan Horse and Syndicate representatives and an independent non-executive director, with full delegated authority to supervise and approve the sale or flotation process.

Certain matters which are likely to have a significant effect on the Company's business will require prior consideration by and the approval of the Board by simple majority, the majority to include, in the case of a sub-set of those matters, the Trojan Horse and Syndicate board representatives. Such matters will include:

- *Approval of the annual budget and business plan;*
- *Establishment and operation of pension or employee benefit plans;*
- *Delegation of Board powers to committees (except as described above);*
- *Changes to accounting policies and practices, or the auditors;*
- *Appointment or removal of any director, officer or senior employee (except pursuant to nomination rights);*
- *Contracts with senior employees or material contracts;*
- *Formulation of key corporate policies (risk management, health & safety, insurance);*
- *Grant of any security interest, indemnity or guarantee;*
- *Material capital expenditure outside the Company's annual budget;*
- *Non-ordinary course of business activities;*
- *Material litigation; and*
- *Public announcements.*

5.3   Shareholder Veto Matters

The Company must obtain the consent of three quarters of the Syndicate (by number of shares held) before it can do certain things which would be likely to be material in the context of the Company's business, including:

- *Changes to the share capital;*
- *Changes to the Company's articles of association;*
- *Distributions by or any winding-up or dissolution of the Company;*
- *Major disposals, acquisitions, mergers or joint ventures;*
- *Material transactions with related parties;*
- *Material changes in the nature of the business;*
- *Borrowings, sale & lease backs, factoring or hire purchase arrangements;*
- *Grants of any security interest, indemnity or guarantee;*
- *Sale or flotation of the Company or its business.*

5.4   Shareholder Information Rights

The Syndicate will have the right to receive, in a format and to a level of detail agreed in advance with Trojan Horse: (i) unaudited monthly management accounts within 30 days of the month end, (ii) audited annual accounts within 90 days of the year end and (iii) an annual business plan and budget within 30 days prior to the next year. In addition, the Syndicate will have the right to receive all information provided to the members of the board, and any and all other material general information concerning the Company. The Company will also deliver any information reasonably requested by, allow inspection of properties by, financial records by, and discuss its business and finances with, the Syndicate from time to time.

6   Equity Capital Structure[6]

We propose that the existing capital structure be left intact, with management and senior employees continuing to hold Ordinary Shares and the Syndicate investing in the A Shares. It is proposed that the relative share rights will be as described below:

6.1   Voting Rights

The Ordinary Shares and the A Shares will vote together as a single class of shares, except where the A Shares have specific veto or other voting rights, where they will vote as a separate class. However, in order to ensure that only individuals with an ongoing interest in the Company continue to have the right to vote their shares at meetings of the Company, any director, officer or employee of the Company will cease to be entitled to any voting rights upon ceasing to remain a director, officer or employee of the Company for any reason, provided that this provision shall not apply to Simon Barnes' shareholding unless and until he comes to hold less than 10% of the Company's issued equity share capital.

6.2   Company Distribution Rights

<u>*Dividend Rights:*</u> *To compensate for the time value of the monies committed to the Company by the Syndicate, the A Shares will accrue a preferential dividend at the rate of 10% per annum on the A Share issue price and on all accrued but unpaid dividends, compounding annually (the "Special Dividend").*

---

[6] Chapter 18 – Equity Participation.

No dividend will be declared or paid on any of the Company's shares until the accrued Special Dividend has been paid on the A Shares. The accrued Special Dividend will:

 (i) *become payable to A Shareholders immediately prior to completion of the liquidation or sale of the Company or its business, in priority to payments to any other shareholders; and*
(ii) *be applied automatically in the subscription of new Ordinary Shares at the same time and on the same basis as the A Shares, if and when they are converted into Ordinary Shares (as described below).*

Except for the preferential dividend rights of the A Shares, no class of shares will have any entitlement to a pre-determined dividend and all shares will have equal rights in terms of dividend entitlement.

Capital Distributions: In relation to any proposed payment by the Company to its shareholders (for example on the solvent liquidation of the Company or in a distribution by the Company of the net proceeds of the sale of its business or any of its material assets), the A Shareholders will first be entitled to receive an amount equal to two times the aggregate subscription price paid up on their A Shares, plus any accrued but unpaid Special Dividend, in priority to any payment to be made to the Ordinary Shareholders. After such a preferential payment entitlement has been satisfied in full, any residue left over will be shared among the Ordinary Shareholders and the A Shareholders equally (pro rata to shareholdings and on an as-if-converted basis with regard to the A Shares). However, if on a notional allocation of the proposed payment equally between all shareholders (pro rata to shareholdings and on an as-if-converted basis with regard to the A Shares) the A Shareholders would receive an aggregate amount greater than six times the aggregate subscription price for the A Shares, then the A Share preferential payment entitlement shall drop away and instead the proposed payment will be made equally between all shareholders (pro rata to shareholdings and on an as-if-converted basis with regard to the A Shares).

6.3   Sale Proceeds Re-allocation Rights

In the event that:

 (i) *the issued share capital of the Company is acquired by a bona fide third party purchaser (the "Sale"); or*
(ii) *the Company merges with another entity in a manner which means that following the merger the shareholders of the Company in aggregate no longer control the merged or surviving entity (a "Merger");*

then the cash and/or non-cash consideration payable/deliverable to the Company's shareholders under the Sale, or the cash and/or non-cash consideration payable/deliverable to (or remaining held by) the Company's shareholders in the merged or surviving entity pursuant to the Merger (in each case, the "Consideration") will be allocated as follows: the A Shareholders will first be entitled to receive an amount of the Consideration valued at the aggregate subscription price paid up on their A Shares, plus any accrued but unpaid Special Dividend in priority to any allocation to be made to the Ordinary Shareholders. After such a preferential allocation has been satisfied in full, any remaining Consideration left over will be allocated among the Ordinary Shareholders and the A Shareholders equally (pro rata to shareholdings and on an as-if-converted basis with regard to the A Shares). However, if on a notional allocation of the Consideration equally between all shareholders (pro rata to shareholdings and on an as-if-converted basis with regard to the A Shares) the A Shareholders would be allocated Consideration to an aggregate value greater than six times the aggregate subscription price for the A Shares, then the A Share preferential allocation shall drop away and instead the allocation of the Consideration will be made equally between all shareholders (pro rata to shareholdings and on an as-if-converted basis with regard to the A Shares).
    The above will not be triggered by a group reorganisation.

6.4   Buy-back or Redemption Rights

Trojan Horse and the other Syndicate members require guaranteed liquidity in their investment in the Company after a reasonable period of time. We believe that an appropriate period for the Company to develop its business plans to an appropriate exit (IPO or sale) at full value is five years following Initial Completion. Therefore, we propose that A Shareholders may elect to require the Company to buy-back or to redeem the A Shares in three equal tranches at any time following the fifth anniversary of the issue of such shares or at any time following the occurrence of an Event of Default, in each case at their initial subscription price plus the accrued Special Dividend.

For such purposes "Event of Default" includes: (i) failure by the Company to make any required buy-back or redemption payment; (ii) breach by the Company of any of the terms of any of the Financing documentation or the terms of any indebtedness; or (iii) the occurrence of a classic insolvency or default event relating to the Company – such as the onset of insolvency, bankruptcy or receivership, the acceleration of third party obligations, an assignment for the benefit of creditors, or an unsatisfied judgment in excess of an agreed amount.

Should the Company be in default of its buy-back or redemption obligations for any reason, the unpaid amount will accrue interest at the rate of 10% per annum, compounded quarterly, and if the default continues for more than 30 days, the Syndicate will become entitled to elect a majority of the Board, to facilitate the work-out of their buy-back or redemption rights.

6.5   Conversion Rights

It is proposed that the A Shareholders will generally have an unfettered right to convert their A Shares into Ordinary Shares in their absolute discretion, enabling them to take advantage of specific liquidity opportunities such as an IPO. In addition, it is proposed that the Company will have the ability to force the A Shareholders to convert their A Shares into Ordinary Shares, where an IPO meets certain minimum criteria, in order for the Company to be able to implement such an IPO even in the face of minority A Shareholder objections (the Syndicate generally having the power of veto over any IPO, however).

Accordingly, A Shareholders will have the right voluntarily to convert their A Shares at any time into Ordinary Shares in the capital of the Company. The conversion ratio will initially be one for one, but will be adjusted to reflect any share capital reorganisation effected by the Company (e.g. share split, consolidation, etc) in the future or arising pursuant to the operation of anti-dilution rights hereunder (see below).

In the event of a Qualifying Stock Exchange Flotation of the Company or with the consent of 75% of the A Shareholders (by shares held), the A Shares will automatically convert into Ordinary Shares on the basis of the then-prevailing conversion ratio. "Qualifying Stock Exchange Flotation" means an underwritten public offering on a leading international stock exchange (to include the NYSE, Nasdaq or the London Stock Exchange) with net proceeds to the Company or its shareholders of at least $100 million at a price per share that is equal to or greater than five times the A Share subscription price (taking into account any share capital reorganisation prior to flotation).

6.6   A Shareholder IPO Ratchet

An IPO of the Company represents a liquidity event following which the preferential rights of the A Shareholders will in general disappear and accordingly is regarded as an exit event by Trojan Horse. Accordingly, we propose that sale preference provisions be applied in the event of an IPO.

To the extent that the value of the Ordinary Shares (based on the underwritten offer price) at the time of a flotation by the Company is less than five times the highest subscription price for an A Share (as adjusted to reflect any share capital reorganisation effected by the Company or the operation of anti-dilution rights), the conversion ratio applicable to the A Shares shall be adjusted so that A Shares will convert into such number of Ordinary Shares as shall have a value equal to four times the highest subscription price of the A Shares (as so adjusted), fractional entitlements being rounded upwards.

7   Share Ownership and Incentives

Trojan Horse supports appropriate share ownership and incentive programmes designed to align the interests of financial investors in the Company with the interests of those members of senior management whose efforts will have a material impact on the development of the Company's business and to provide all other employees with a modest equity participation in the Company for which they work.

7.1   Employee Share Ownership Plans[7]

Immediately prior to Initial Completion, an all-employee share option plan (the "ESOP") will be created comprising options over 20% of the fully diluted post-Financing equity share capital, of which half will be awarded to the senior management and employees of the Company on a basis to be agreed with Trojan Horse and the remainder will be unallocated and available for issue in the future. All options will be over Ordinary Shares and will vest over a four year period from grant; 25% after one year and the remainder on a quarterly, straight line basis over the following three years. Future option grants will only take place with the approval of the Company's remuneration committee or Trojan Horse. Should an employee leave employment for any reason, all unvested options will lapse and he will be obliged to exercise his vested options within 90 days, or they too will lapse.

7.2   Vesting of Management Equity[8]

The Ordinary Shares held by the members of senior management will be subject to vesting over the four years following Initial Completion: 25% after one year and the remainder on a quarterly, straight line basis over the following three years, such that in the event of the termination of a manager's employment for any reason (except as described below), the unvested part of the manager's Ordinary Shares will be compulsorily acquired by the Company for $1 in aggregate and the remaining Ordinary Shares may (at the option of the Company) be purchased at their aggregate market value at the time of departure.

In the event that the manager's employment with the Company is terminated either by virtue of the manager's death or permanent disability, or by the Company without reasonable cause, the standard vesting period applicable to the shares held by such person shall be halved such that the number of vested shares on departure shall be doubled (up to the ceiling of the number of shares held by such person). In the event that the manager's employment with the Company is terminated by reason of the manager's fraud or gross negligence, or the commission by the manager of a criminal offence, the standard vesting period applicable to the shares held by such person shall be doubled such that the number of vested shares on departure shall be halved.

In the event of an Exit Event, the standard vesting period applicable to the Ordinary Shares held by senior management immediately prior to the Exit Event shall be halved such that the number of vested shares shall be doubled (up to the ceiling of the number of Ordinary Shares held by any such person).

7.3   Management Ratchet

Trojan Horse recognises the vital importance of the management team in developing the Company's business and in seeking and executing an exit for the Syndicate on their investment. We therefore propose that if there is a Sale, Merger or IPO (an "Exit Event") that delivers a certain threshold level of return to the A Shareholders, Ordinary Shareholders will be remunerated by means of a value shift to them on exit. Accordingly, in the event that an Exit Event delivers a five times multiple cash on cash return to the A Shareholders and an Internal Rate of Return of not less than 40% per annum, A Shares will be repurchased by the Company at their par value in accordance with the following formula: [ ].

---

[7] Chapter 19 – Share Incentives.
[8] Chapter 20 – Share Vesting.

8   Share Issues

8.1   Pre-emption over Securities Issues[9]

As described above, the Syndicate will maintain an absolute veto over any securities offerings. However, even where the Syndicate approves the circumstances of a securities offering, except for very limited circumstances, it is vitally important that the Company does not undertake securities issues following the Initial Financing without offering the Syndicate an opportunity to participate in any such issue. Accordingly, if the Company proposes to issue any securities, it must offer the Syndicate the opportunity (but not the obligation) to purchase such securities on a pro rata basis and on the same terms as are proposed for the issue to third parties and such that following such securities issue, the Investors have the opportunity to maintain their percentage interest in the fully diluted issued share capital of the Company.

To the extent that any member of the Syndicate fails to take up all or any part of its pre-emption rights in any instance (the "Pre-emption Shortfall"), other Syndicate members who have taken up their pre-emptive rights in full will have additional pre-emption rights to take up all or any part of the Pre-emption Shortfall and if more than one Syndicate member expresses such interest, then pro rata between them.

The above provisions will not apply to the following securities issues: (i) Ordinary Shares issued as a consequence of the exercise of options under the ESOP, (ii) securities offered or sold to third parties pursuant to an IPO, (iii) Ordinary Shares issued on the conversion of the A Shares, (iv) securities issued pursuant to any group reorganisation, Merger or Sale, (v) securities issued as consideration for the acquisition by the Company of third party assets, or other business or entity, and (vi) securities issued to third parties as part of a commercial collaboration or other arms length commercial undertaking.

8.2   Anti-Dilution Rights[10]

In accordance with standard market practice for investment transactions of this type, Trojan Horse requires a measure of price protection. In the event that equity securities are issued by the Company at a subscription price lower than the price per share paid by the Syndicate for the A Shares in the Financing (as adjusted to take account of any subsequent capital reorganisation) (a "Down Round"), the Company will be required either (i) to issue further A Shares to each A Shareholder by way of bonus, capitalisation or other issue for negligible consideration, (ii) to adjust the A Share conversion rights or (iii) to issue options or warrants over A Shares to the A Shareholders, exercisable for negligible consideration (the "Down Round Adjustment") so that each Investor is compensated for the dilution resulting from the Down Round on a full ratchet basis such that, irrespective of the size of the Down Round, the average subscription price per A Share for each A Shareholder following the Down Round Adjustment is equal to the price per share at which the Down Round took place.

However, the above anti-dilution protection shall only apply to the extent that the relevant Syndicate member has participated in the Down Round at least pro rata to his shareholding in the Company and in the event that any Syndicate member does not comply with such requirement, he will lose any anti-dilution rights attaching to the same proportion of his A Shares. In addition, anti-dilution rights will not apply to the following securities issues: (i) Ordinary Shares issued as a consequence of the exercise of options under the ESOP, (ii) securities offered or sold to third parties pursuant to an IPO, (iii) Ordinary Shares issued on the conversion of the A Shares, (iv) securities issued pursuant to any group reorganisation, Merger or Sale, (v) securities issued as consideration for the acquisition by the Company of third party assets, or other business or entity, and (vi) securities issued to third parties as part of a commercial collaboration or other arms length commercial undertaking.

---

[9] Chapter 21 – Pre-emption Rights on Securities Issues.
[10] Chapter 22 – Anti-dilution Rights.

9   Share Transfers[11]

9.1   Transfer Restrictions

It is very important to Trojan Horse and the Syndicate that securities issued by the Company are locked-up for a protracted period. Therefore, Ordinary Shareholders may not transfer any interest in their shares except for the purpose of normal tax and estate planning purposes (including on the death of any member of management), or with the consent of 75% of the Syndicate (by shareholding), in each case provided that the transferee accedes to the Financing documentation. A Shares held by the Syndicate will be freely transferable. Transfer restrictions will not apply to the transfer of Shares following or pursuant to the operation of the pre-emption, tag-along and drag-along rights described below.

Any director, officer or employee who ceases to be employed by the Company for any reason will be required (at the option of the Company) to sell their vested Shares back to the Company (i) at par value to the Company, if the reason for the departure is fraud, theft, conviction for a criminal offence, breach of a material term of the individual's employment or service contract, or gross misconduct, or (ii) at market value, in any other case.

In the case of an IPO by the Company, all shareholders and optionholders will agree to an appropriate lock-up period in terms agreed between the Company, Trojan Horse and the relevant underwriters, but being no longer than the shorter of (i) six months and (ii) the period ending on the date of publication of the Company's half year or full year (as applicable) financial results next following the IPO.

9.2   Pre-emption on Securities Transfers

Even where the Syndicate are prepared to approve of a transfer of securities to a bona fide third party purchaser, it is vitally important that a transfer takes place only after Syndicate members have been offered the opportunity to acquire the shares proposed to be sold. Accordingly, if any shareholder proposes to transfer any securities, it must offer the Syndicate the opportunity (but not the obligation) to purchase such securities on a pro rata basis and on the same terms as are proposed for the sale to a bona fide third party purchaser.

To the extent that any member of the Syndicate fails to take up all or any part of its pre-emption rights in any instance (the "Transfer Pre-emption Shortfall"), other Syndicate members who have taken up their pre-emptive rights in full will have additional pre-emption rights to take up all or any part of the Transfer Pre-emption Shortfall and if more than one Syndicate member expresses such interest, then pro rata between them.

In order to ensure that the above pre-emption process does not derail the sale opportunity for the transferring shareholder, the process will be operated under a 30 day fast-track procedure under which Syndicate members will elect both for core and additional pre-emption rights in one round. In addition, unless all the shares to be sold are taken up under such pre-emption process, the sale may proceed free of pre-emption rights on the same price and terms as notified to shareholders within 60 days period from the end of the 30-day period.

Pre-emption rights on transfer will not apply to (i) transfers by management shareholders for the purpose of normal tax and estate planning purposes (including on the death of any member of management), (ii) transfers by Syndicate members, in each case provided that the purchaser accedes to the Financing documentation or (iii) transfers of Shares pursuant to the operation of pre-emption, tag-along or drag-along rights.

9.3   Tag-Along Rights

In the event that the Syndicate are prepared to permit another Shareholder to transfer its shares to a bona fide third party purchaser, nonetheless we propose that all other Shareholders should have the

---

[11] Chapter 23 – Provisions Relating to Share Transfers.

right to participate in such a liquidity opportunity. Therefore, upon any transfer of Shares to a third party, pro rata "tag-along" rights in favour of the other Shareholders will apply to ensure that no such transfer will be permitted unless the purchaser acquires an equivalent proportion of Shares from the Shareholders on the same terms. Such rights will operate on a 30-day fast-track procedure which will run simultaneously with the transfer pre-emption rights described above. In such a case, the purchaser will be at liberty to elect either (i) to increase the size of the purchase transaction to accommodate all elections for tag-along rights or (ii) to maintain the size of the purchase transaction, in which event the selling shareholder's participation in the transaction will be scaled back to accommodate tag-along elections.

Tag-along rights will not apply to (i) transfers by management shareholders for the purpose of normal tax and estate planning purposes (including on the death of any member of management), (ii) transfers by Syndicate members, in each case provided that the purchaser accedes to the Financing documentation or (iii) transfers of Shares pursuant to the operation of pre-emption, tag-along or drag-along rights.

9.4   Drag-Along Rights

It remains vital that the Syndicate are, with sufficient shareholder support, able to initiate and complete an IPO, Sale (including a sale of business for such purpose) or Merger transaction, to carry out an exit of their investment in the Company. Accordingly, a majority of the Shareholders (by shareholding, on an as-if-converted basis) may, with the prior written consent of 75% of the Syndicate (by shareholding), require the initiation of an IPO, or a Sale or Merger of the Company or of all or substantially all of its business or assets, and in such circumstances all shareholders will be obliged to do all things as may be necessary and desirable to permit the flotation, sale or merger of the Company or its business or assets.

10.   Deal Management Considerations[12]

In order to implement the Financing terms set out above, it will be necessary to agree the following key implementation items.

10.1   Financing conditions

Implementation of the above-described Financing will be conditional upon:

(i) *completion by Trojan Horse of its remaining items of due diligence, to its full satisfaction and sign-off by the incoming members of the Syndicate. Trojan Horse will agree with the Company a plan for the completion of outstanding items of due diligence and will manage the process of ensuring that incoming members of the Syndicate complete their own due diligence requirements in a timely manner. The Company will provide all reasonable assistance and access to Trojan Horse, potential members of the Syndicate and their legal and other professional advisers for such purpose.*

(ii) *the grant of all approvals and the waiver of share issue pre-emption rights by the Company's current shareholders and the completion of any and all other necessary corporate formalities to permit the Financing (including the Reorganisation) to be completed. Trojan Horse will agree any and all such approvals, waivers, etc, in advance with the Company.*

(iii) *no material adverse change in the Company's position or prospects having occurred or having become likely to occur between the date of this term sheet and completion of the Financing. In the event that any such event does occur or becomes likely to occur, the Company must notify Trojan Horse immediately.*

---

[12] Chapter 24 – Deal Management Terms.

(iv) Trojan Horse investment board approval and such investment, advisory board or other required entity approval(s) as may be required to be obtained by other members of the Syndicate as a pre-condition to their participation in the Financing. The Company agrees to provide Trojan Horse and each member of the Syndicate with all such assistance as they may reasonably require for the purposes of seeking and obtaining any such consents or approvals etc.

(v) the Reorganisation is completed in a manner satisfactory to Trojan Horse.

(vi) the Company puts in place (i) key man insurance on the senior management team and (ii) patent litigation insurance (covering pursuit, defence and commercial agreements), in each case in an amount, on terms and to an extent agreed with Trojan Horse.

10.2   Exclusivity

It is vital that Trojan Horse be granted a reasonable period of exclusivity, during which it may commit the potentially significant resources (including the incurral of costs) necessary to progress the Financing to completion. Therefore, in consideration of Trojan Horse committing such resources, the Company grants Trojan Horse the exclusive right (together with the Syndicate chosen by Trojan Horse) to invest in the Company on the terms set out in this term sheet (as varied by agreement) for a period of three months from the date of this term sheet (the "Exclusivity Period").

During the Exclusivity Period, neither the Company, nor any director, officer, employee nor shareholder of the Company will, directly or indirectly, without Trojan Horse's prior consent (i) share any information regarding the Company, or its business or financial affairs, with another potential investor or lender, whether strategic or financial, or (ii) issue or agree to issue any Company securities (including securities having rights over the Company's capital or assets), in each case without Trojan Horse's prior written consent.

10.3   Confidentiality

The Company agrees to keep confidential the terms of this document, the Financing and the fact that discussions are on-going between the parties hereto in relation to the proposed Financing, except with the prior written consent of Trojan Horse.

10.4   First Right of Refusal

If within twelve months following the later of (i) the breakdown of negotiations between the Company and Trojan Horse relating to the Financing and (ii) the expiry of the Exclusivity Period, the Company enters into negotiations with a third party with respect to the raising of equity or debt financing for the Company (the "New Financing"), the Company will give Trojan Horse an opportunity to participate in an amount of up to $5 000 000 in the New Financing on the same terms as are made available to other third party institutional investors.

10.5   Documentation Production

The definitive legal agreements documenting and implementing the Financing will be prepared and administered by legal counsel to Trojan Horse and will contain such other terms and conditions not contained in this term sheet which are standard for a deal of this type. Legal counsel to the Company will be approved by Trojan Horse, such consent not to be unreasonably withheld. The governing law of these definitive legal agreements will be New York law.

10.6   Reimbursement of Expenses

The Company agrees to be responsible for Trojan Horse's and the Syndicate's legal and other professional fees and expenses (including the fees and expenses of legal counsel, accountants, and any and all *consultants employed in the conduct of technical, commercial and regulatory due diligence) incurred by them in connection with the closing of the Financing, whether or not the Financing closes. These fees and expenses will be reimbursed in full by the Company monthly not more than 10 days following the delivery of monthly invoices by Trojan Horse to the Company.*

10.7 Conduct of Due Diligence

It is obviously critically important that the remaining pieces of Trojan Horse's due diligence are completed in a timely fashion. The Company, the current shareholders and senior management will provide all reasonable assistance to Trojan Horse to facilitate the completion of its pre-completion due diligence process.

In order to support the due diligence process, warranties and indemnities customary for a transaction such as the Financing will be provided by the Company and senior management, both at Initial Completion and at each subsequent draw-down of capital commitments.

10.8 Regulatory Requirements

The Company will enter into a registration rights agreement with the Syndicate on standard market terms. For the purposes of Trojan Horse's and/or any Syndicate member's mandatory compliance with the US ERISA legislation, a "management rights letter" in a standard form will be entered into between such person(s) and the Company. For purposes of compliance with applicable anti-money laundering regulations, as soon as practicable following signature of this term sheet, the Company will supply written confirmation in standard form of the identities of (i) the Company, (ii) each investor in the round (institutional or individual) and (iii) each director of the Company.

This term sheet is not legally binding save that paragraph 10 will be fully binding immediately upon the Company countersigning this term sheet.

The proposal contained in this term sheet will expire at midnight ten business days following the date on this term sheet, unless signed by the Company and Simon Barnes and returned to Trojan Horse prior to that time.

If you have any questions regarding any of the above, please do not hesitate to contact Sherman Patton or Randy Avalon at Trojan Horse.

Yours sincerely

———————————

Sherman Patton
Senior Executive General Partner
for and on behalf of Trojan Horse Ventures

Accepted and agreed

———————————   ———————————

SilicoLabs Limited   *Simon Barnes*

SilicoLabs $20 000 000 Equity Financing

Shareholders	Ordinary Shares	%	First Tranche $5 000 000	Interim	% Undiluted	% Diluted	Second Tranche $5 000 000	Final	% Diluted
Simon Barnes	7 000 000	50.00%		7 000 000	36.84%	28.00%		7 000 000	23.33%
Management 1	1 750 000	12.50%		1 750 000	9.21%	7.00%		1 750 000	5.83%
Management 2	1 750 000	12.50%		1 750 000	9.21%	7.00%		1 750 000	5.83%
Management 3	1 750 000	12.50%		1 750 000	9.21%	7.00%		1 750 000	5.83%
Management 4	1 750 000	12.50%		1 750 000	9.21%	7.00%		1 750 000	5.83%
Management Total	**14 000 000**	**100.00%**		**14 000 000**	**73.68%**	**56.00%**		**14 000 000**	**46.67%**
Trojan Horse			2 500 000	2 500 000	13.16%	10.00%	2 500 000	5 000 000	16.67%
Syndicate 1			1 000 000	1 000 000	5.26%	4.00%	1 000 000	2 000 000	6.67%
Syndicate 2			1 000 000	1 000 000	5.26%	4.00%	1 000 000	2 000 000	6.67%
Syndicate 3			500 000	500 000	2.63%	2.00%	500 000	1 000 000	3.33%
Syndicate Total			**5 000 000**	**5 000 000**	**26.32%**	**20.00%**	**5 000 000**	**10 000 000**	**33.33%**
ESOP			6 000 000	6 000 000		24.00%		6 000 000	20.00%
Total	**14 000 000**		**11 000 000**	**25 000 000**			**5 000 000**	**30 000 000**	

Figure 1.1 Example capitalisation table

The above "cap table" shows the investment proposal described in our pro forma term sheet from Trojan Horse. In this example we have assumed that three additional VCs have joined the overall investment syndicate. The cap table also shows that in addition to Simon Barnes the lead entrepreneur, there are four other founding members of the management team who between them own 50% of the initial equity. We can see how their equity holdings are diluted over two tranches of investment and how the stock option pool (ESOP) impacts equity ownership and effectively lowers the pre-money valuation of the company.

13
Business Valuation

We understand that you are hoping to raise $20 000 000 to fund the next stage of the development of the Company. However, for the reasons we have shared with you during our initial due diligence, we continue to believe that $10 000 000 is a more suitable ambition for the Company, in light of its immediate business objectives and the state of the private equity funding markets and we therefore propose a Financing at this aggregate level.

We have shared valuation information with you during the initial stages of this potential transaction. We confirm that we are willing to implement the Financing on the basis of a fully-diluted pre-money valuation for the Company of $20 000 000, which we believe represents a very attractive valuation for the Company at this time in the prevailing marketplace. This valuation assumes that there is established immediately prior to the Financing an employee stock option programme over 20% of the fully-diluted post-Financing equity share capital, of which not less than one half of the programme remains unallocated on completion of the Financing.

We enclose with this term sheet a detailed capitalisation table spread sheet which illustrates the pre-Financing and post-Financing share capital position of the Company (as well as all intermediate steps), based on the terms set out herein, which we trust clarifies the impact of the above valuation and below investment terms.

The term sheet will include several sections on the valuation of the investment proposition. Typically, the term sheet will describe both the pre-money and post-money valuations, as well as the bases on which those valuations are made (undiluted, partly diluted, fully diluted, etc) and will enclose a capitalisation table for the company demonstrating, share by share, the exact impact of the financing on the issued and to be issued share capital of the company.

Business valuation issues are dealt with in detail at Chapter 11 and we do not propose to rehash these here. But as a practical matter, the entrepreneur must, as a bare minimum:

(1) evaluate whether the VC firm is committing enough money to make the financing worthwhile and strategically advisable in the context of the entrepreneur's ambitions for his business and its development profile over the medium term – getting the sizing and timing of the business's capital raisings positioned optimally is fraught with difficulty;

(2) read the valuation assumptions carefully and correlate them to the capitalisation table (and if no capitalisation table is supplied, insist that one is supplied), to better understand the "real" pre- and post-money valuations – and conduct research to figure out whether those valuations broadly intersect with the prevailing private equity marketplace. It is important to take note here of the use of "pre-money" and "post-money" valuations and "fully diluted" share capital terms – all issues that we discussed in Chapter 11;

(3) identify any and all conditions precedent (or subsequent) to the deliverability of the promised valuation and investment commitments, so that the entrepreneur can fully understand the risks inherent in accepting the private equity investment commitment; and

(4) identify and understand the viability of any "plan B" proposals, should the investment transaction fail to close or be significantly delayed.

14

Investment Structure

Following a preliminary review, we believe that the current group structure should be reorganised (in as tax-efficient a manner as possible) prior to Initial Completion of the Financing by (i) creating a new Delaware holding company for the business and operations (ii) relocating the group headquarters to the United States, (iii) developing a US sales and marketing activity in the United States and (iv) relocating research and development activities to the Republic of Ireland. The terms set out herein assume that such a reorganisation (the "Reorganisation") is completed prior to the first draw down under the Financing.

In the event that the VC firm has determined that it wishes to engineer an evolution of the corporate or group structure to optimise the development of the business or its investment in the business, the term sheet will contain a description of the broad parameters of the proposal, completion of which will usually be conditional to completion of the financing (although it may sometimes be possible to convince the VC firm to delay implementation of any such reorganisation until after the financing, or at least until after the first tranche of the financing, but only where the reorganisation is deliverable by the shareholders relatively easily and there are no material third party consents (e.g. customers, suppliers, tax authorities, etc) needed that would mean that implementation would be highly risky and of uncertain outcome.

Investment structure issues are dealt with in detail in Chapter 11. But as a practical matter, the entrepreneur must, as a bare minimum:

(1) understand in detail the timing and risk implications of the restructuring proposal made by the VC firm, in terms of the investment transaction;
(2) evaluate the relative merits of the proposal and any potential adverse impact on the current shareholder base, or restraints on the development of the business; and
(3) push hard to get the VC firm to agree to the implementation of the reorganisation as soon as reasonably practical following initial closing of the investment transaction, to ensure that the overall transaction is de-risked in a step by step process and that the reorganisation is not undertaken in a vacuum, but following the contribution of meaningful funds by the VC fund.

15

Syndication

15.1 INTRODUCTION TO SYNDICATION

> *Trojan Horse is therefore willing to lead an investment syndicate (the "Syndicate") which will invest $10 000 000 in aggregate in the Company, subject to the pre-completion group reorganisation specified in paragraph 2 above. Trojan Horse itself is willing to invest up to $5 000 000 in the Company as a cornerstone investment around which the Syndicate will be formed. Trojan Horse will use all reasonable efforts to procure investment commitments from future Syndicate members to provide the balance of the Financing not otherwise provided by Trojan Horse.*
>
> *Trojan Horse may in its absolute discretion elect to increase or decrease its aggregate investment commitment to the Company, depending on the level of Syndicate demand. Members of the Syndicate proposed by Trojan Horse must be pre-approved by the Company but allocations of investment commitments among the Syndicate members will be made in the absolute discretion of Trojan Horse.*

As discussed in Part II, it is extremely common to see a VC firm retain the ability to lead manage the syndication of a financing opportunity, under which the VC firm will market the investment opportunity to third party investors and bring them into the deal around its own fund's "cornerstone" investment (the pros and cons of syndication are discussed in more detail in Chapter 5). In our example capitalization table attached to the pro forma term sheet we can see that three other VCs have joined the syndicate. With regard to syndication, an entrepreneur must at a minimum ensure that he or she reviews the following items:

(1) The minimum commitment undertaken by the VC fund as syndicate leader and whether this commitment is conditioned on a minimum additional commitment from syndicate joiners, so that the entrepreneur understands exactly what the minimum shortfall currently is in funding terms and the extent to which the VC fund may dominate the funding round. Note here that in the opening paragraphs of the term sheet, one could easily misunderstand that Trojan Horse will invest $10 000 000, and it only becomes clearer later that the commitment is in fact $5 000 000. This is not a deliberate attempt to deceive but the layout of the term sheet does mean that entrepreneurs need to read carefully before jumping to conclusions;

(2) Whether the VC fund has the right unilaterally (i) to increase its commitment beyond the minimum level (which the entrepreneur may be concerned would cause the VC fund to become dominant) or (ii) to decrease its commitment below its minimum commitment (which the entrepreneur may be concerned would cause the VC fund to become too peripheral to warrant the powers of a syndicate leader, or enable other new syndicate members to become dominant), usually meaning that the entrepreneur will want to set the parameters of the VC fund's minimum and maximum capital commitment;

(3) Whether the entrepreneur has the ability to approve any syndicate member joining the syndicate and the level of its capital commitment. The entrepreneur should invariably insist that this is the case, to ensure that all syndicate members are credible, have a sufficient

investment in the business and will add value as investors. This is a particularly important point because as we have discussed earlier, equity investors become business partners for the entrepreneur and management team. Nobody wants a partner they don't respect or don't like.

15.2 REWARD FOR SYNDICATE LEADERSHIP

> *In recognition of Trojan Horse's services as cornerstone investor and Syndicate leader as described above, the Company will grant Trojan Horse warrants to subscribe 200,000 new A Shares (with the rights as described below), exercisable in whole or in part at any time in the five years following the completion of the Financing, at the discretion of Trojan Horse, at a subscription price of $1 per A Share.*

It is increasingly becoming the case that syndicate leaders are seeking recompense from investment opportunities for the value that they add through their syndication function, even though it is arguable that the VC fund benefits as much from the syndication process as the entrepreneurial company receiving the investment. Nonetheless, it is incontrovertible that the skills and networks of the lead investor can be extremely valuable for the entrepreneur in finding and evaluating potential syndicate members and bringing them into the deal on the back of the syndicate leader's negotiated investment terms. In the absence of some reward to the syndicate leader, this value-add goes unrecognised and all syndicate members will typically invest on the same terms. In truth, the picture in the marketplace is somewhat mixed, as although to some extent there exists a small coterie of syndicate leaders who may invite "members of their exclusive club" into each others' deals, it is equally the case that there exists a large number of other investors who specialise in being "me too" syndicate members, coming into others' deals once terms have been formed around a lead investor's due diligence and deal structuring. There are several ways in which a VC firm acting as a syndicate lead might try to negotiate an improved position including:

(1) investing at a lower price per share in the investment opportunity than other syndicate members – this is attractive but still requires the VC fund to put the same amount of capital to work as it originally committed, albeit that it receives an enhanced equity participation to reflect its position as syndicate leader;

(2) making a smaller investment commitment, but receiving an unchanged equity participation – this is the flip side to investing at a lower price and is also attractive but means that (a) the VC fund will put less capital to work in the investment, which may not be optimal, and (b) its position as syndicate leader never creates an enhanced equity participation; or

(3) having the ability to enhance its equity participation at its option in the future (on an agreed basis that may be costless, low-cost or at market rates, depending on the relative bargaining position between the syndicate leader and the entrepreneur) – this is usually the ideal outcome for a syndicate leader, as it provides the VC fund with the option, but not the obligation, to enhance its equity participation in the investment, possibly by contributing further capital to a performing investment. This is the structure set out above in the example above and in the pro forma term sheet.

15.3   THE ENTREPRENEUR'S RESPONSE

For the reasons discussed in detail at 15.1 above, an entrepreneur should strongly support the syndication process; albeit making sure that the company's legitimate interests are protected.

The entrepreneur may get away without having to reward the VC fund for its syndicate leadership role, and lack of remuneration is the market norm. However, pressure from the VC firm to recognise their value-add may be difficult to resist. If so, the entrepreneur should consider whether to support the grant of a market rate option to the VC firm, at a suitable level (1% of funds produced by the syndication?) and also whether no grant whatsoever should be made unless the VC firm has reached pre-agreed, measurable targets in terms of (e.g.) capital raised, and the diversity and quality of investors in the syndicate.

16
Investment Milestones

"Investment milestones" are no more than conditions for the staged draw down of financing commitments. Typically, milestone–driven provisions will stipulate the number of milestones that are applicable, what those milestones are (their nature and their timing) and what happens if they are satisfied or not satisfied.

16.1 INTRODUCTION TO INVESTMENT MILESTONES

The Financing will take place in two phases, the first phase being unconditional and the second phase being conditioned upon the achievement of certain key business development steps by the Company.

On completion of the Financing, tentatively targeted for a date not later than six weeks following the date of this term sheet, ("Initial Completion") the Syndicate will contribute $5 000 000 in aggregate to the Company by way of the subscription of 5 000 000 new A Ordinary Shares ("A Shares"), at $1 per A Share. This initial investment contribution will be unconditional.

In the event that the Company completes the business development milestones described below (the "Milestones") by the first anniversary of Initial Completion, the Syndicate will contribute a further $5 000 000 in aggregate to the Company by way of the subscription of a further 5 000 000 new A Shares at $1 per A Share.

Investment milestones are strongly preferred by VC firms, because they enable VC funds to drip-feed capital into an investment opportunity over a protracted period, with each commitment (a "tranche") being measured against and conditional upon the business achieving certain performance criteria. As a consequence of this, VC funds are able to manage their operational risk in the investment very carefully and are in particular able either to pull out quickly from an investment that "stumbles" or otherwise does not perform to expectations, or continue to commit capital (at the original entry price) into an investment that gains successful traction against those expectations. Both of these features are important risk management tools for a VC firm and many firms will, as a matter of policy, not invest in opportunities that are not tranched in this way.

16.1.1 Milestone definitions

In the event that the Company completes the business development milestones described below (the "Milestones") by the first anniversary of Initial Completion, the Syndicate will contribute a further $5 000 000 in aggregate to the Company by way of the subscription of a further 5 000 000 new A Shares at $1 per A Share. The relevant Milestones are: (i) an agreed level of progress in the development of the product prototype; (ii) recruitment of an agreed Vice President of Sales and Marketing; and (iii) enrolment of the Company's first customer for a paid trail.

The "milestones" against which tranche commitments are conditioned can come in every shape and size. Usually they are financial, commercial, technical or operational conditions extrapolated from an agreed business plan (and therefore by agreeing to the business plan as part of the investment process, there is a risk that the entrepreneur will be held to ransom by it later on – hence the temptation to under-promise in that document and then over-deliver against those promises). If the milestones are met, then the VC investors are obliged to contribute their capital commitment to the company. Note that the price per share at which the subsequent investment is made is usually the same as in the initial unconditional investment. This may seem counter-intuitive: the VC fund has decreased its risk as the milestones are passed and in theory the business should have become more successful and therefore valuable (after all, in the term sheet example the business has progressed its prototype, hired a key sales executive and convinced a customer to trial its product on a paying basis)... and yet the VC fund is contributing capital at an unchanged price. It is very rare that a VC fund can be convinced to adjust the subscription price of future tranches, however. There is value to the entrepreneur in the commitment (see below), both in terms of the certainty of that commitment and the price at which that commitment is made – and these are the balancing factors. In addition, of course, the VC fund is offering to make a *commitment* today (albeit conditionally) and therefore there is a strong argument that the only basis on which it can fairly make any such commitment is today's open market valuation. Anything else would be enormously speculative and of little value to either side.

16.1.2   Milestone waivers

Trojan Horse, on behalf of the Syndicate, may agree to defer or delay any Milestone deadline, or even to waive any Milestone, in its absolute discretion. Whether or not any or all of the Milestones have been completed at any time, Trojan Horse may, on behalf of the Syndicate, at any time after Initial Completion decide to accelerate the contribution of all or any part of the further $5 000 000 investment commitment described above, in which event the Company will be obliged to issue new A Shares as described above as though the Milestones had been satisfied in full.

In addition to the above tranching structure, it is extremely common for VC investors to give themselves the power to extend or waive a milestone. Whilst this may appear to be altruistic and good-hearted – it is not entirely so! While on the one hand this power is indeed useful to deliver a fair outcome to a business that misses a milestone by inches (or perhaps even rightly prioritises other matters for legitimate business reasons), or to curtail discord among an investment syndicate on whether or not a milestone has been satisfied (these are "good" uses of a waiver power): on the other hand the ability to waive a milestone can be extremely useful for the syndicate if the valuation of the business has risen markedly and the entrepreneur begins to feel that it may actually suit him or her to have the business miss the milestones set for it (potentially allowing the old financing to fall away, enabling the entrepreneur to raise replacement finance more cheaply elsewhere), or should an attractive exit opportunity present itself more quickly than expected – which in each case would potentially leave the syndicate "underweight" in the company, in terms of the aggregate amount of capital contributed to the business (particularly as they will have had their remaining, undrawn capital commitment "locked up" awaiting draw down, and yet de facto uninvested). In these latter instances, the VC investors will want to have the ability to pre-empt the situation by waiving any milestones and "putting" (aka forcing) their capital commitment onto the company compulsorily, frustrating a cheaper capital-raising opportunity or ensuring their participation to the maximum extent possible in the exit opportunity, reflective of their original capital commitment.

Is this unfair? Well, a VC fund would argue not, as its capital commitment is made up front – albeit subject to milestones being passed – and the VC fund capital matching that commitment is ring-fenced and allocated towards draw-downs on that commitment, and is therefore unavailable for investment in other opportunities. In other words, the VC firm's capital commitment represents a quasi-equity position. The VC fund would argue that it would be very unfair then for the VC fund to be denied the ability to invest those committed funds at its option. Conversely, the entrepreneur will argue that the VC fund has already garnered significant economic and strategic benefits from tranching its investment (see below) and that these factors significantly compensate the VC firm should circumstances change and render the later tranches undrawable. A compromise position would be to allow the waiver of milestones generally by the syndicate with the consent of the non-Syndicate shareholders (or the Board, if it is independent), but to provide that this additional consent is not required where the company can be shown not to have used all reasonable endeavours to achieve the relevant milestones – meaning that situations where the company's development track is genuinely overtaken by events (a sudden sale or IPO opportunity, or a major and attractive change in the business model) can be grasped by the company without providing a windfall benefit to the VC firm ("having its cake and eating it"), but that deliberate and unreasonable sloth by the company designed to miss a milestone (for example to benefit from an improved funding climate to raise money on improved terms) could be pre-empted by the VC fund. This would be an innovative approach likely to be resisted by a VC firm, of course.

16.2   ATTRACTIONS FOR THE VC FIRM

As already mentioned above, the principal attractions of milestone-based tranching of investments for the VC fund are that the structure:

(1) enables the VC firm to hold an increased share in the investment opportunity without increasing its risk – further money is contributed to the investment by the VC fund only after risk-retiring milestone events have been passed – and yet the investment opportunity remains locked-up exclusively for the VC fund;

(2) facilitates the dynamic capital allocation process that lies at the heart of the venture capital business model, by enabling the VC fund to keep back a significant proportion of its overall investment funds and to allocate those funds towards (i) those companies that progress their businesses successfully through milestones, becoming less risky and more attractive investment propositions, and (ii) follow-on investments (potentially on significantly improved terms) in those businesses that have failed to pass milestones, but in which the VC fund (perhaps taking a longer term or opportunistic view) wishes to continue to invest nonetheless;

(3) improves IRRs on the VC fund's investments, because it delays the input of new capital until it is actually required. Indeed it is not uncommon to see "milestones" which are in fact merely time-based or triggered automatically once the cash resources of the business fall beneath a set threshold (see the example below), which have only a positive IRR impact for the VC fund and no other protective effect, but is still seen as attractive for a VC fund nonetheless. This is because the later that capital is contributed to an investment, the faster it will be turned around in the eventual exit, as compared to the contribution of

that capital in one fell swoop at the outset, and therefore the lower the discount applied to that cash flow cycle in the IRR calculation;

> *Upon the earlier of the first anniversary of Initial Completion and the date on which the Company's cash reserves fall below $50 000, the Syndicate will contribute a further $5 000 000 in aggregate to the Company by way of the subscription of a further 5 000 000 new A Shares at $1 per A Share*

(4) may permit acceleration of the VC fund's investment in any event (by a waiver of the milestones and ability to force a contribution of the capital to the investment – see above), should that prove to be an attractive option – for example if the value of the business should increase unexpectedly, or should an attractive exit opportunity present itself out of the blue.

16.3   ATTRACTIONS FOR THE ENTREPRENEUR

The attractions for the VC community of milestones are obvious and expected features, given that the VC syndicate will tend to be in the driving seat. What is less expected is that a milestone-based, tranching approach is not necessarily unattractive to the entrepreneur either. The reasons for this are as follows:

16.3.1   Protected committed funding

If the business performs to plan, the passing of milestones will ensure that the entrepreneur will gain access to committed funds sufficient to fund his or her operations for a protracted period – probably much longer than for a conventional fund-raising. This is a classic "is the glass half empty or half full?" issue: it is often the case that entrepreneurs feel cheated by milestone-based tranches, because (using the term sheet example) they treat the commitment of $10 M to have been given with one hand ("We're happy to commit $10 million!") and then $5 M to have been immediately withdrawn with the other ("Er, but you won't get your hands on $5 million of it for a long while" . . .) and made subject to conditions (. . . "and you're going to have to jump through all sorts of hoops to get it."). That's to see the glass as half empty. One could equally describe the situation in a completely different fashion – the marketplace has determined that only $5 M can be committed unconditionally at the outset given the circumstances of the company's business, not more: however, the syndicate has in addition been generously prepared to commit a further $5 M, conditional upon the business meeting reasonable stretch goals (which in all probability have been set by reference to an agreed business plan and so have the tacit support of the entrepreneur and his or her management team) – in other words they have been prepared to substantially over-commit capital, subject to reasonable conditions. That's to see the glass as half full, but it's probably the more appropriate analysis if the investment opportunity has been properly marketed, so that the entrepreneur can be sure that there really is no market appetite to put in more than $5 M on an unconditional basis (at least at the valuation proposed).

   If the entrepreneur does not like this reality, he or she may always choose either to raise more unconditional funding, but at a lower valuation (price being a proxy for risk and therefore potentially capable of doing away with much of the reason for milestones) or fix the first $5 M in place and reject the conditionally committed additional $5 M, in the hope that it is possible to raise additional funding in the future on better terms (e.g. after satisfying the milestones in any event). In the latter case, as explained at 16.3.2 below, the entrepreneur takes on both operational and market risk (the latter being a factor most entrepreneurs do not fully recognise). There is also a low-level risk that the entrepreneur may find that the initial $5 M investment is no longer available on the same terms, as most pieces of a VC firm's term sheet are inter-dependent – in particular a VC fund will usually want to see a pathway to put significant amounts of money to work in a high performance investment, an important feature of the VC business model. Of course, this issue may be fixable if the entrepreneur is willing to offer the VC fund a first run at future financing opportunities on the best terms obtainable in the open market.

16.3.2   Guaranteed subscription price

If the business meets the milestones, the company has guaranteed committed additional funds *at an agreed price*. Once again, this is a classic "glass is half empty/full" issue: entrepreneurs often feel that it's unfair that the subscription price for the new shares following satisfaction of the milestone(s) is the same which prevailed in the original unconditional tranche – they believe that if the milestones are satisfied, the valuation of the company must inevitably have risen and that therefore they are being asked to commit to issue equity at an undervalue in the future. However, this is to miss a highly important issue.

As we have seen in the discussion on valuation at Chapter 11, one of the most significant elements of volatility in pre-money pricing is the prevailing public and private equity funding marketplace. It is perfectly possible that the funding marketplace will have moved *adversely* for the business, even while it has made operational progress, ensuring that even if the business manages to complete several important milestones, its pre-money value in corporate finance terms may have stood still or even reduced from the pre-money valuation at initial closing. This is precisely what happened in the recent period from 1999 to 2004: companies effectively had to run extremely hard in operational terms, just to stand still in valuation terms. Many companies did everything right in operational terms, only to find that they were worth, in investment terms, a fraction of their value in years past (and meanwhile many of their publicly-quoted compatriots were becoming members of the "95% club" – companies that had shed more than 95% of their market value since IPO). When this consideration is taken into account, it should be recognised that a commitment at a *fixed price in advance* (even on a conditional basis – and after all the milestones will have been accepted by the entrepreneur and the management team as reasonable stretch goals) takes away any market risk over the relevant period (which may be a number of years) and is therefore of very significant value to the entrepreneur.

16.3.3   Fund-raising without milestones

As mentioned above, the entrepreneur's alternatives to a milestone-based approach would be:

(1) to take more money on board on an unconditional basis, but at a lower valuation – using the term sheet example, to raise $10 M at a $15 M pre-money valuation. The entrepreneur could still offer the VC fund the IRR benefits of a tranched investment, but the tranching would simply be time-based, or matched to the cash thirst of the company. Clearly, this is a defensive move, but also one that avoids the entrepreneur storing up trouble for the future. Generally, an earn-in should be preferred to this course of action (see 16.4.6 below).

(2) to take only the $5 M offered unconditionally and then seek to raise new funding on the back of the milestones being passed. Leaving aside the market risk issues and the question of whether the same terms would be available on this basis (discussed above – significant areas of risk), this course of action assumes two additional items of risk related to the subsequent fund-raising, which the entrepreneur will need to plan for very carefully:

(a) the entrepreneur needs to be confident that the $5 M raised unconditionally will take the company not only through the milestone events (which will no longer trigger an automatic infusion of new capital) but also through a subsequent fund-raising period/plan B period, to ensure that the company will be able to retain control over the entire subsequent fund-raising/plan B process and not fall prey to investors because it runs out of money half way through. When a thorough analysis is carried out on this issue, it is often found that the initial $5 M is NOT enough to render the company master of its destiny, even when it has been operationally successful (failure is considered below). So the entrepreneur may need to raise further initial unconditional funds, which may be difficult in the prevailing market at the same valuation level.

(b) the act of raising capital through a subsequent round could be long and arduous and will almost certainly disrupt management materially from their highly important day job of running a successful business. Many entrepreneurs take the view that the immediate and automatic availability of a second tranche of capital upon satisfaction of the milestones, even at a flat pre-money valuation, is a small price to pay to avoid having to go into fund-raising mode again.

16.4   AREAS TO WATCH OUT FOR

Entrepreneurs will form their own view on the relative attractions of milestone-based tranched deals, but if they are in the end part of a financing proposal there are several key areas that need to be considered, in order to optimise the situation:

16.4.1   Sizing each tranche

It is extremely important that each tranche is carefully evaluated to ensure it is of an appropriate size (i) to enable the company to achieve the milestone(s) that release the next capital infusion in the time permitted AND (ii) to enable the company to go through the usual period of uncertainty and strategic recalibration that would follow any failure to pass, or delay in passing, any milestone(s), which would prevent or defer the release of the next investment tranche. The latter issue is a point often missed – the entrepreneur needs (a) to have a plan B for failure as well as a plan A for success and (b) to ensure that the company at all times has the resources to remain in control of its destiny.

The above analysis inevitably leads to a vigorous debate with the VC firm around the number and sizing of investment tranches (particularly the first, unconditional investment), the number and nature of milestones, their inter-action and potentially also the freedom of the company to implement a plan B in the event that it fails to pass critical milestones (for example, should existing shareholders have a lock on fund-raising activity in such circumstances, or just pre-emption rights, or no rights at all?).

We have already discussed planning for failure in several instances with regard to milestones. However, it is important to recognise that in the event that the company does not pass a milestone, not only should the company ensure that it has the resources, unaided, to take appropriate action, but it should also ensure that it has the ability to garner support from even a small sub-set of investors who remain willing to contribute capital to the company, which may bulk up its remaining resources and provide it with strategic options not otherwise available to it. Ideally, investors should not have a lock on financing rescue options (see 16.4.3 below), as this could put an unscrupulous investor in an overwhelming position of strength.

16.4.2 Careful drafting of milestones

It is absolutely vital to ensure that the milestones themselves are as objective and clearly measurable as possible – a milestone that has an element of subjectivity or uncertainty can only operate to the disadvantage of the entrepreneur and the business, as it renders the syndicate's commitment incapable of guaranteed enforcement (whereas, conversely, if the syndicate wish to put their commitment on the company, even where a milestone is not satisfied, they can – through the medium of the waiver of the milestone). Great care should be taken in the negotiation and drafting of each milestone to ensure that no room is left for doubt or subjectivity and, in areas where either of these factors lurks, the entrepreneur should provide for some form of third party evaluation of the situation (ideally by a professional body or agreed appropriately qualified arbitrator) to ensure maximum fairness in the event of disagreement between the parties.

Looking at the term sheet example, there are three milestones specified: (1) an agreed level of progress in the development of the product prototype, (2) recruitment of an agreed vice-president of sales and marketing, and (3) enrolment of the company's first customer for a paid trial. Only the latter milestone immediately has the potential to be truly objective (and even then, there are grounds for a fertile debate over the status of "customer", the nature of "enrolment", and threshold levels and criteria for a trial to qualify as "paid"). The first milestone will require very careful drafting concerning the technical development of the prototype, to ensure that passing the milestone becomes as automatic as possible – but the more detailed the defined development pathway to satisfy the milestone, the less easy it may be for the entrepreneur to decide to deviate from that pathway for valid commercial or operational reasons (market developments, developing customer requirements, competitive pressures, improved technological solutions/architectures, etc), and so the entrepreneur must be careful not to be so prescriptive in drafting the milestone as to preclude value-added tactical and strategic decision-making – a difficult balance to get right. The second milestone is going to be almost impossible to make entirely objective – however detailed the recruitment specification, both sides will always want to maintain some kind of subjective criteria in dealing with complex skills and personality issues.

16.4.3 Syndicate decision-making

Where the investment is made by an investment syndicate, it is very important that the mechanism by which that syndicate makes decisions is clearly addressed and can operate to ensure that the majority in the syndicate can carry the minority, so that no small minority of the syndicate can effectively hold up the rest. In addition, it is worth considering enabling individual members of the syndicate unilaterally to commit funds in any event voluntarily, as this may reduce the pressure on the company of unreasonable syndicate "cartel" behaviour (in the absence of this power, the company would not be able to issue equity to a syndicate member, because of other conventional restrictions in the investment terms), perhaps allowing the company a crucial breathing space to operate a plan B scenario with the support of a sub-set of investors.

16.4.4   Enforcement teeth

Unfortunately, following the shake-out of the VC industry in the first half decade of the twenty-first century, it can no longer be taken for granted that, when an investment milestone has been satisfied, every syndicate member will have retained sufficient capital to satisfy their triggered investment obligations. Equally, the entrepreneur may find him or herself in a situation in which the relevant milestones have been passed, and yet the investment syndicate, or a significant minority of the syndicate, take the position that the milestones have not been passed or that they are simply not going to contribute capital in any event. Both of these scenarios present real problems for the entrepreneur. In the event that the syndicate (or any member of it) fails to comply with its obligations to contribute additional funds, it is extremely important that the investment documentation both has enforcement "teeth" and a mechanism to enable the company to rescue itself in the short-term. In the absence of such powers, there is little downside to a syndicate member walking away from its subsequent commitment and, much more importantly, the company may collapse through lack of funding while any dispute is settled.

> *To the extent that any Syndicate member fails to subscribe its pro rata share of the further $5 000 000 investment commitment upon either (i) the Company passing in full the Milestones by the relevant date or (ii) the Syndicate deciding to waive the Milestones (a "Defaulter"), then the same proportion of the A Shares held by the Defaulter as represents the proportion of the Defaulter's capital commitment not made will automatically convert into economically worthless deferred shares and the Defaulter will have no further rights as a shareholder or investor in the Company (without prejudice to the Company's right to enforce all legal rights and remedies against the Defaulter in respect of such default).*

In terms of enforcement "teeth", conventional structures recognise that it is unlikely that a law suit by the company will provide a suitable remedy or incentive to good behaviour (too little, too late and in most jurisdictions damages have to be proven – which may not be straightforward) and focus instead on severe punishment of a defaulter. The typical mechanisms involve the downgrading or elimination of the defaulter's initial investment, for example by converting the defaulter's shares either to common stock, or even to economically worthless deferred stock.

> *In the event that the size of Defaulters' aggregate defaulted commitments is not more than $500 000 (or is greater than $500 000 but the Company's funding shortfall is brought below such threshold following the procurement of new investors as described below), the non-defaulting Syndicate members agree that they will each increase their investment commitment pro rata between them to fill the amount of such defaults and ensure that $5 000 000 in aggregate is contributed to the Company. In the event that the size of such defaults is greater than $500 000 in aggregate, then the non-defaulting Syndicate members agree that the Company will be permitted three months to procure additional investors to fill the amount of such defaults (and Trojan Horse shall use all reasonable endeavours to assist the Company in procuring commitments from such investors) on the same terms as set out in this term sheet.*

In terms of freeing the entrepreneur's hand to progress a plan B, conventional structures operate a combination of asking the remaining investors to fill any modest funding gap created by "one of their own" (although any funding gap above 10% of the aggregate commitment is unlikely to be susceptible to being filled in this way), permitting the draw down of piecemeal commitments (from those investors who are prepared to comply with their legal obligations) and supporting the company in its efforts to secure additional financing commitments to fill the hole.

16.4.5   Negotiation approaches

It is always worthwhile for an entrepreneur to try to resist a milestone waiver right for investors, and/or to try for a modest pre-money valuation hike upon satisfaction of a milestone (even if only to reflect the value of the investors' money previously contributed). Don't count on succeeding, but who knows?

16.4.6   Earn-ins and ratchets as an alternative

> *Upon the earlier of the first anniversary of Initial Completion and the date on which the Company's cash reserves fall below $50 000, the Syndicate will contribute a further $5 000 000 in aggregate to the Company by way of the subscription of a further 5 000 000 new A Shares at $1 per A Share provided that in the event that the Company fails to complete the business development milestones described below (the "Milestones") by the first anniversary of Initial Completion, the subscription price for the new A Shares referred to above shall be reduced to $0.50 per A Share. The relevant Milestones are: (I) An agreed level of progress in the development of the product prototype; (II) Recruitment of an agreed Vice President of Sales and Marketing; and (III) Enrolment of the Company's first customer for a paid trial.*

Whenever confronted by milestone provisions in a term sheet, an entrepreneur should always consider whether it would be more attractive to turn the whole thing around – into an "earn in" or "ratchet", whereby the investment capital is all contributed up front on closing (or, to give the VC fund the IRR benefits of tranching, contributed in tranches purely against time or cash resources triggers), but there is a re-pricing of the whole round either (i) downwards (an "earn-in") in the event that certain agreed milestones are NOT met or (ii) upwards (a "ratchet") in the event that such agreed milestones ARE met. Which option is chosen will depend on the price at which the initial equity is issued (low or normal). This creates a whole new set of issues and dynamics for the entrepreneur, but the attractions are that although the fundamental business risk in the milestones remains the same for the entrepreneur, this time the money is in the bank or at least available when needed and therefore can be used to assist the entrepreneur in getting to the milestones all the quicker and, better still, those funds remain available to finance alternatives (e.g. a pathway to plan B) if things should go off-track, greatly reducing the influence of the VC fund in any such work-around strategy and ensuring the company is fully stabilised should adverse events hit it in the run-up to a milestone event. Therefore the company has an enhanced ability to retain control of its destiny.

The downside of this approach, of course, is that the entrepreneur has pre-wired the downside impact on the company's valuation should the business fail to deliver on the milestones – a downside that (in theory) might not have been present in a conventional milestone scenario, either because the nature of the missed milestone is not significant (but then why would the VC fund not invest anyway, so long as the company has left itself the ability to produce third party funds, to keep the market honest?) or because the financing market may have improved in the interim and lessened the cost of failure (although in practice, a failure to pass a milestone would probably cause a financial crisis engendering a reconstruction and rescue financing of the company, simply because of the time and cost implications of implementing a new financing). Essentially the entrepreneur is swapping two uncertainties (will the company hit the milestones? What will happen if it doesn't?) for a single certainty (he or she knows exactly what will happen under each outcome). The entrepreneur has accepted a pre-wired dilution in equity interest in the company in the event of a failure to pass a milestone as the price of keeping the company alive.

From the VC fund's perspective, it is notionally protected from the implications of failure by the re-pricing mechanism. However, the workability of this structure for a VC firm much depends on the nature of the milestones missed and/or its ability to predict the value impact on the company should a milestone not be passed by a given date. For example, most VCs would prefer to have the option of abandoning their first \$5 M and "saving" their next \$5 M commitment, rather than retain, or ratchet up, their percentage interest in a problem company on the back of an unconditional \$10 M investment. Equally, a VC firm may fancy its chances in the kind of uncontrolled, emergency situation that often arises upon the failure to pass a milestone and unlock a financing tranche – in such a situation a VC firm may find itself with an opportunity to take advantage of the company's short-term weakness, to drive an aggressive bargain on it's fund contributing further capital opportunistically. Much depends on the relative sizing of the VC fund's initial investment and conditionally committed follow-on investment and on the stage of development of the company. So, an entrepreneur may meet resistance to this proposal in some cases, but it is usually worth considering and discussing with the company's lead investor.

17
Corporate Governance

17.1 INTRODUCTION TO CORPORATE GOVERNANCE

This chapter on corporate governance draws together all those elements of a conventional term sheet which touch on the way in which the business is managed and governed, both from the perspective of day to day operations (typically by means of provisions operating at the board level) and from the point of view of the interface with shareholders in areas such as information flows and over-arching controls.

Three core areas are examined – board powers and procedures, veto rights, and information systems and controls.

17.2 VC BOARD REPRESENTATION

There are three key areas of concern to a VC investor that relate to the operations and activities of the board of directors (or other appropriate governance body): matters of composition, matters of nomination, and process and veto.

17.2.1 Composition of the board

> *The board of directors (the "Board") will be composed of a maximum of seven persons, of which a majority will always be non-executive directors. On Initial Completion, the Board will be composed of three executive directors (the Chief Executive Officer, the Chief Financial Officer and the Chief Technical Officer) and four non-executive directors (a Trojan Horse representative, a Syndicate representative, an independent non-executive director and an independent non-executive Chairman).*

The first area of focus for a VC firm will be to ensure that the size of the board is tightly constrained, not only to ensure that the discussion at board meetings can be efficient and productive, commensurate with the size and nature of the business itself, but also to ensure that at no time can the executive directors on their own come to control the board process, ensuring that public company-style board processes can be built into the company's governance, through which the VC firm will expect to be able to minimise business risk both through these checks and balances, but also through introducing a broader range of debate and discussion on key issues between persons who come to the board table with a diverse range of skills, experiences and perspectives. It is therefore entirely typical for the term sheet to provide that the majority of the board must at all times be non-executive directors.

From the entrepreneur's perspective, it may come as a surprise to discover that the minority shareholders wish to impose this kind of change on the governance of the company, and also that the controlling shareholder(s) (which may be the entrepreneur) will not also continue to control the board – although direction and control of the day to day management of the business in its ordinary course may not change materially, as this is the sole preserve of the executive directors. Nonetheless, it is extremely unlikely that the entrepreneur will be able to deflect the VC firm from this approach.

17.2.2   Nominations to the board

> *Both Trojan Horse and the Syndicate as a whole will each have the right to nominate one non-executive director to the Board, and both Trojan Horse and each other Syndicate member committing more than $1 000 000 in aggregate to the Financing will have the right to send a non-voting observer to Board meetings. The two independent directors will be nominated by Board agreement, by means of a bare majority to include the agreement of the Trojan Horse and the Syndicate board representatives.*

Not surprisingly, VC investors will insist on the ability to appoint and replace their nominees to the board (this right is known as a nomination right): they need this in order to be able adequately to monitor their investment and to play an active part both in developing the investment opportunity and in protecting their downside risk. Many VC firms also need a board seat for US regulatory reasons (in order to qualify their fund as a Venture Capital Operating Company under the US Investment Advisors Act). Quite how many nominees will be requested will depend in large part on the prevailing board dynamics, the stage of development of the company and the amount of capital being subscribed by the VC syndicate. At the very least, a significant minority will be requested – at least one director for the lead VC fund and at least one further director for the rest of the investment syndicate (it is a moot point whether the syndicate as a whole will want nomination rights or whether a senior member of the syndicate will itself appropriate the nomination rights).

In addition, it is common for a VC fund to demand "observer rights", which is simply the right to bring someone along to board meetings in an ex officio capacity (non-voting, as such a person is not a director or officer of the company). To some extent this demand has to be worked through with the VC firm by the entrepreneur, to confirm that this right will be used sparingly and productively for the company: at one end of spectrum, some VC firms can use this power to bring along "bag carrying" associates as part of their professional development (not a great value-add from the board's perspective): at the other end of the spectrum, other VC firms will deliver real added-value by bringing thought-leaders or industry experts to the board, to add real value to specific debates, etc.

These nomination rights are not unreasonable and should form part of a productive dialogue with the VC firm around corporate governance. One area that the entrepreneur should consider, however, could be more problematic: the entrepreneur should consider how nomination rights change (if at all) in the event that a VC fund goes passive on its investment and/or allows its stake in the company to fall to a relatively low level. Many VC funds in such a situation would do the decent thing and resign from the board in any event, but it may be sensible for the entrepreneur to insist that nomination rights should fall away once the VC fund's interest in the company falls below an appropriate threshold (conventionally, somewhere in the range of 10% of the fully diluted share capital).

When it comes to the appointment of independent non-executive directors, a whole range of choices are available, including any of the following:

(1) A VC fund may ask for the right to appoint one or more of such persons, so long as it can demonstrate that they are both independent of the VC firm and of high quality, of if either criteria is not satisfied, then approval of the whole board may be required;
(2) One or more of (or the remaining) independent non-executives may be appointed by the board as a whole, without any veto powers by any constituency;
(3) One or more of (or the remaining) independent non-executives may be appointed by the board as a whole, but subject to a veto power in any case exercisable by the VC fund or its nominated director;
(4) Special arrangements may apply as regards the appointment of the non-executive chairman of the board, particularly if that person has a casting vote on deadlocked decisions (they usually won't, unless prevailing law requires that they must do).

From the entrepreneur's perspective it matters most that the non-executive directors are both of the highest quality and independent and fair-minded – people who can be relied on as colleagues, collaborators, mentors and friends. Nonetheless, it is important to make sure that the nomination system gives due weight to each important shareholder constituency, respecting the balance of powers, and cannot be abused to take control of the company.

> *If the founder of the Company, Simon Barnes, shall for any reason cease to hold a position conferring automatic representation on the Board (Chief Executive Officer, Chief Financial Officer or Chief Technical Officer), then for so long as he holds at least 10% of the fully diluted equity share capital of the Company, he will have the personal right to nominate one non-executive director to the Board. In such circumstances, Trojan Horse may stipulate in its absolute discretion that either the Chief Financial Officer or the Chief Technical Officer will cease to serve on the Board.*

One area that is often (surprisingly) missing from board nomination rights is the right of a founder to appoint a nominee (usually him or herself). The reason for this is that entrepreneurs often take it for granted that they will remain on the board in an executive capacity, or that if they do not, then in some way their position on the board will remain entrenched after they cease to be executives. The truth is that without separate and personal nomination rights, the entrepreneur's seat at the board table is not entrenched at all, and is at the mercy of the board's whim once he or she ceases to qualify in an executive capacity (indeed there is no guarantee of a board seat even for the chief executive officer).

It is therefore vital that the founding entrepreneur negotiates at the outset with the VC firm to establish the basis on which his or her interests will be represented at the board going forward. So long as the entrepreneur retains a significant ownership (the rough rule of thumb is 10%+ of the fully diluted share capital), a request for entrenched nomination powers will be very difficult to resist by the VC. In addition (and this is discussed generally as a separate matter at Chapter 20 below), it may be difficult for a departed founding entrepreneur who no longer remains either an executive or an employee to maintain other levers of control inherent in his or her shares (e.g. voting rights and veto rights).

17.3   BOARD PROCESS

Once composition and nomination has been agreed, attention will turn to the most critical part of the board governance mechanics – establishing board process, which will cover every aspect of board activities, including committees, regularity of meeting, quorum and decision-making powers and processes.

17.3.1   Regularity and quorum

> *Board meetings will be held at least six times a year at intervals of not more than ten weeks and the quorum will be any two directors, to include the representative of either Trojan Horse or the Syndicate. However, in order to ensure that non-attendance by Trojan Horse's or the Syndicate's representatives does not prejudice the deliberation of important Company business, in the event that a quorum is not present at the time that any Board meeting is due to start, the business (and only the business) of that meeting may, in the discretion of the attending Board members, be adjourned to a date not less than a week later and no minimum quorum requirements will apply to the adjourned Board meeting. Board meetings may take place in person, by telephone or by webcast.*

The VC firm will want to establish that board meetings occur with reasonable regularity, to ensure that it is able to exercise its monitoring powers properly. Board meetings every month or every two months are the norm. In addition, the VC firm will want to insist that board meetings cannot be quorate without its fund's nominated director present, to ensure that important business cannot be conducted without it. Equally the entrepreneur will want to insist on adjournment powers to ensure that a disorganised VC cannot prejudice the legitimate conduct of business, and that a VC cannot play "dog in the manger" by its nominated director deliberately not participating in important board meetings (either of which behaviour would in fact put the individual director in danger of breaching his or her fiduciary duties to the company).

17.3.2   Committees

> *On Initial Completion, the Company will establish: (i) a remuneration committee of the Board, to be composed exclusively of the Trojan Horse and Syndicate representatives and an independent non-executive director, with full delegated authority to determine the remuneration of all directors and senior employees and the creation, amendment and issue of any and all employee incentive programmes; (ii) an audit committee of the Board, to be composed exclusively of the Trojan Horse and Syndicate representatives and an independent non-executive director, with full delegated authority to supervise the Company's budget, financial planning and audit functions and the Company's financial controls, reporting and procedures; and (iii) a nominations committee of the Board, to be composed exclusively of the Trojan Horse and Syndicate representatives and the Chairman, with full delegated authority to nominate members of the Board. In the event that any director becomes aware of an opportunity for the Company or its business to be sold or floated on a stock exchange, the Board shall forthwith establish an exit committee of the Board, to be composed exclusively of the Trojan Horse and Syndicate representatives and an independent non-executive director, with full delegated authority to supervise and approve the sale or flotation process.*

It is becoming increasingly common in this post-Enron, post-Sarbanes Oxley world, for VC firms to insist that their portfolio companies put in place quasi-public company supervision and compliance programmes. In the context of board governance, this is often seen in the form of remuneration and audit committees with full delegated power to supervise and monitor the key areas of:

(1) pay, benefits and conflicts of interest involving senior managers (remuneration committees); and
(2) financial controls and procedures, information flows and the audit and budget process (audit committees).

It is also increasingly common to see nomination committees empowered to deal with nominations to the board, and provision for exit committees, which deals with the analysis and implementation of exit opportunities such as a sale or IPO. These bodies are usually comprised exclusively of non-executive, independent directors (which includes the VC firm and fund for these purposes – although such persons may be unlikely to qualify as "independent" for London Stock Exchange, SEC, Nasdaq or Sarbanes Oxley purposes) and these bodies will often have full delegated authority to make decisions as though they were the full board of directors. Where this is not possible under applicable laws (e.g. in many Continental European jurisdictions), these bodies will have supervisory functions only and will report back to the full board.

To some extent, the entrepreneur should resist this encroachment of public company-style governance, because it may be inconsistent with the demands of a small and fast-moving business that needs to remain nimble in its decision-making. In addition, the entrepreneur may feel uncomfortable at the thought of matters as sensitive as executive pay and incentives being put into the hands of the non-executives alone. On the other hand, the entrepreneur should recognise that if the company has ambitions to be a public company one day, then the earlier that it embraces public company-style governance and controls, the easier it will be to migrate to public company status subsequently.

17.3.3   Board veto rights

Certain matters which are likely to have a significant effect on the Company's business will require prior consideration by and the approval of the Board by simple majority, the majority to include, in the case of a sub-set of those matters, the Trojan Horse and Syndicate board representatives. Such matters will include: (i) Approval of the annual budget and business plan; (ii) Establishment and operation of pension or employee benefit plans; (iii) Delegation of Board powers to committees (except as described above); (iv) Changes to accounting policies and practices, or the auditors; (v) Appointment or removal of any director, officer or senior employee (except pursuant to nomination rights); (vi) Contracts with senior employees or material contracts; (vii) Formulation of key corporate policies (risk management, health & safety, insurance); (viii) Grant of any security interest, indemnity or guarantee; (ix) Material capital expenditure outside the Company's annual budget; (x) Non-ordinary course of business activities; (xi) Material litigation; and (xii) Public announcements.

It is extremely common for VC firms to insist that early stage venture-backed companies have veto rights at board level, in some cases requiring in addition to a general board approval that the VC fund's nominated director (acting within his or her fiduciary responsibilities) is part of the approving majority. This ensures that important business decisions attract the focus of the board rather than being decided by the management team outside the board process (tightening corporate governance still further and supporting the fiduciary responsibilities of the directors) and that material items that may affect the VC fund's equity interest can be blocked by the VC fund. Accordingly, the governance structure within the company will be constructed so that a defined list of activities will require the prior approval of the board of directors, and a subset of those activities will require the prior approval of the director nominated by the VC fund.

The VC fund will inevitably require shareholder vetos over certain matters and this is perfectly reasonable, given that they will be a significant shareholder. It is in the interest of the entrepreneur to make sure that as many as possible of these vetos are operated at the level of the board. This is because the exercise of vetos will then move from a position where they can be exercised selfishly and arbitrarily without penalty (a shareholder veto) to a position where the individual director nominated by the VC fund must exercise vetos subject to his or her over-riding duty as a director of the company. In other words, a director is legally required to act at all times in the best interests of the company, not the individual shareholder who appointed them. By the same token, the VC fund will insist that any vetos that are of particular importance to its interests as a shareholder are embedded as shareholder vetos, not director vetos. Clearly, the "fun" is to be had at the margins between these two concepts – which is where the vigorous debate in negotiation will be focused.

In practice, director vetos tend to focus on significant, but day to day matters such as the matters that fall generally to the remuneration and audit committees – the appointment or removal of directors and officers, material disputes, the determination of the annual business plan and budgets, material contracts, changes to the company's advisers, etc. Often issues will only be raised to the level of VC director veto if they are sufficiently large to become material in the context of the business taken as a whole. The entrepreneur should simply ensure that this list is sensible in the context of the state of development of the company and the experience of management and also that there is provision for these items gradually to fall away as the company becomes more mature and capable, so that eventually the board activities can be unfettered by specific process requirements or director vetos.

17.4   SHAREHOLDER INFORMATION

As we have discussed in detail previously (Chapter 5) it is absolutely vital to a VC fund that it receives timely and high quality information regarding its investment. Much of the focus in this area goes on ensuring that information systems, particularly financial controls and procedures, are high quality and effective, but it is still necessary for the VC fund to have specific rights as a shareholder to receive and use the information it needs. This is because, in the absence of specific contractual rights, company law in most jurisdictions will give a shareholder relatively little access to information about the company and its operations, and the information flows that the VC fund will be receiving indirectly through the medium of its nominated board director (board papers, etc) may not be utilised freely by the VC fund or the VC firm without risking breach of duties by the director. Of course, in reality this information flow happens all the time illustrating the conflict of interest that most VCs face when nominated as directors on behalf of their fund.

> *The Syndicate will have the right to receive, in a format and to a level of detail agreed in advance with Trojan Horse: (i) unaudited monthly management accounts within 30 days of the month end, (ii) audited annual accounts within 90 days of the year end and (iii) an annual business plan and budget within 30 days prior to the next year. In addition, the Syndicate will have the right to receive all information provided to the members of the board, and any and all other material general information concerning the Company. The Company will also deliver any information reasonably requested by, allow inspection of properties by, financial records by, and discuss its business and finances with, the Syndicate from time to time.*

Accordingly, the VC fund will insist on having specific rights to receive certain routine financial information on a timely basis and all information provided to the board (thereby enabling the director-appointee to pass on the board papers within his or her organisation). In addition, the VC firm will often ask for a "sweeper" clause that allows it to make reasonable requests for information and access from time to time. Some VC firms will specify with more particularity their general need to receive sufficient information to construct their own reports to their LPs and monitor other important matters peculiar to the VC fund.

As discussed before, while the entrepreneur should not resist legitimate and reasonable demands for information by the VC fund, it is extremely important that these information flows are closely monitored and controlled, that it is made clear that no information provided to the VC fund is warranted or in any way gives rise to obligations or liabilities on the company or its managers, and that the use and dissemination of the information received is tightly proscribed (e.g. through a standard confidentiality agreement) – to ensure that the information cannot be misused and will not fall into the wrong hands.

17.5   SHAREHOLDER VETO POWERS

> *The Company must obtain the consent of three quarters of the Syndicate (by number of shares held) before it can do certain things which would be likely to be material in the context of the Company's business, including: (i) Changes to the share capital; (ii) Changes to the Company's articles of association; (iii) Distributions by or any winding-up or dissolution of the Company; (iv) Major disposals, acquisitions, mergers or joint ventures; (v) Material transactions with related parties; (vi) Material changes in the nature of the business; (vii) Borrowings, sale & lease backs, factoring or hire purchase arrangements; (viii) Grants of any security interest, indemnity or guarantee; and (ix) Sale or flotation of the Company or its business.*

As prefigured above, the VC fund will insist on shareholder veto rights over a defined list of items that are regarded as so material to the value of the VC fund's investment in the business that to carry the item out would be tantamount to varying the rights of the VC fund in the deal. It is important to realise that these powers will be in addition to the general protections that the VC fund will have as a minority shareholder under the applicable law under which the company has been incorporated (for example, core share rights, class rights, etc), which may of themselves be very extensive and almost amount to separate vetos in themselves (for example under German law).

These shareholder veto items will typically include areas such as:

(1) the issue of securities/shares by the company or rights over securities;
(2) constitutional changes such as changes to share rights, or the repurchase or redemption of shares, or any other type of capital reorganisation or reconstruction;
(3) the flotation or sale of the company or its business, or any significant collaboration, joint venture or merger transactions, or the purchase or sale of any material asset out of the ordinary course of business;
(4) transactions between the company and related parties (catching all conflict of interest situations);
(5) the liquidation, winding up or other form of creditor composition, etc by the company;
(6) significant borrowings or security arrangements by the company;
(7) the declaration or payment of dividends or any other form of distribution by the company.

As far as the entrepreneur is concerned, the goal in this area is threefold:

(1) to ensure that the complete list of veto items is as short as possible;
(2) to downgrade as many agreed veto items as possible to director veto issues (see above); and
(3) to ensure that the mechanics for exercising the veto powers are reasonable. In some cases, this may be a fait accompli, for example if the veto is granted solely to a single VC fund. However, where the veto is granted to an investment syndicate (much more common), it is very important that the mechanism by which that syndicate makes decisions on vetos is clearly addressed and can operate to ensure that the majority in the syndicate can carry the minority, so that no small minority of the syndicate can effectively hold up a consensus approach.

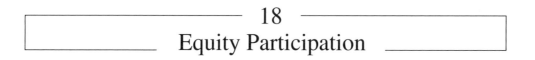

18

Equity Participation

18.1 INTRODUCTION TO EQUITY PARTICIPATION

The nature of the equity participation taken up by the VC fund is really where the "rubber hits the road" in the term sheet – these are the provisions which detail the fundamental economic rights of the VC fund vis à vis the other shareholder constituencies and they are enormously important to each of those constituencies. They also have the potential to be extraordinarily complicated.

There are certain basic concepts for the shares commonly issued to VC funds in venture financings, but within those concepts lurk a multitude of issues. The shares most likely to be issued to a VC fund in a venture capital financing will contain certain inevitable features – voting rights, participation rights, redemption rights and conversion rights. In order to keep things as simple and as clear as possible, this chapter examines the core features of a VC fund's equity ownership in any company it backs by discussing the market-standard "participating preferred redeemable convertible share" (or "Preferred Share" to use its simpler name), as set out in the pro forma term sheet. We will also discuss the potential variations from the Preferred Share, examining the flex in each individual feature and come to some preliminary conclusions.

18.2 VOTING RIGHTS

18.2.1 Introduction to voting rights

> *The Ordinary Shares and the A Shares will vote together as a single class of shares, except where the A Shares have specific veto or other voting rights, where they will vote as a separate class. However, in order to ensure that only individuals with an ongoing interest in the Company continue to have the right to vote their shares at meetings of the Company, any director, officer or employee of the Company will cease to be entitled to any voting rights upon ceasing to remain a director, officer or employee of the Company for any reason, provided that this provision shall not apply to Simon Barnes' shareholding unless and until he comes to hold less than 10% of the Company's issued equity share capital.*

Voting rights are an easy aspect of Preferred Shares to describe – they are merely the rights of a shareholder to attend and vote, in person or by proxy, at general meetings of shareholders.

18.2.2 Attractions of voting rights to the VC firm

Not surprisingly, the VC firm will insist that the VC fund's shares have voting rights that are in all respects *at least* equal to the rights of any other shareholder in the company, and in particular the ordinary or common shares that form the core share capital constituency. This is inevitable, as the VC fund will aim to be an active investor and, as a representative of the

LPs in the fund, the VC fund will want to have the normal and usual levers of shareholder influence, which are principally exercised through the medium of voting rights. This right will usually be one vote for every share held by the VC fund.

In addition, there will be two areas in which the voting rights of the VC fund may be enhanced above and beyond the standard "one vote per share" approach embedded in most systems of corporations law. Firstly, many systems of corporations law will provide additional voting rights to shareholders in specific circumstances, either generally or to a specific sub-set of shareholders. For example, the shares held by the VC fund/syndicate will usually constitute a separate class of shares to other shares in issue (because they will have distinct and different economic rights to the other shareholders, as discussed below). In such a case "class rights" will apply such that any change to the rights to those shares – whether directly or indirectly (by means of a change to the rights of any *other* class of share that impacts, directly or indirectly, the class of shares held by the VC fund) – will require the *separate* approval of the class of shares held by the VC fund. Because the VC fund (or the syndicate investing together in a financing round) will usually hold the entirety of a new class of shares issued specifically for that financing round, it means that in practice the VC fund/syndicate will hold an effective veto over a diverse range of corporate actions that directly or indirectly impact their underlying share rights – sometimes well beyond the formal veto rights discussed above at Chapter 17. This is a point that is often missed by entrepreneurs when planning for change.

In addition, because the applicable law will often specify the majority level at which class consents must be given, the entrepreneur should also consider carefully the consequences – in terms of shifting the balance of power towards the VC fund or a significant minority of the syndicate members – for example, under English law, a 75% class approval is required, meaning that a syndicate member holding 25.1% of the relevant class of shares will have negative control over a significant set of matters, which in practice may lead to a disproportionate influence over the company. Note that this approval threshold applies to the proportion of the relevant class of shares, not the entire company, which can often mean that a very small shareholder in absolute terms can frustrate a corporate action – using the example term sheet, a person holding less than 8.4% of the company through the A shares (e.g. 2 510 000 A Shares), would hold more than 25% of the A Shareholders class and be able unilaterally to block matters affecting the class of A Shareholders differently from other classes. The entrepreneur must identify such risks and seek legal advice as to how they may be countered.

The Company must obtain the consent of three quarters of the Syndicate (by number of shares held) before it can do certain things which would be likely to be material in the context of the Company's business, including: (i) Changes to the share capital; (ii) Changes to the Company's articles of association; (iii) Distributions by or any winding-up or dissolution of the Company; (iv) Major disposals, acquisitions, mergers or joint ventures; (v) Material transactions with related parties; (vi) Material changes in the nature of the business; (vii) Borrowings, sale & lease backs, factoring or hire purchase arrangements; (viii) Grants of any security interest, indemnity or guarantee; and (ix) Sale or flotation of the Company or its business.

Secondly, the VC fund will usually specify a list of material matters where it demands specific veto powers as a shareholder. We have discussed these at 17.5 above.

As a structural matter, there is no reason why voting rights have to follow, or be embedded in the security that provides the VC fund with any part of its economic protection or return in the investment opportunity: instead they may from time to time be held in separate securities.

18.2.3   Attractions for the entrepreneur

It is an impossible and unreasonable task for an entrepreneur to resist the grant of voting rights to a VC fund. However, the entrepreneur should take great care to ensure that these voting rights do not extend too far, or give rise to dangerous conflicts of interest in particular situations, or even give rise to a situation where the VC fund or syndicate may ride rough-shod over the interests of another group of shareholders. As such, in agreeing a position as regards voting rights, the entrepreneur should:

(1) understand the application of class rights under applicable laws (indeed the location of incorporation of the company may have been deliberately chosen by the VC fund to benefit it in this regard) to figure out whether the list of items that would be subject to VC fund/ syndicate class rights are suitable and appropriate. If they are not, there may be ways in which a defined outcome in specific circumstances can be engineered (for example by using weighted voting rights or other structural solutions – including, in some jurisdictions, simply "deeming" each class of shares to be a single class);
(2) as discussed at 17.5, deal appropriately with any and all specific shareholder veto requests; and
(3) consider carefully whether there are any circumstances within the veto items in which the interests of the shareholders, or any sub-set of them, are likely to be fundamentally divergent, creating a potential schism that could significantly disrupt the company – in particular, the entrepreneur should try to avoid a situation where any individual shareholder or small sub-set thereof without a material economic investment in the venture could come to have a unilateral veto over a corporate action or event.

18.2.4   Voting rights – areas to watch out for

Once an entrepreneur has evaluated the reasonableness and practical application of the veto powers requested by the VC firm, as well as the hidden veto powers that arise under applicable laws, pretty much all relevant issues are covered. However, one issue that is easy to miss in this area is the possibility that the *absence* of veto powers, particularly class veto powers, may operate against the entrepreneur's own interests. In other words, the entrepreneur may spend too much time focusing on the VC fund's veto powers and forget to ensure he or she is included in the constituencies required for some vetos, or is protected under the applicable laws in any event. By way of example – two key areas:

(1) the entrepreneur will obviously want to ensure that the founder shareholders as a group, either have the ability to veto any sale (almost certainly unachievable, as it would fetter the exit potential for the VC firm) or that a reasonable sub-set of the founder shareholders are required to support the exit opportunity (for example a significant minority sufficient for a substantial majority of the shareholders overall to be in favour of the sale), before a sale of the company or its business can take place – this is important, because without this express veto, many jurisdictions would permit a bare majority of the shareholders (and often the board alone, without reference to the shareholders) to sell the company's business, or even merge the company or transfer the issued share capital to a buyer, in each

case without separate special approvals being required from different shareholder constituencies or classes, who may be very differently affected in economic terms by the sale.

(2) The entrepreneur will also want to ensure that shares cannot be issued by the company without the support of each separate interested constituency, particularly as he or she will be likely to be holding a junior security in the company's share capital. Again, this is important, because without this express veto, many jurisdictions would permit a bare majority of the shareholders (and often the board alone, without reference to the shareholders), to permit the company to issue new shares, without separate special approvals being required from different shareholder constituencies or classes, who again may be very differently affected in economic terms by the share issue.

18.3   DIVIDEND RIGHTS

18.3.1   Introduction to dividend rights

> *To compensate for the time value of the monies committed to the Company by the Syndicate, the A Shares will accrue a preferential dividend at the rate of 10% per annum on the A Share issue price and on all accrued but unpaid dividends, compounding annually (the "Special Dividend"). No dividend will be declared or paid on any of the Company's shares until the accrued Special Dividend has been paid on the A Shares. The accrued Special Dividend will: (i) become payable to A Shareholders immediately prior to completion of the liquidation or sale of the Company or its business, in priority to payments to any other shareholders; and (ii) be applied automatically in the subscription of new Ordinary Shares at the same time and on the same basis as the A Shares, if and when they are converted into Ordinary Shares (as described below). Except for the preferential dividend rights of the A Shares, no class of shares will have any entitlement to a pre-determined dividend and all shares will have equal rights in terms of dividend entitlement.*

Dividend rights are rights for a shareholder to receive an income return on an investment in the company, by means of a payment on the shares held in the company.

18.3.2   Attraction of dividend rights to the VC firm

A dividend right performs two fundamental functions for a VC fund – it ensures that cash cannot leak out of the company through dividends or other distributions on the shares without the VC fund at least participating equally and ratably, and it provides a mechanism whereby a basic level of return on the VC fund's investment (often akin to the time value of the money committed by the VC fund) can be built into the investment structure.

The fundamental protection that a VC firm will invariably seek for the VC fund's shares is that they have dividend rights (covering every form of dividend or distribution that can be made by the business) which are *at least equal* to those of any other class of shares, in particular the common stock of the company (typically held by the founders and management). That essentially means that the company can never pay a dividend or make any other form of distribution to any other category of shares without also including the shares held by the VC fund. In practice, "leakage" of value away from the company, through the payment of dividends, is not a major risk for VC funds, not only because it is usual for such an action to be subject to a director or shareholder veto (see Chapter 17 above), but also because young, high-growth businesses tend not to be distributing their free cash flow, but reinvesting it furiously in future growth.

However, in addition to this kind of core dividend protection for a VC fund, it is not uncommon for VC firms also to require that the money their VC fund contributes to the investment opportunity bears, effectively, a rate of interest representing a notional "cost of money" return (typically taken as being in the range of 5–15% per annum, although of course the real cost of money to a VC fund may be much higher, based on the return expectations of its investors). This notional return will generally be applied through the medium of a preferential dividend on the shares subscribed by the VC fund ("preferential" meaning that it is paid exclusively to the class of shares held by the VC fund and not to any other class of shareholder). Such a preferential dividend can be either:

(1) "non-cumulative", meaning that if a dividend is ever paid, the VC fund will have first call on the dividend to the fixed or pre-defined preferential level, but the right lapses if the dividend is not made in any period; or

(2) "cumulative", meaning that the VC firm's shares will bear a fixed or pre-determined level of preferential dividend return each year, which if not paid in any period will "roll-up" (i.e. be retained as an obligation of the company, often compounding with the "principal" underlying subscription proceeds at regular intervals) and eventually be paid on a defined event – which could be anything from the date on which the company finally has the cash resources and legal ability to pay the accrued dividend entitlement, or an exit event such as a sale of the business or of the company itself (in which event the accrued preferential dividend entitlement could be paid out in cash, or could be converted into new shares participating in the exit opportunity – for example in an IPO).

The dividend entitlement can be set by any means – the rate can be fixed, or it can vary ("float"), or step up or down at regular or irregular intervals by reference to any number of internal or external factors such (interest rates, corporate developments, time, etc).

18.3.3 The entrepreneur's response

Obviously, it is true that a VC's committed funds have a time value and at first glance it appears reasonable for that value to be reflected in a preferential dividend, essentially as an interest cost – but that is conveniently to forget that the VC fund will almost invariably negotiate an uncapped upside participation (see 18.4 below), and this basic equity feature sits uncomfortably alongside the debt-like feature of the guaranteed minimum "interest" return and should generally be resisted for this reason. However, the terms of many VC funds include a cost of capital allocation as a priority return to their LPs (known as a "hurdle rate"): this is a conventional feature of private equity funds, but less so for VC funds. Where such a feature is in place for the VC fund, it does not seem unreasonable for the VC firm to ask its portfolio companies to meet the same minimum return on capital invested, to match the hurdle rate embedded in its fund terms.

The degree of reasonableness in a given situation will depend on the overall features of the equity structure – which should be considered together as a package and not separately. For example, if the VC fund's equity is in the form of a preference share with a capped return (see 18.4.1 below), then it will be perfectly reasonable to have a fixed or floating coupon rate accrue on the shares, which will be quasi-debt. Conversely, if a preferred dividend rate is proposed with an uncapped return, the entrepreneur should try to keep the absolute level of the "interest rate" as low as possible, for obvious reasons. The starting point for an entrepreneur should therefore be to resist any rate at all, particularly if the VC fund does not have a hurdle rate in its terms or if other features of the preferred return (see 18.4 below) are already strongly favourable to the VC fund.

If a preferential dividend is conceded, then the entrepreneur will naturally focus on keeping the rate as low as possible. However, it also important to try to ensure that the dividend is non-cumulative, but this battle will almost certainly be lost unless it can be demonstrated that the company's cash-generation and dividend paying abilities are generally sufficient to pay the dividend (extremely unusual for venture-backed companies). In this case the VC fund may be prepared to take the risk of a non-cumulative dividend. With a cumulative preferential dividend, the entrepreneur's focus should simply be on keeping the interest rate as a "simple" rate (i.e. non-compound) and if the entrepreneur cannot win that argument, then it is important to try and ensure that the regular points at which compounding occurs (known as "rests") are far apart (e.g. annual rests, as opposed to quarterly or even monthly rests).

18.4   THE PREFERENCE CASCADE

The preference cascade refers to the relative rights of the shareholders to participate in *any* capital return on their investment in the company. Typically such a capital return would arise on (i) a sale of the business (or any asset) and subsequent distribution of the net proceeds of sale to the shareholders or (ii) a sale of shares by the shareholder. In addition, increasingly, the marketplace is treating both a private sale of shares and the creation of an *opportunity* to sell shares via an IPO as the same thing – an exit – and applying the preference cascade rules to both situations.

There are many and various ways in which the preference cascade can be applied, but fundamentally we are talking about two core concepts – the extent to which the VC fund may be "preferred" in terms of initial allocations of capital return, and what happens after this preference is satisfied. In this debate, two fundamental "animals" exist – the preference share and the preferred share – and increasingly we are seeing the emergence of a third concept (essentially a compromise concept), the "high watermark" preferred share. Each of these alternatives is discussed in turn below with a focus on their essential features and pros and cons. When dealing with this area, the entrepreneur should first identify the type of security being proposed by the VC firm and then address the issues raised by the peculiar features of that security type.

18.4.1   Preference shares

> *In relation to any proposed payment by the Company to its shareholders (for example, on the solvent liquidation of the Company or in a distribution by the Company of the net proceeds of the sale of its business any of its material assets), the A shareholders will first be entitled to receive an amount equal to the aggregate subscription price paid up on their A Shares, plus any accrued but unpaid Special Dividend, in priority to any payment to be made to the Ordinary Shareholders, following which the A Shares shall carry no further participation and therefore any residue will be distributed among the Ordinary Shareholders alone.*

A preference share has a defined, capped but priority participation in the profits of the business – the "preference" – which may arise in the form of capital dividends or distributions from the company, or as a contractual right of first participation in the net proceeds of the sale of the company by shareholders themselves. After that priority payment has been made (typically a return of the amount advanced, together with notional interest on such amount that may be paid at regular intervals or may roll up and accumulate), the preference stock will not participate further.

Therefore, a preference share has many of the features of debt – a pre-determined and capped return (essentially a repayment of the debt: the equity infusion made by the VC fund) together with an interest return that will be payable at intervals or roll up for the duration of the "loan" period and be payable on an exit. However, for accounting and legal purposes, a preference share is part of the share capital of the company (and sometimes even the equity share capital of the company, for technical reasons).

With a preference share, the VC fund has secured its downside – although not a creditor, it is the first shareholder to be able to exit its investment, which may be particularly valuable in a situation where the company decides to wind itself up or is sold in a "fire sale" at little aggregate value. The preference share itself has no upside potential, and so that feature is usually created through the ability of the preference share to be converted into fully participating ordinary shares at any time at the option of the VC fund (see 18.6 below). As such, a VC fund holding preference shares will be watching the value of the business carefully as an exit opportunity approaches, to establish whether the crossover point – at which its shareholding is more valuable in the form of ordinary shares than preference shares – has been passed. Once that crossover point has been passed, the VC fund will be expected to convert its shares into ordinary shares and participate in the exit opportunity accordingly (pro rata and equally with all shareholders), having given up the comfort and protection of the preference share status (the defined, capped return plus downside protection) for the racier upside, but unprotected downside, of an ordinary share.

This type of share is extremely common in venture funding and very neatly meets the concerns of both the entrepreneur and the VC fund. The VC fund is usually concerned to embed three features in any equity security – reasonable downside protection, a stretch goal for management performance, and full upside participation. The preference share features all of these criteria to a greater or lesser extent – in particular management will recognise that they will receive nothing from a sale until an amount significantly in excess of the preferential return is capable of being returned to the VC fund – at that inflection point, the VC fund will convert to common shares and everyone will participate together equally in the proceeds.

Entrepreneurs should note, however, that this crossover point is *not* the moment when the company can be sold for $1 more than the preference right: it is the point at which the pro rata participation by the VC fund in the exit proceeds would be $1 greater than the maximum amount recoverable under the preference right, which may create a higher crossover point than the entrepreneur expects. In the term sheet example (where the VC syndicate commits $10 M and owns one third of the fully diluted share capital at $30 M post-money valuation – NB we assume that the options that are issued can be exercised into shares which will participate in the sale), the crossover exit valuation point would be a little above $30 M. Therefore, management will not be rewarded until they have added value over and above the post-money of the financing: neatly demonstrating the downside protection feature – hardly unfair commercially, although it is immediately clear that the preference share structure does not provide much of a stretch goal of itself for management to deliver high performance and demonstrate ambition (unless the preference feature contains a principle multiple above 1, which is rarely seen). Hence the use of preferred share structures described below.

It is typical for each round of financing to be in the form of a separate class of preferred or preference share.

18.4.2 "Double-dipping" preferred shares

> In relation to any proposed payment by the Company to its shareholders (for example on the solvent liquidation of the Company or in a distribution by the Company of the net proceeds of the sale of its business or any of its material assets), the A Shareholders will first be entitled to receive an amount equal to two times the aggregate subscription price paid up on their A Shares, plus any accrued but unpaid Special Dividend, in priority to any payment to be made to the Ordinary Shareholders. After such a preferential payment entitlement has been satisfied in full, any residue left over will be shared among the Ordinary Shareholders and the A Shareholders equally (pro rata to shareholdings and on an as-if-converted basis with regard to the A Shares).

A preferred share has a defined priority participation in the profits of the business in a similar fashion to a preference share. The difference is that the participation is not capped at the priority amount but, after that priority payment has been made (typically a return of the amount advanced, or a multiple thereof), the preferred stock will participate pari passu in any residue along with the common stock, without limit. This double participation – first on a preferential basis and then again on an equal basis with the common shareholders – is known as the "double dip".

As with a preference share, a VC fund holding a preferred share has secured its downside protection (absolutely essential in a VC firm's portfolio management), but unlike the preference share, the preferred share also contains full upside participation without the need to convert the shares to common stock. The benefits of this are both enhanced downside protection and the beginnings of the creation of a genuine stretch goal for management. This significantly strengthens the performance of the VC fund's portfolio performance in the middle ground (the c 40%+ of the portfolio that will "bump along the ground" in performance terms, but which must be worked to pay for the c 70%+ of the portfolio that will not out-perform). For this reason, the preferred share remains highly popular for VCs in investment term sheets.

The absolute level of the double dip multiple can vary, largely according to risk, stage of investment and market cycle. For early stage or very high risk investments, or at the bottom end of the market cycle (when investors are bearish and perhaps looking for "payback" for overpaying at the top of the cycle), multiples can go as high as 3–6×. However, in more usual times, multiples in the range of 1–2× should be expected (meaning that – e.g. at 2× – the entrepreneur will have to return twice the VC fund's financial investment before beginning to participate in any residue). Even at the lower end of these double dip multiples, however, the preferred share features are extremely useful for the VC firm to create enhanced downside protection and a perfectly legitimate stretch goal for management (in a way that the preference share does not), in order to try to ensure that management's ambitions are suitably aggressive – as has to be the case for the out-performing investments in a venture capital portfolio.

The actual term sheet example from Trojan Horse uses a double dipping preferred share structure.

(1) Using a 1× double dip, at a $30 M exit value (the "crossover" point for the preference share in the previous example) the syndicate would receive $16.67 M in proceeds. This is equivalent to 55.6% of the net proceeds, not the 33.3% of the equity that the syndicate actually owns (again, assuming that management are able to exercise their options and participate in the sale as to the shares issued on their exercise). This is because the first $10 M goes immediately to the syndicate and of the remaining $20 M the syndicate receives its 33.3% share of the residue. Compare this with the $10 M received by the syndicate (and the $20 M received by management) under a conventional preference share structure.

1× Preferred Share Worked Example		Preferred	Ordinary
Net proceeds	$30 000 000		
First distribution	$10 000 000	$10 000 000	–
Residue	$20 000 000	$6 666 000	$13 334 000*
Total		$16 666 000	$13 334 000

* includes entitlement arising from options exercised into ordinary shares

(2) Using a 2× double dip, at a $30 M exit value the syndicate would receive $23.33 M (77.8% of the net proceeds). This is because the first $20 M goes to the syndicate and of the remaining $10 M the syndicate receives 33.3% ensuring that the VC fund will take very much the lion's share of the net proceeds of sale at the lower end of investment performance. The net effect of this super-allocation of low-side exit proceeds to the VC syndicate, in addition to enhanced downside protection, is to increase the stretch goal modestly for management before they start to participate materially: it would take a 1.37× exit multiple at a 1× double dip (a $40 M sale) and a 1.7× exit multiple at a 2× double dip (a $50 M sale) for management to recover the $20 M that they would have obtained in a $30 M exit under a conventional preference share, identical to an all ordinary share scenario, as the exit valuation is exactly at the crossover point at which it would make commercial sense for the holder of the preference shares to convert to ordinary shares. These are modest stretch goals indeed (the impact of the double dip tool is greater where large sums in absolute terms are being raised from VC syndicates) but they are helpful nonetheless in terms of portfolio management by VC firms.

2× Preferred Share Worked Example		Preferred	Ordinary
Net proceeds	$30 000 000		
First distribution	$20 000 000	$20 000 000	–
Residue	$10 000 000	$3 333 000	$6 667 000*
Total		$23 333 000	$6 667 000

* includes entitlement arising from options exercised into ordinary shares

In the case of a double-dipping preferred share, it is perfectly possible to sever the preferred return component from the pro rata participation component – for example by converting the former into a debt security (usually termed a "subordinated preference certificate", which rolls up interest at the Special Dividend rate) and leaving the latter as an ordinary share participation. Economically, the VC fund is in the same position as it would be with a preferred share, but structurally this has the benefit (i) to the VC fund, of ensuring junior creditor status for the bulk of the VC fund's financial contribution to the company (a modest enhancement in a downside scenario to a preferred equity status) and (ii) to the company, of enabling the interest return element (the Special Dividend) to be tax deductible (whereas a dividend on shares is payable out of the post tax income of the company and is not tax deductible). While this structure is highly prevalent in private equity financing structures, it may be only a matter of time before this innovation passes across into the VC environment.

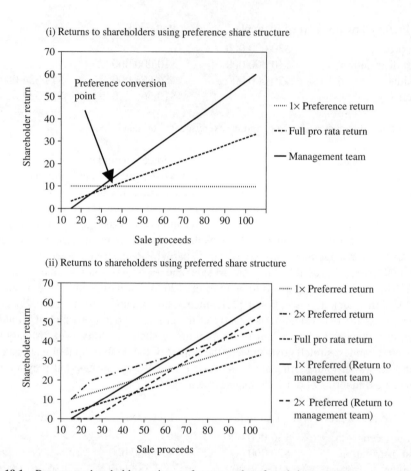

Figure 18.1   Returns to shareholders using preference and preferred share structures

The diagrams show the relative impact of (i) preference shares and (ii) preferred shares on the returns to the VC syndicate, and the founding management team. Diagram (i) shows clearly that the simple preference share affords downside protection below the cut off point, but offers no upside potential unless converted to ordinary shares. Diagram (ii) shows that the preferred share approach offers the best of both worlds: downside protection and upside participation. Note the effect of the 1× and 2× double dipping mechanism. Under a 2× preferred return it takes the management team much longer to "catch up" in terms of pay off for a successful exit.

18.4.3 "High watermark" preferred shares

> ... However, if on a notional allocation of the proposed payment equally between all share-holders (pro rata to shareholdings and on an as-if-converted basis with regard to the A Shares) the A Shareholders would receive an aggregate amount greater than six times the aggregate subscription price for the A Shares, then the A Share preferential payment entitlement shall drop away and instead the proposed payment will be made equally between all shareholders (pro rata to shareholdings and on an as-if-converted basis with regard to the A Shares).

Under the classic double dip methodology, the management team will never recover their true pro rata position (as though all parties had always held ordinary shares) – they will always cede the preferred return (the first 1–2×, etc) of the VC syndicate's financial contribution ($10–20 M in our term sheet example) as a first slice of the net proceeds of any exit, meaning that however successful the eventual investment exit, management's participation will always be below their pro rata ownership of the company. As a consequence of this perceived unfairness, and also to seek to continue at the same time to drive reasonable stretch goals for management teams, a variation to the classic preferred share has developed in VC term sheets in recent years, which addresses this perceived unfairness by including a term which disqualifies the double dip provided that a specified overall return has been reach of the VC fund's investment (known the "high watermark"), often at a return level in the range of a 5–6× multiple on the money invested.

In other words, if the specified return threshold would be earned by the VC fund on a *notional* pro rata allocation of the exit proceeds among all shareholders (treating all shareholders as though they all held ordinary shares – i.e. as though the preferred shares were converted to common shares in accordance with their rights), then the first preferential return right otherwise allocable to the VC fund (the first element of the double dip) will be disregarded and the proceeds will instead be distributed entirely on a basis that is simply pro rata to shareholdings (on an as-if-converted basis). Looked at from the perspective of the preferential rights of a preferred shareholder, it means that the double dip feature drops away and management are able to participate in the net proceeds of sale on an equal footing with the investors in every dollar of exit proceeds.

Using the term sheet example, the high watermark at 6× would be $60 M (six times the $10 M investment contribution by the VC syndicate) and therefore the point at which the preferential rights of the A Shareholders would drop away entirely would be at an exit value of $180 M – creating a very significant stretch goal for management before they can recover the double dip element "lost" to the VC syndicate. The attraction of this feature is that it creates a significant "carrot" at the end of the stretch goal (the recovery of the pro rata participation lost in the preference – $10 M in the case of a 1× double dip: $20 M in the case of a 2× double dip), unlike the double dip feature alone, which operates more as a "stick" than a "carrot".

The key problem with this type of feature (one often missed in VC term sheets) is that the structure can create an artificial barrier to exit at certain exit values – a point of dislo-cation in the interests of each shareholding constituency – because as the high watermark level is crossed, the VC syndicate will suddenly drop back onto a shallower return participation profile which will prejudice it in absolute terms – potentially causing a conflict of interest between the different shareholder constituencies between certain exit value parameters. For example, again using the term sheet example of a 6× high watermark and a 2× double dip: at a $179 M exit value, the VC syndicate would receive $73 M in net proceeds (a $20 M first preference, plus $53 M in pro rata participation in the residue), whereas at a $181 M exit, $2 M more of net proceeds, the syndicate would receive only $60.3 M in proceeds (entirely in pro rata participation of the full amount, as there is no longer a 2× first preference), because by then they would have moved through the 6× high watermark threshold in absolute terms and would participate on a different basis. This would mean, perversely, that the VC syndicate would have no incentive to support an exit price higher than $179.9 M (indeed a strong disincentive) until that exit price exceeded $220 M – a $40 M value gap – at which point they would then be better off applying the high watermark provision. This return dislocation is demonstrated pictorially below.

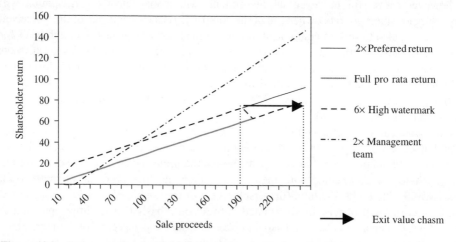

Figure 18.2   Returns to shareholders using a high watermark preferred share

The high watermark approach allows the management team to catch up with the VC syndicate in terms of pay off at exit. The "exit value chasm" can however create a disconnect in the incentives for the VC to support an exit above a certain valuation.

The best way to fix this problem is usually to provide that, instead of falling back to a full pro rata position immediately at the high watermark trigger, the VC syndicate simply does not participate thereafter (or participates only modestly – usually a modest compensation is necessary to encourage the VC firm to aim high) until all other shareholders have caught up to a full pro rata position in aggregate, whereupon further distributions are then made pro rata without limit: this kind of "flip-flop" approach will ensure that the VC syndicate will never be worse off under any high watermark trigger and therefore will be incentivised along with the management team to seek the best possible exit price at all times. The cost of this to management is a slight deferral in their "catch-up" to full pro rata status, but it is usually a price worth paying in order to align everyone's interest on an exit at full value. Appropriate wording is included below.

> *...However, if on a notional allocation of the proposed payment equally between all shareholders (pro rata to shareholdings and on an as-if-converted basis with regard to the A Shares) the A Share- holders would receive an aggregate amount greater than six times the aggregate subscription price for the A Shares, then (i) firstly, the A Shareholders will be entitled to receive an amount equal to two times the aggregate subscription price paid up on their A Shares, plus any accrued but unpaid Special Dividend, in priority to any payment to be made to the Ordinary Shareholders, and thereafter (ii) secondly, the A Shareholders and the Ordinary Shareholders will participate in the residue of the proposed payment in the ratio of 20:80 until such time as the Ordinary Shareholders have received in aggregate an amount equal to the amount they would have received had the aggregate distributions under paragraphs (i) and (ii) been made equally between all shareholders (pro rata to shareholdings and on an as-if-converted basis with regard to the A Shares), and thereafter (iii) thirdly, any remaining residue (if any) of the proposed payment shall be made equally between all shareholders (pro rata to shareholdings and on an as-if-converted basis with regard to the A Shares).*

It can be extremely complex to administer this kind of instrument and prevent economic anomalies if it is part of a complex capital structure involving several classes of preferred equity, but, nonetheless, the entrepreneur may consider in the circumstances that it is an appropriately sophisticated security to balance the interests of financial investors and the founders in all situations and avoid a situation where the financial investors invariably make off with a priority return that is never shared with the founders.

18.4.4   The best type of preference?

There is simply no "best" type of preference in any given situation.

The entrepreneur will immediately understand that this is a highly complex area, where there is no absolutely right or wrong answer. The most critical issue is to understand the different approaches available, the nuances in each approach and the potential consequences for the entrepreneur and his or her business in each situation. Thereafter, which type of equity the entrepreneur ends up agreeing on will depend on relative negotiating positions. So long as the crucial components of downside protection, upside participation and the creation of legitimate stretch goals for management are fully respected, the VC firm is likely to be supportive of the solution.

18.4.5   Application of the preference

The final area that an entrepreneur must consider in relation to the preference is the breadth of the transactions to which the preference should apply.

It is axiomatic that the preference feature should apply in any downside scenario, which invariably means the liquidation of the business, and it is for this reason that the preference is often referred to as a "liquidation preference". However, it is almost invariably the case that this liquidation preference will also be applied to any exit scenario, for obvious reasons. But where do we draw the line on what is an exit and what is not an exit, for these purposes? A sale of the business (and the distribution of the net proceeds to shareholders) or a sale of the company itself are both easy to accept as conventional exits that should trigger the preference – which will operate in the first case through the share rights that will allocate the eventual liquidation distribution between shareholders, and in the second case through the shareholders agreement that will re-allocate the net proceeds of sale received by each shareholder on completion of the share sale (usually with the company managing the process). However, there are three areas where the line is particularly blurry:

> *In the event that: (i) the issued share capital of the Company is acquired by a bona fide third party purchaser (the "Sale"); or (ii) the Company merges with another entity in a manner which means that following the merger the shareholders of the Company in aggregate no longer control the merged or surviving entity (a "Merger"); then the cash and/or non-cash consideration payable/ deliverable to the Company's shareholders under the Sale, or the cash and/or non-cash consideration payable/deliverable to (or remaining held by) the Company's shareholders in the merged or surviving entity pursuant to the Merger (in each case, the "Consideration") will be allocated as follows: the A Shareholders will first be entitled to receive an amount of the Consideration valued at two times the aggregate subscription price paid up on their A Shares, plus any accrued but unpaid Special Dividend, in priority to any allocation to be made to the Ordinary Shareholders. After such a preferential allocation has been satisfied in full, any remaining Consideration left over will be allocated among the Ordinary Shareholders and the A Shareholders equally (pro rata to shareholdings and on an as-if-converted basis with regard to the A Shares). However, if on a notional allocation of the Consideration equally between all shareholders (pro rata to shareholdings and on an as-if-converted basis with regard to the A Shares) the A Shareholders would be allocated Consideration to an aggregate value greater than six times the aggregate subscription price for the A Shares, then the A Share preferential allocation shall drop away and instead the allocation of the Consideration will be made equally between all shareholders (pro rata to shareholdings and on an as-if-converted basis with regard to the A Shares). The above will not be triggered by a group reorganisation.*

(1) *A sale of part of the business* – to what extent, if at all, should the preference be triggered by a *partial* sale – for example the sale of a substantial division of the business? Should the company be obliged to distribute the proceeds of the sale, or will it be empowered to reinvest the proceeds of sale in developing its existing remaining operations, or in acquisitions of new assets? Fortunately, this is a rare problem for the kind of early-stage company typically backed by the venture capital community, because these issues present intractable questions that can only be answered in a sophisticated way on a case by case basis, based on the particular fact pattern. In the absence of specifics, the best approach is to adopt an approach whereby the preference will be triggered only on the sale of *all or substantially all* of the business. It will also be important to specify that a group reorganisation (which may require some careful defining to ensure that the qualification is not abused) should not trigger the preference, which should merely follow the reorganisation, ensuring that the VC fund is put in an equivalent position in the new group structure.

(2) *A merger* – in principle, whether the consideration payable on the sale of the company is cash or shares (or any other form), it should not affect the implementation of the preference. But where does a merger fit into this approach? At one end of the spectrum, a sale of the company which is dressed up for presentation reasons as a "merger" (big company acquires much smaller company) or which for tax or other reasons is structured as a merger or even a reverse take-over (big company reverses into much smaller company), clearly should trigger the preference. But at the other end of the spectrum, if the company is buying a much smaller business, but for tax or other reasons it is decided that the transaction be effected by a reverse take-over (under which the smaller target "acquires" the company), then it seems equally clear that the preference should not apply.

In the middle are many transactions which come much closer to mergers of equals, whichever way they may be implemented structurally. Once again, there is no easy line to draw, but a conventional approach is to specify that the preference will only be triggered by a merger transaction (howsoever structured) in the event that the shareholders of the company, taken together, do not control the enlarged entity following the transaction (in other words, one way or another, the merger transaction engenders a change in the control of the assets comprising the business).

> *An IPO of the Company represents a liquidity event following which the preferential rights of the A Shareholders will in general disappear and accordingly is regarded as an exit event by Trojan Horse. Accordingly, we propose that sale preference provisions be applied in the event of an IPO. To the extent that the value of the Ordinary Shares (based on the underwritten offer price) at the time of a flotation by the Company is less than five times the highest subscription price for an A Share (as adjusted to reflect any share capital reorganisation effected by the Company or the operation of anti-dilution rights), the conversion ratio applicable to the A Shares shall be adjusted so that A Shares will convert into such number of Ordinary Shares as shall have a value equal to four times the highest subscription price of the A Shares (as so adjusted), fractional entitlements being rounded upwards.*

(3) *An IPO* – is an IPO an exit or not, for purposes of triggering the preference? Many constituencies will regard an IPO as an exit, and (perhaps more importantly) it is generally the last occasion when holders of preferred shares will be able to crystallise their preference ratchet to reconfigure the economic ownership of the business (as all shareholders will almost invariably convert to common stock on an IPO, for reasons of liquidity and because no institutions will invest in the public company if the preferred shares remain outstanding), so even if an IPO is not an exit event, it can be construed as an event of great importance for the preference feature. The countervailing view is that an IPO is *not* an exit in any shape or form, merely another capital-raising opportunity which also offers shareholders the prospect (afar off, usually) of liquidity and that the release of the preference, on conversion, is a perfectly appropriate price to pay for these significant benefits. However, as discussed below at 19.4, the private equity industry often operates "IPO ratchets" in flotation scenarios – whereby the relative ownership interests of investor and management are essentially reviewed with regard to the valuation of the company at IPOs – and in a similar vein such ratchets are now becoming more common in venture capital terms too. Therefore, the entrepreneur can expect the preference features to be applied in an IPO scenario as though flotation was a sale of the business at the enterprise value implied by the IPO offer price.

It will be up to the entrepreneur to be aware of these issues and ensure both that his or her legitimate interests are adequately protected and that the overall arrangements are entirely fair to each key constituency.

18.4.6 Legal considerations

It should be understood that the preference share and preferred share concepts are largely creatures of US and UK law and other common law legal systems. Some European jurisdictions may not countenance separate share classes or preferential rights of this type. In such cases the essential features of the preference may have to be contractual (in the shareholders agreement) rather than constitutional (in the share rights), which may impact at the margins on the enforceability of the preference provisions, although most European jurisdictions have evolved work-around solutions – effectively implementing preference and preferred share concepts – that have been blessed by the marketplace.

18.5   REDEMPTION FEATURES

A redemption right is a right in the share terms for the shareholder to present his or her shares to the company at a defined point in time and to require the company to repurchase those shares and pay the shareholder a defined amount.

> *Trojan Horse and the other Syndicate members require guaranteed liquidity in their investment in the Company after a reasonable period of time. We believe that an appropriate period for the Company to develop its business plans to an appropriate exit (IPO or sale) at full value is five years following Initial Completion. Therefore, we propose that A Shareholders may elect to require the Company to buy-back or to redeem the A Shares in three equal tranches at any time following the fifth anniversary of the issue of such shares or at any time following the occurrence of an Event of Default, in each case at their initial subscription price plus the accrued Special Dividend. For such purposes "Event of Default" includes: (i) failure by the Company to make any required buy-back or redemption payment; (ii) breach by the Company of any of the terms of any of the Financing documentation or the terms of any indebtedness; or (iii) the occurrence of a classic insolvency or default event relating to the Company – such as the onset of insolvency, bankruptcy or receivership, the acceleration of third party obligations, an assignment for the benefit of creditors, or an unsatisfied judgment in excess of an agreed amount.*

18.5.1   Attractions of a redemption feature to the VC firm

As discussed in several places in this book, it is fundamental to a VC firm that it is able to generate a liquidity event within a reasonable period following investment by its fund – the earlier the better, but the conventional venture capital "sweet spot" is five to seven years following initial investment. Having a redemption right in the investment terms is a "belt and braces" approach to this issue – it provides a long term right, in theory, to force an exit, either by virtue of the very right to have its shares redeemed (forcing the entrepreneur to take the exit planning very seriously) or in actual fact by triggering the redemption right itself.

The redemption right is highly theoretical and rarely used, for two principal reasons: firstly, the redemption right usually operates in the same manner as a preference share, providing the right to be paid back the capital invested plus a modest return in the form of the special dividend. In the case of a company that is performing well, but where the exit opportunity is still a little way off, this is not going to be remotely attractive for the VC fund and it will consider other ways to generate liquidity in its investment at a price nearer full value (for example by selling its shares to a buyer), or it will hold tight and sit things out until the exit event materialises. Secondly, in a situation where the company is not performing well, it is highly unlikely that the company will be able either legally or practically to redeem the VC fund's shares, except out of the proceeds of a fresh issue of shares – which is just the kind of situation where new finance will be jealously guarded by the company and any offer to buy out the VC fund will be at a very low valuation. This leaves redemption as being applicable to that mythical "middle road" company that is sufficiently successful to have free cash sloshing around to redeem the VC fund's shares, but not successful enough to be likely to generate a medium term exit opportunity better than a non-participating preference share return ... it's not common!

In light of these practicalities, entrepreneurs should probably not get too excited about redemption rights as a practical matter.

18.5.2 Events of default

Redemption features are also seen in event of default-type scenarios, just in the same way that pre-payment can be used as a protective measure by lending banks where breaches of banking covenants arise. Events of default of this type might include a cross default provision (triggered by breaches by the company of any material contract), breaches of covenants or warranties, or the onset of insolvency or similar event. To some extent, this is consistent with the use of quasi-equity such as preference or preferred shares in the investment structure, but the obvious concern from the company's perspective is that the VC fund may be retaining an unfair ability to jump out of a situation sooner rather than later – essentially to decide that it is a creditor not a shareholder – and this is inconsistent with the equity features. For this reason, the entrepreneur should resist this kind of provision.

18.5.3 Default

> *Should the Company be in default of its buy-back or redemption obligations for any reason, the unpaid amount will accrue interest at the rate of 10% per annum, compounded quarterly, and if the default continues for more than 30 days, the Syndicate will become entitled to elect a majority of the Board, to facilitate the work-out of their buy-back or redemption rights.*

Where redemption provisions are in place, a critical knock-on issue will be enforcement of the provision – essentially, what happens if the company does not redeem the shares when it is obliged to? It is very common for onerous provisions to be put in place for this eventuality, creating the "teeth" for the company to comply with its obligations. This is normal, but these teeth can on occasion operate unfairly: for example, unless the company's obligation to redeem the shares is specifically qualified by reference to its ability to do so under applicable laws (see 18.5.5 below), then it may be placed into breach of the provisions by prevailing company law – at which point the teeth (typically super-voting powers to take control of the board and work out the investment) will bite and the redemption mechanism becomes a lot rougher on the company than it was intended to be.

18.5.4 The decision-making process

The decision-making structure for triggering the redemption feature is important to get right. One option of course is an automatic trigger if the shares are still in issue and the company has not gone public by a defined long-stop date (e.g. seven years) – but this is rarely attractive, as it represents a sword hanging over the company in an arbitrary manner (although of course that very fact enables the company at least to plan for the event from a long way out). Another alternative at the other end of the spectrum is to permit unlimited voluntary redemptions by any member of the VC syndicate at any time after a defined long-stop date – again the potential chaos that could be caused by such an uncontrolled situation is probably not optimal either. Two or three factors are important in this area:

(1) While voluntary redemption is in theory an attractive thing (because one would hope that some syndicate members at least would elect not to trigger their rights), it is equally important to have a sensible "gating" mechanism to ensure that a right which has been put in place many years in advance of the actual situation is not operated in an unfair or arbitrary manner (and that the company therefore has the ability to make representations, suggest alternatives, etc in a controlled environment). It is therefore common for the redemption feature to be dormant and only triggered by a sufficient vote of the VC syndicate – and calibrating the majority required to effect a trigger, to ensure that it is difficult but not too difficult to effect the trigger, will require some measure of skill.
(2) Equally, whether the redemption decision arising on the long-stop date has to be made prior to or at that moment only, or becomes a general "live" right lurking in the background and capable of being activated at any time is another decision to take. The once-only approach is better for the company, but the VC syndicate are likely to press for a general right.
(3) When a redemption right is triggered, it is usually sensible to control the flood of redemptions into a manageable process over a sensible period. Accordingly, it is common practice to develop pre-determined windows following the trigger when redemptions can be requested, with maximum redemptions during each window – for example redemption over two years at quarterly intervals.

18.5.5   Legal issues

This book is not intended to be a legal textbook. However, the entrepreneur should be aware, when negotiating redemption rights that:

(1) many jurisdictions (particularly those in the EU) require that a company can only redeem or repurchase its shares out of distributable reserves (accumulated trading profits less accumulated trading losses) or out of the proceeds of a fresh issue of shares – this is the case, for example, in the UK;
(2) for some other jurisdictions, the whole concept of a share redemption or repurchase is a civil law anathema and can be extremely difficult to achieve under the prevailing law – this is the case, for example, in Germany and to a lesser extent in France; and
(3) in the US, the flexibility is such (redemptions and repurchases out of capital are possible) that sufficient cash is in practice the only issue.

18.5.6   Alternatives to redemption

> *In the event that VC fund comes to believe that it is not possible to implement the economic effect of the above provisions under the applicable law to the benefit of the A Shareholders, the A Shareholders will instead, at the request of VC fund be granted rights to initiate and conclude a liquidity event after five years.*

Because of the various legal restrictions that can severely delimit the implementation of the redemption route in many cases (see 18.5.5 above), it is increasingly common that the redemption right is replaced in such circumstances by an alternative liquidity solution, or such an alternative is inserted as a back-up to the core redemption right. The example provided above is typical – something "warm and woolly" that proposes that the VC syndicate take a more proactive approach to engineering an exit for their investment in the near term.

18.6   CONVERSION RIGHTS

A conversion right is a right in the share terms for the shareholder to present his or her shares to the company at a defined point in time and to require the company to "convert" those shares into a new class of shares (usually ordinary shares). Usually, the mechanism for doing this is not strictly a conversion but either a re-designation of the shares (e.g. from preferred shares to ordinary shares) or their redemption, repurchase or cancellation in return for the issue of the new class of shares, or even their consolidation and subsequent split and re-designation.

> *It is proposed that the A Shareholders will generally have an unfettered right to convert their A Shares into Ordinary Shares in their absolute discretion, enabling them to take advantage of specific liquidity opportunities such as an IPO. In addition, it is proposed that the Company will have the ability to force the A Shareholders to convert their A Shares into Ordinary Shares, where an IPO meets certain minimum criteria, in order for the Company to be able to implement such an IPO even in the face of minority A Shareholder objections (the Syndicate generally having the power of veto over any IPO, however).*

18.6.1   Voluntary conversion rights

> *A Shareholders will have the right voluntarily to convert their A Shares at any time into Ordinary Shares in the capital of the Company. The conversion ratio will initially be one for one, but will be adjusted to reflect any share capital reorganisation effected by the Company (e.g. share split, consolidation, etc) in the future or arising pursuant to the operation of anti-dilution rights.*

The final core economic feature of the VC fund's equity ownership is a conversion right – the right to convert its equity (then either a preference or preferred share) into common shares in the company. Indeed, as discussed above, for a holder of preference shares this conversion right is the only mechanism by which he or she is able to ensure full upside participation in a liquidity event. But while a holder of preferred shares has in theory such full upside participation inherent in the share rights, there are many circumstances in which a conversion right is extremely attractive – for example on an IPO by the company.

There are no circumstances in which the VC fund will be willing to consider a fetter on this conversion right, which is fundamental to its equity.

This right will generally be a one-for-one conversion feature, but of course if as the company progresses the share capital structure changes, it is possible that (like any equity derivative feature) the conversion ratio may have to be adjusted to reflect those changes. For example, it is extremely common for the ordinary share capital to be reconfigured in the run-up to an IPO (usually by means of a share split designed to ensure that the trading price for the company's stock is at a sensible level for the marketplace chosen): equally, some economic adjustment features (e.g. the anti-dilution feature discussed at Chapter 22 below) may operate by adjusting the conversion ratio to achieve their ends.

18.6.2   Compulsory conversion rights

> *In the event of a Qualifying Stock Exchange Flotation of the Company or with the consent of 75% of the A Shareholders (by shares held), the A Shares will automatically convert into Ordinary Shares on the basis of the then-prevailing conversion ratio. "Qualifying Stock Exchange Flotation" means an underwritten public offering on a leading international stock exchange (to include the NYSE, Nasdaq or the London Stock Exchange) with net proceeds to the Company or its shareholders of at least $100 million at a price per share that is equal to or greater than five times the A Share subscription price (taking into account any share capital reorganisation prior to flotation).*

However, there may be circumstances in which the VC fund will be prepared to countenance a mandatory conversion of its equity – a feature which may be highly attractive to an entrepreneur. For example, if a company is approaching an IPO, it will be very important to the prospects of the IPO that the equity structure is simplified and that there are no classes of equity lying ahead of the ordinary shares to be subscribed by institutions and/or the general public. It cannot be guaranteed that a VC fund (or, at least every member of the syndicate) would be fully supportive of an IPO – for example at "borderline" pre-money valuations – and so it has become common practice in VC terms for a mandatory conversion right to operate once certain IPO transaction thresholds have been satisfied. These thresholds are commonly:

(1) that the IPO takes place on a leading international stock exchange, so that what occurs is a genuine listing on an exchange that will attract top quality investors – it is not uncommon for qualifying exchanges to be listed;
(2) that the IPO raises sufficient funds or sells sufficient numbers of shares to generate effective post-flotation liquidity, to ensure that there is a genuine after-market in the stock enabling the investors (eventually, after all lock-up periods have ended) to exit in a sensible fashion;
(3) that the pre-money valuation of the company on IPO meets certain minimum criteria, to ensure that there is a minimum deliverable exit return for investors and that the company is of sufficient scale to warrant decent analyst coverage and post flotation interest.

It is also worth considering whether there may be merit in adding in the power for a defined majority of the VC syndicate to require the minority to convert along with them into common stock – a "drag-along" power into conversion (see the above term sheet example). This may be valuable if there is a recalcitrant minority of VC funds (or other constituencies) who wish to prevent an IPO going ahead where the threshold is not quite reached, but the majority take a more sanguine view. Clearly, the level at which the binding majority will operate may be subject to vigorous debate.

> *In the event that more than 90% of the A Shares originally in issue have been converted into Ordinary Shares, then the Company may elect by notice in writing to the remaining A Shareholders mandatorily to convert all remaining A Shares into Ordinary Shares, at the then-prevailing conversion rate.*

Equally, it may make administrative sense to provide for a "low watermark" mandatory conversion feature, which would be triggered when only a small number of preference/ preferred shares remain in issue (the rest having converted to ordinary shares), so that the residual shares would then be compulsorily converted to ordinary shares.

18.6.3 Adjustment to conversion rights

There are several situations in which the basic one to one conversion ratio may be subject to adjustment. Each of these is discussed below.

> *To the extent that the value of the Ordinary Shares (based on the underwritten offer price) at the time of a flotation by the Company is less than five times the highest subscription price for an A Share (as adjusted to reflect any share capital reorganisation effected by the Company or the operation of anti-dilution rights), the conversion ratio applicable to the A Shares shall be adjusted so that A Shares will convert into such number of Ordinary Shares as shall have a value equal to four times the highest subscription price of the A Shares (as so adjusted), fractional entitlements being rounded upwards.*

In 18.4.5 above, we discussed the potential for an "IPO ratchet" to be applied, effectively to operate the preference right by reference to the pre-money valuation of the company at IPO. The classic way of operating an IPO ratchet is to adjust the conversion ratio automatically to "compensate" the VC firm for the under-performance against the expected multiple (the threshold often being the same as the level at which an IPO becomes a "Qualifying Stock Exchange Flotation" in mandatory conversion terms).

> *In accordance with standard market practice for investment transactions of this type, Trojan Horse requires a measure of price protection. In the event that equity securities are issued by the Company at a subscription price lower than the price per share paid by the Syndicate for the A Shares in the Financing (as adjusted to take account of any subsequent capital reorganisation) (a "Down Round"), the Company will be required... to adjust the A Share conversion rights... (the "Down Round Adjustment") so that each Investor is compensated for the dilution resulting from the Down Round on a full ratchet basis...*

In addition, it is very common (particularly in the US) for the anti-dilution mechanism itself (see Chapter 22 below) to be effected generally by means of an adjustment to conversion rights. This approach works without a hitch only in jurisdictions which permit "nil par value shares" to be issued (shares which have no "par" or base value whatever and which can be issued for no consideration whatsoever – e.g. the US), or which require only a negligible economic amount as a minimum "par" or base value (e.g. the UK, where par values can be tiny fractions of any currency – e.g. 0.0000001 penny): other jurisdictions which demand an economically significant minimum "par" or base value on issue (e.g. €1 – as is the case for several European jurisdictions) may find that this mechanism is not sufficiently flexible to be used for the anti-dilution mechanism, and other approaches may be preferred.

19
Share Incentives

19.1   INTRODUCTION TO SHARE INCENTIVES

It is often assumed that VC firms will be against share incentive programmes because of the dilution of their ownership interest. In fact nothing could be further from the truth: VCs are strongly in favour of generous share incentive programmes for the following key reasons:

(1) Share incentive programmes align the interests of the key value drivers in the business (the employees) with the needs of the VC fund, focusing everyone on growth in capital gains and eventual exit at full value.

(2) There is usually no cash cost to the company in implementing a share incentive programme, ensuring that the cash committed by the VC fund to the business can be focused solely on the development of the underlying business itself. In accounting terms, this advantage has been significantly eroded in recent years, as many generally accepted accounting practices (e.g. UK GAAP, IAS, IFRS and US GAAP) have come to require that the "cost" of share incentive programmes (usually the market value of the share incentive at the time it is granted to the employee) is expensed through the profit and loss account: however, this is only an accounting impact and during the early stages of a company's growth and development, cash is usually "king" and cash flow is usually "queen", and accounting considerations are very much of tertiary importance. In addition, share incentive programmes that involve the acquisition by business founders of shares or stock at (usually negligible) market value upon the creation of the business do not generally have any adverse accounting impact and may have many attractions in tax terms for the shareholder.

(3) Share incentive programmes can be structured to create long-term stretch goals for the management team and key employees and as such are excellent tools to retain valuable staff over protracted periods. Such programmes are also often capable of being enlarged easily or even of "recycling" incentives to incoming or replacement members of management, should an initial participant in the programme leave the business for any reason or as junior employees become more senior and come into positions of significant responsibility.

(4) Share incentive programmes are often highly tax efficient, so that in effect the relevant government shares in the cost of providing the incentives. In many countries, share ownership of itself may be tax efficient, as the realisation of these shares will usually attract capital gains tax on the capital gain, as opposed to income tax on earnings, in the hands of the shareholder – and capital gains (particularly long-term capital gains) are often taxed internationally at lower rates than income. Many governments have committed themselves to encourage employee share ownership by offering attractive tax-spared programmes for share incentives: for example the Enterprise Management Incentive Scheme in the UK, which broadly provides share options with the same tax treatment as actual shares, or the Plan d'Epargne en Actions programme in France, which lowers tax rates materially on eventual share realisations. If these programmes are available to a growing business, it is foolish not to employ them.

19.2   SIZING OF INCENTIVE PROGRAMMES

Immediately prior to Initial Completion, an all-employee share option plan (the "ESOP") will be created comprising options over 20% of the fully diluted post-Financing equity share capital, of which half will be awarded to the senior management and employees of the Company on a basis to be agreed with Trojan Horse and the remainder will be unallocated and available for issue in the future. All options will be over Ordinary Shares and will vest over a four year period from grant; 25% after one year and the remainder on a quarterly, straight line basis over the following three years. Future option grants will only take place with the approval of the Company's remuneration committee or Trojan Horse. Should an employee leave employment for any reason, all unvested options will lapse and he will be obliged to exercise his vested options within 90 days, or they too will lapse.

The sizing of the incentive programme for a business is obviously a critical issue, to ensure that a sufficient incentive is created for current and future management and employees, whilst at the same time not diluting unnecessarily the owners of the business, including the entrepreneur, other founders and the VC fund.

The typical sizing range seen in venture capital situations is 10–20% of the fully diluted share capital, but obviously within this range the optimal allocation will depend on a range of common-sense factors, such as the equity already owned by the key value drivers in the business (founders' stock), the growth profile of the business and the volatility risk inherent in this profile, and market, sector and cultural practice (some are more equity-oriented than others). Over the last ten years, we have seen an explosion in the equity culture, with remuneration structures through the mid to late 1990s being substantially driven by equity incentives which spread deep within organisations, so that for a time all-employee share option programmes distributing stock ownership throughout the corporation became prevalent. Conversely, in the early years of the twenty-first century, we have seen a re-calibration of remuneration structures, with far more emphasis being placed on traditional cash-based incentives such as base salary and discretionary bonus and share option programmes typically being more targetted.

It is essential that an entrepreneur gets expert advice concerning the design, structure, sizing and allocation approach for his or her share incentive programmes. The relevant expertise can be found in specialist benefits consultancies, as well as in accountancy firms and employment and benefits specialists within law firms. On the back of such advice, the entrepreneur will be well-armed to agree the way forward with the VC firm. Above all, two factors must be fully understood and carefully considered in relation to the design and implementation of any share incentive programme:

(1) Share incentive programmes are not a zero sum game – there is a cost to the company and its shareholders in their implementation, both in terms of the non-availability of a limited equity allocation for other purposes (there is only so much equity to share around for incentive purposes) and in terms of the very real negative impact on earnings (owing to the accounting of the cost of incentive programmes through the profit and loss account). As such, it is very important that all affected constituencies understand that equity incentives are one element of an employee's total compensation package of salary and benefits and that, therefore, in being awarded a larger equity incentive allocation, the employee must necessarily be receiving a smaller piece (salary, bonus, benefits)

elsewhere. In principle, equity incentives should not be ladled freely on top of a total compensation package that is already fully benchmarked to the marketplace in value terms.

(2) Not surprisingly, equity incentive programmes involve equity! Equity is an extremely complex instrument, comprising a highly volatile, long term and illiquid incentive arrangement: shares can go up, as well as down (sometimes for reasons having nothing to do with the business); it can take many years for the value of an equity allocation to become realisable at fair value and in the interim equity incentives tend to be forfeited if individuals depart employment (see below); and the eventual realisation of an equity allocation at fair value requires a marketplace and a willing buyer, as well as, increasingly, a window of opportunity taking into account extremely complex and restrictive international securities laws that may apply in any given situation. Such a sophisticated and long-term instrument demands a recipient who is equally sophisticated and who above all can genuinely appreciate the long-term over the short-term (put plainly – the faint prospect of significant sums in three to four years, over a nice bonus cheque in the hand today). If allocations are made to individuals who are not fully able to appreciate the risks of equity and value in the longer term, there will be a value dislocation between the grantor (the company, which values its equity very highly) and the grantee (the employee, who does not value the equity at all and wonders why he or she's not getting paid more), which inevitably means that the impact of the equity incentive programme will be wasted.

19.3   WHO BEARS THE DILUTION?

> *We have shared valuation information with you during the initial stages of this potential transaction. We confirm that we are willing to implement the Financing on the basis of a fully-diluted pre-money valuation for the Company of $20 000 000, which we believe represents a very attractive valuation for the Company at this time in the prevailing marketplace. This valuation assumes that there is established immediately prior to the Financing an employee stock option programme over 20% of the fully-diluted post-Financing equity share capital, of which not less than one half of the programme remains unallocated on completion of the Financing.*

The reader may have spotted the subtle impact of this wording earlier (see Chapter 13). A VC firm approaching an investment opportunity will take the view that a sophisticated and market-standard share incentive programme should already be in place, and if it is not, then the entrepreneur should bear the dilution resulting from putting such a scheme in place. The VC's financing offer will, therefore, be priced as though the share incentive programme had been put in place immediately before its money is contributed to the business (so that the pre-existing shareholders bear all of the dilution arising on the implementation of the programme).

However, it has become common practice for a VC firm to demand not only that this take place, but also that any increase in the share incentive programme to maintain adequate absolute levels of incentive in light of the VC fund's *own* investment, is also borne entirely by the pre-existing shareholders (essentially the entrepreneur and the other founders). What this amounts to, of course, is a subtle reduction in the "real" pre-money valuation of the business – in other words, the VC syndicate is presenting the best possible pre-money valuation interpretation, but it is in fact largely "window dressing". In the term sheet example, the headline pre-money value is $20 M – but the fact that existing shareholders are being asked to bear exclusively the additional dilution required to enlarge the share incentive programme (in the term sheet example, 6 000 000 options – a size equal to 20% of the enlarged equity, which itself is growing markedly from 14 million shares to 24 million shares pursuant to the Financing), means that the "real" pre-money value could in fact be said to be only $14 M, being the value of the shares that the founders end up owning in the Company post Financing (calculated at the $1 per share subscription price for the Syndicate). Looked at another way, the founders will end up with a 46% share ownership, on a fully diluted basis, of a business with a post-money value of $30 M. It's an easy trick to miss, even if it may not in fact be possible to change the VC syndicate's pricing. The capitalisation table will always tell the unvarnished truth.

Demonstrably, this approach does not appear fair and an entrepreneur should be extremely careful, firstly, to position the company's share incentive programme optimally in advance of a venture capital financing and, secondly, to ensure that all shareholders, including those coming in at the time of the financing, bear equally (pro rata to their shareholdings) the dilution caused by any increase in the company's share incentive programme at that time – after all, incentive programme awards are not about rewarding the past but about incentivising future successes – meaning that the benefits of the programme will be enjoyed equally in the future by all shareholders. It therefore makes sense that all shareholders "pay" (through dilution) for such a programme. Come what may, it is essential that the entrepreneur looks very carefully at the denominators in the fully-diluted pre-money valuation and tracks these through into the capitalisation table, so that he or she fully understands the dynamics and the real value placed on the business by the VC firm.

19.4   RATCHETS

Trojan Horse recognises the vital importance of the management team in developing the Company's business and in seeking and executing an exit for the Syndicate on their investment. We therefore propose that if there is a Sale, Merger or IPO (an "Exit Event") that delivers a certain threshold level of return to the A Shareholders, Ordinary Shareholders will be remunerated by means of a value shift to them on exit. Accordingly, in the event that an Exit Event delivers a five times multiple cash on cash return to the A Shareholders and an Internal Rate of Return of not less than 40% per annum, A Shares will be repurchased by the Company at their par value in accordance with the following formula: [ ].

One form of incentive arrangement that often finds favour in venture capital term sheets is a management "ratchet". This mechanism rewards management for delivering a successful exit to the VC fund, by effecting a defined value shift from the VC fund (or defined shareholding constituency) to the management shareholders. The size of this value shift is related to the return on investment received by or attributable to the VC fund. For example, once the return on investment to the VC fund exceeds four times cost of investment there might be a value shift that increases management's participation in the excess exit proceeds.

Ratchet mechanisms typically operate by "retiring" a defined proportion or value of the shares held by the VC fund (or defined shareholding constituency) – essentially defined shares held by persons other than the management team are cancelled, bought back by the company or converted into economically worthless deferred shares, meaning that, proportionately, the shares held by management become more valuable. It is of course also possible to transfer these shares to management, but in some jurisdictions this creates tax problems.

Ratchets are of course extremely attractive for an entrepreneur and from the VC's perspective they can be useful in aligning interests in a high-value and rapid exit. However, they are also extremely complex both to draft and to operate and almost inevitably will give rise to arbitrary outcomes that means that in practice their implementation in the specific exit circumstances will have to be explicitly negotiated. This could disrupt an exit opportunity unless handled calmly and creatively.

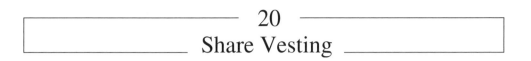

20
Share Vesting

20.1 INTRODUCTION TO SHARE VESTING

> *The Ordinary Shares held by the members of senior management will be subject to vesting over the four years following Initial Completion: 25% after one year and the remainder on a quarterly, straight line basis over the following three years, such that in the event of the termination of a manager's employment for any reason (except as described below), the unvested part of the manager's Ordinary Shares will be compulsorily acquired by the Company for $1 in aggregate and the remaining Ordinary Shares may (at the option of the Company) be purchased at their aggregate market value at the time of departure.*
>
> *In the event that the manager's employment with the Company is terminated either by virtue of the manager's death or permanent disability, or by the Company without reasonable cause, the standard vesting period applicable to the shares held by such person shall be halved such that the number of vested shares on departure shall be doubled (up to the ceiling of the number of shares held by such person). In the event that the manager's employment with the Company is terminated by reason of the manager's fraud or gross negligence, or the commission by the manager of a criminal offence, the standard vesting period applicable to the shares held by such person shall be doubled such that the number of vested shares on departure shall be halved.*
>
> *In the event of an Exit Event, the standard vesting period applicable to the Ordinary Shares held by senior management immediately prior to the Exit Event shall be halved such that the number of vested shares shall be doubled (up to the ceiling of the number of Ordinary Shares held by any such person).*

It is conventional in the design of share incentive programmes for the exercisability of (e.g.) share options or warrants to be graduated over several years (typically between three and five years, often with an initial period of one year or more during which no options can be exercised – known as the "cliff" period), to ensure that the programme operates on a long-term basis. This period, during which a share incentive programme holds back the economic benefits of share ownership (because an option may not be exercised and a share may not be sold), is known as the "vesting period" and the mechanics by which vesting is designed and operated lie at the heart of the key issues worthy of debate in an investment term sheet.

An entrepreneur may naturally assume that the concept of vesting could not possibly apply in the case of shares held by themselves at the time of the venture capital financing. After all, the equity was subscribed at the outset of the life of the company and the entrepreneur may be undertaking significant risks in taking on the business opportunity. Think again! One of the first things that a VC firm will look to do will be to apply many of the vesting features inherent in a share incentive programme to these founders' shares.

20.2 ATTRACTIONS OF VESTING TO THE VC FIRM

Clearly, a VC firm examining an investment opportunity will want to create a strong community of interest between its fund and the other shareholder constituencies in the investment to use the infusion of venture capital funding to build the business they believed they were investing in, and the vesting mechanism is this tool.

For the VC firm, not only does vesting ensure that the actual ownership interests are closely aligned with economic reality (as the value of the business grows over time, so it becomes fair to recognise the value contributed in the form of "sweat equity" by the founders and management), but the mechanism also ensures that founders and key members of management are powerfully motivated to remain with the business for the longer term (just like other staff through the share incentive programme) – once again tightly aligning the interests of the different equity constituencies.

Why is vesting needed to achieve this goal? As discussed above (Chapter 13), the post-money valuation of a venture capital investment opportunity is not intrinsic – it is all about the subtle inter-action of different hopes, needs, expectations and risk models that throw out a reference point at a particular moment in time that motivates all shareholders adequately. If the founders' shares were fully vested immediately following the completion of the financing transaction, then this "spectral" post-money valuation would become real for them – and that could be very dangerous for the VC syndicate, whose money contributed to the business is very real, though little else in the business is more than an idea at this stage.

Under the term sheet example – the founders will hold, on completion of the $5 M first tranche of the Financing, 73% of the Company on an undiluted basis and even following the contribution of the $5 M second tranche and taking into account the option pool, they will hold 46.67% of the Company. This is a company whose only valuable and readily realisable asset may well be the $5 M of cash sitting in its bank account (i) immediately following the Initial Completion and (ii) immediately following the contribution of the second tranche (assuming that the first $5 M has then been spent and ignoring for the moment any increase in value attributable to the passing of the milestones)... in other words the founders would own, pro rata, (i) $3 650 000 in cash immediately following Initial Completion, without having had to build a business, and (ii) $2 333 500 immediately following the contribution of the second tranche. This of course neatly demonstrates the effect that investment milestones have in terms of smoothing this disconnect – if the whole $10 M was contributed in a single tranche, then the founders would on Initial Completion be sitting on shares worth $7 300 000 – the founder would be a multi-millionaire immediately and there would almost be a disincentive to build the business, even though checks and balances like the preferred status of the VC's shares would prevent them realising this value!

But there is a further reason why vesting mechanisms are favoured by VC firms. In the event that a member of senior management departs the company for any reason, the owners of the business (principally the VC firm) will need quickly to hire a replacement person of suitable quality. Such an individual will expect a market-standard equity remuneration package and in such circumstances it can be extremely useful to be able to recycle unvested equity entitlements arising on the departure back into a new incentive structure for the incoming person.

20.3   THE ENTREPRENEUR'S RESPONSE

In the first visceral negative reaction by an entrepreneur to vesting provisions in a term sheet – and the first reaction will naturally be that vesting is a form of theft – the potential attractions of vesting will often be ignored. However, so long as the issues discussed at 20.4 below are carefully weighed and dealt with, vesting can also be highly attractive to an entrepreneur too, for the same reasons that the feature is attractive to a VC firm. Vesting provisions, like many provisions in a term sheet, can seem unpleasant when applied to one's own situation, but entirely fair and reasonable when applied to another shareholder.

It is highly likely that the entrepreneur will be part of a small group of founder shareholders that may contain persons with potentially disparate interests – for example:

(1) Disparate ownership interests – it is not uncommon for the founding group to contain a leading player or two, and then a group of "also rans" whose equity interest, though significant, is not of the same order of magnitude of the other founders.

(2) Disparate financial interests – it is very common for a sub-set of the founders to provide (often quite substantial amounts of) start-up capital to found the business and get it through its first crucial months and it is equally likely that this group of "founders" will have been supplemented by the time of the venture capital financing by one or more additional investors ("angel investors") who have contributed further growth capital to the business as an interim measure, but whose involvement with the business may be essentially passive or at best patchy. By contrast, other founders may have contributed little to the business directly in financial terms, but their contribution may be of an operational nature, or they may have contributed indirectly financially, by coming on board with minimal salary and benefits, or they may have made "soft" contributions in the form of intellectual property, know-how or contacts.

(3) Disparate age and ambition – almost invariably, the entrepreneur will find that the founding group will be composed of individuals with different ages and ambitions – in particular those persons may have entirely different outlooks on how long "long term" is, on how far they are prepared to commit themselves to the future of the company and, above all, on how much risk they are prepared to shoulder in driving the company forward.

(4) Disparate roles in the organisation – stating the obvious, not everyone can be CEO and the founding group will generally share out the range of senior roles – but these roles will have different risk profiles, time horizons and relative value (and their relative value will change as the company develops and becomes successful). For example, the Chief Technology Officer role may be the most important at the outset, whereas five years later the key development metrics may be supported principally by the VP of Sales and Marketing and in the lead-up to a flotation or sale the Chief Financial Officer's role will be of critical importance.

So, it would be mistaken to assume that the founding group will in all situations possess common interests. Indeed, it is far more likely that as the company's business develops, fractures in the founding group will materialise and at that point is may be extremely attractive to be able to align those interests, or at least deal with the fall-out from such disagreements, through the medium of share vesting provisions. The logical consequence of this situation is of course that an entrepreneur should not assume that all founders should be treated the same. For example, it might seem perfectly appropriate to focus vesting provisions on those founders (i) who have not put significant financial or other capital to work in the business, (ii) with shorter-term investment horizons, (ii) with lower risk tolerance, or (iii) whose role only becomes pivotal in subsequent years. However, the entrepreneur will often find that (except in the case of (i) above – see 20.4 below) triaging the founders in such a way is either perceived as invidious or simply ensures that everyone falls in to the "to be vested" category under one heading or another and so often the easiest approach is simply to submit everyone to standardised vesting provisions.

Even more than for a VC firm, the entrepreneur will have a powerful interest in ensuring that the departure of a co-founder is managed properly. This will often mean that a proportion of the departing founder's shares will be clawed back on the basis that they are "unvested". For the entrepreneur, not only will this be necessary in order to free up equity with which to attract a replacement executive to the business (without diluting the current shareholders by a new issue of equity), but the remaining founding team may feel quite negative about a departing colleague "riding on their backs" in the future, as they build the company in the coming years, particularly if the company is at a pivotal moment in its development when the founder departs. When an entrepreneur looks at his founding colleagues and asks the question "what would I want to happen if one of these colleagues leaves me in the lurch?" the concept of vesting starts to look pretty attractive.

20.4   VESTING – AREAS TO WATCH OUT FOR

Vesting techniques relating to options and stock are many and various and each element has important choices to be considered. It is an extremely complex area. However, at the heart of this area is a very simple goal – to be able to judge fairly the contribution of an individual at the point of his or her departure, taking into account all of the relevant circumstances, and to reflect the value of that contribution in the form of vested equity which enables the departing individual to maintain an appropriate and fully-earned equity ownership in the company going forward.

Of course, although this goal is, in theory, extremely straight-forward, its application is fraught with difficulty, leading the marketplace to adopt sweeping mechanics to counter this complexity. In some cases the value of the particular contribution is very simple (for example the contribution of significant financial capital on arm's length terms) but in general calibrating value is extremely difficult. For example, when does a CTO deliver real value to a company – when the technology is built, when that technology is patented and becomes defendable, or when that technology turns its first dollar of revenue? Or is it only when the company goes cash flow positive and it can be demonstrated that the technology can actually support a genuine business?

These enormously difficult issues permeate the areas to watch out for.

20.4.1   Pace and level of vesting

> *The Ordinary Shares held by the members of senior management will be subject to vesting over the four years following Initial Completion: 25% after one year and the remainder on a quarterly, straight line basis over the following three years ...*

As discussed above, it is common for vesting to be stretched over some three to five years. The period chosen will depend on relative bargaining positions, of course but most of all on the state of development of the company and the future development profile lying ahead. Because of the enormous complexity in terms of defining the value of each individual's contribution to the company at any moment in time, particularly when looking several years ahead, the vesting period will principally be driven more off the investment cycle lying ahead for the VC firm, than off individual goals and metrics. In other words, the VC firm's primary goal is to ensure that the founders are committed and incentivised through the vesting mechanic to grow the company and deliver to the VC fund an exit at full value within the time horizon required for the VC fund given its stage of investment (early stage, late stage, etc).

For example, for an early stage company with a five to seven year development profile to a viable exit opportunity for a VC fund, the longer period of five years may be appropriate: conversely for a company which has made substantial progress by the time it raises venture funding and maybe only has some three years to a viable exit opportunity, a much shorter period will be appropriate. The VC firm won't be concerned that the founders will be fully vested towards the end of those periods, because at that point the interests of all shareholders will have been fully aligned around finding an exit opportunity from which to realise value. Somewhere towards the end of the vesting period this "tipping point" occurs.

Once the period has been agreed, then it will be necessary to agree at what level vesting will start from completion of the financing transaction. It is by no means certain that vesting should commence at zero on that date, for two reasons: firstly, it may be that the founders have been with the company already for a protracted period and have delivered real value during that time – and that should be reflected in a fair initial vested entitlement. Secondly, it is perfectly possible that the stock subscribed by the founders when they established the company or otherwise joined the business, was acquired for real value (real cash contributions or real assets such as intellectual property) and not just for a nominal sum – and again this should be reflected in a fair initial vested entitlement. These two considerations may even take initial vesting in some cases up to 100% and it is not uncommon to see initial vesting on completion of an early-stage financing at 25–30% levels, recognising these kinds of contribution. Obviously, subsequent financings should not reset the level of initial vesting. There is no reason why a term sheet cannot differentiate between different categories of founder in setting initially vested levels.

The third element to consider in any vesting schedule is the design of the "vesting line" – in other words the smoothness or otherwise of the progress from initial vesting to full vesting (ignoring special circumstances such as good/bad leaver provisions, or acceleration on exit, both of which are discussed below). The simplest approach is to adopt a straight line, with regular and equal vesting points through the vesting period, but it is increasingly common with zero vesting initiation to see an initial "cliff" period of six months to one year, which is generally seen as the minimum period through which a person must remain with the company following its financing, in order to continue to participate. However, it may well be that the company's development profile suggests irregular vesting periods tied to particular corporate events, although this would be unusual in the venture capital context, not only because of its complexity and potentially binary outcomes, but also because individuals like to feel that they are adding value to the business every day – and the straight-line approach supports that outlook.

Even with a simple, straight line approach it is still necessary to decide on the inflection points – will the vesting steps occur daily, monthly, quarterly, semi-annually or annually? Obviously there's a huge difference between each end of this spectrum, in terms of the impact on the person whose shares are vesting, the perception of fairness or unfairness, and in particular the creation of a series of stretch goals through any particular year. In practice, monthly or quarterly steps seem to be the most popular and the entrepreneur should press for monthly steps if possible, so that the vesting "line" is as smooth as possible.

20.4.2   Good/bad leaver provisions

> *In the event that the manager's employment with the Company is terminated either by virtue of the manager's death or permanent disability, or by the Company without reasonable cause, the standard vesting period applicable to the shares held by such person shall be halved such that the number of vested shares on departure shall be doubled (up to the ceiling of the number of shares held by such person).*

Of course, it is one thing to agree upon a standard vesting approach, but as soon as that is done, the entrepreneur will start to be extremely concerned at the potential for being ejected from his or her own company for no good reason before having a chance to deliver value to the company. It is therefore extremely common for an entrepreneur to question the application of the standard, straight-line approach to vesting in circumstances where he or she may be fired for no good reason, or the contract is terminated due to his or her death or long-term illness/disability. This is where the concept of a "good" leaver and a "bad" leaver can arise.

An entrepreneur will want to argue that if he or she is a "good leaver" then the vesting schedule should either not apply at all (so that shares are automatically fully vested) or should be accelerated on a pre-agreed basis, awarding the entrepreneur a larger number of vested shares than would otherwise have occurred at that point in time. Of course, the concept of a "good" leaver can hide a multitude of sins: at one end of the spectrum it might refer purely to a "departure" solely due to death (which simply amounts to accelerated vesting on compassionate grounds) and at the other end of the spectrum, to any departure for any reason other than being fired for gross incompetence or a criminal act. Nonetheless, somewhere in the middle there would seem to be a perfectly reasonable ground for argument.

Usually, however, this argument falls on stony ground, as far as the VC firm is concerned, simply because, from the VC firm's perspective the vesting schedule has been created on the basis that departing members of management *would* be "good" leavers, not "bad" leavers. Philosophically, the VC firm recognises that a perfect vesting arrangement would be closely calibrated to each individual manager's value-add, day to day, week to week, but equally the VC firm knows full well that, because of the practical impossibility of ever approaching such a perfect arrangement, the next best thing is an arbitrary, straight line vesting approach that may operate generously or unfairly in specific circumstances. Although up front no one has any idea what the outcome will be (fair or unfair) they may be fairly confident that in general the possibility of over or under-rewarding the individual is likely to be within tolerable limits and that the longer the vesting runs on, the more attuned to the underlying value the vesting is likely to be (assuming that the business does not suffer fools in its midst for too long). Indeed it is far more likely that a good leaver acceleration provision will operate unfairly in the circumstances – to those left behind to deliver real and lasting value creation in the business.

The other problem with good leaver provisions is the difficulty in deciding exactly where to draw the line and, even where a line is agreed, determining in the particular circumstances that arise which side of the line the affected individual falls. Death is clearly an easy one, as it is a very definite event, but things become much less difficult once one moves into territory such as "dismissal without reasonable cause", etc. Even the concept of permanent disability can be problematic – at what point does chronic back pain, etc become an event that merits accelerated vesting? This might be an area of fluidity that VC firms and entrepreneurs would be happy to live with in the scheme of things, but, unfortunately, the blurred lines can easily be a recipe for damaging, costly and disruptive disputes and even litigation, particularly where large sums of money are involved. The entrepreneur must always remember that it is probably more likely that he or she will be in the camp of those remaining rather than the departing employee. In such a situation both the VC firm and the company concerned will be keen to have clear, bright lines demarking an individual's entitlement, to eliminate any possibility of employment disputes that would divert management's attention from running the business (or even derail an exit opportunity). Those members of management who remain will generally feel the same way. Hence the reason why simple, straight-line vesting remains the market norm.

> *In the event that the manager's employment with the Company is terminated by reason of the manager's fraud or gross negligence, or the commission by the manager of a criminal offence, the standard vesting period applicable to the shares held by such person shall be doubled such that the number of vested shares on departure shall be halved.*

Conversely, a "bad leaver" provision can often seem very attractive to a VC firm. A bad leaver provision is simply the exact opposite of a good leaver provision: the VC firm will want to argue that if an employee is a "bad leaver" then the vesting schedule should be decelerated on a pre-agreed basis, so that the individual exits with a smaller number of vested shares than otherwise would have occurred or, perhaps if the actions are particularly egregious, the individual's shares are forfeited altogether. Once again, the concept of a "bad" leaver can hide a multitude of sins: at one end of the spectrum it might refer to summary dismissal for a criminal act (fraud, theft, etc) or gross incompetence; in the middle ground to dismissal by the company on reasonable grounds (e.g. in a redundancy programme); and at the other end of the spectrum, to any voluntary departure by an employee (the "rats leaving a sinking ship" analogy). Nonetheless, somewhere in the middle there would seem to be a perfectly reasonable ground for argument that a bad leaver approach makes sense – particularly to those left behind to grow the company.

The idea that the company has the ability to penalise a departing person who has damaged the company in some way (e.g. fraud, embezzlement, gross negligence) or is seen as a "rat leaving a sinking ship", by divesting stock from the individual, is very attractive in theory. Once again, however, unless the defined circumstances are extremely narrow and objective, these kinds of provisions are a recipe for dispute and disruption in the same way as good leaver provisions and in general should be resisted by the entrepreneur.

20.4.3   Acceleration on exit events

> *In the event of an Exit Event, the standard vesting period applicable to the Ordinary Shares held by senior management immediately prior to the Exit Event shall be halved such that the number of vested shares shall be doubled (up to the ceiling of the number of Ordinary Shares held by any such person).*

Another classic area for debate regarding vesting is whether, and the extent to which, vesting should accelerate in the event of an exit opportunity (a trade sale, IPO, etc) emerging unexpectedly. As we have seen, vesting mechanisms, particularly for those who are funda-mental to the business development process (founders and senior management), are designed to drive the business towards an exit opportunity at full value: therefore if an opportunity emerges earlier than the end of the vesting schedule, it would seem churlish not to deem vesting to have been completed in such circumstances. Indeed, an entrepreneur should push hard to include an automatic acceleration for key (specified) members of senior manage-ment upon any exit. VC firms will often be happy to accommodate such a request, because they understand the community of interest that this brings – in particular an incentive on senior management to keep an eye out for, and make the most of, any legiti-mate exit opportunity.

There are countervailing views of course. A VC firm may argue against this approach on three fronts:

(1) That the earlier an exit opportunity arises, the more that the VC fund's own money should be seen as driving the exit, as opposed to the sweat and labour of senior management – and therefore the less that acceleration is appropriate. That approach gives rise to an interesting debate about the inter-relationship of those two factors (cash versus sweat) – which in many circumstances leads back to consensus around a "quick and dirty" straight line approach to vesting in all circumstances.

(2) In the case of an IPO, there is a perfectly respectable argument that an IPO is not an exit for existing shareholders, merely a liquidity event (and oftentimes not even that), and that accordingly acceleration should not apply to this type of "exit". It may be possible to defeat this argument by reference to a defined concept of "qualifying IPO" which incorporates agreed dynamics such as identity of the exchange, size of the pre-money value, size of the primary capital-raising, aftermarket liquidity and duration of lock-up, to ensure that the IPO event genuinely is approximate to an exit for the VC fund.

(3) In the context of a trade sale, acceleration may have damaging knock-on effects not only for the institutional shareholders, but also in some respects for the management seeking acceleration. The argument runs that the buyer of the business will expect to inherit the ongoing incentive programmes that are outstanding in the business, which will in principle include the vesting programme: if the vesting programme is accelerated for the senior management, then in theory the buyer will pay less for the business, because the buyer will have to create new incentive packages in the acquired business to replace the accelerated amount. In other words, in the circumstances it may not be a zero sum game for selling shareholders.

It is important that the entrepreneur is aware of all the issues and all the arguments that will need to be considered in this area, in order to be able to drive the parties towards an elegant solution or compromise. For example, where acceleration proves to be very contentious in the circumstances, often a sensible solution is to provide the board or a committee of the board (e.g. the remuneration committee) with the power to accelerate vesting in their absolute discretion and on a case by case or general basis, if the circumstances warrant, thereby placing the issue in the hands of a body that has to make decisions in the best interests of the company as a whole, and subject to fiduciary duties, and can be expected to be relatively impartial and independent.

20.4.4 Treatment of vested shares

> *... and the remaining Ordinary Shares may (at the option of the Company) be purchased at their aggregate market value at the time of departure*

The final commercial issue which needs to be considered in this complex area is the treatment of *vested* shares on the departure of an employee. The options are, either to leave things where they are, or to have the company or its shareholders buy out the departing employee's vested shares such that he or she departs richer but with no ongoing ownership interest in the company.

Once the unvested shares have been acquired for no, or a nominal consideration, the vested shares will remain the property of the departing employee, with the normal participation in the future upside of the company that this connotes. But is this fair? The departing employee would argue that it is manifestly fair, that the vesting mechanism itself is designed to deal with fundamental issues of value over time and that he or she should be allowed the privilege of continuing as a passive shareholder in the business until eventual exit. In particular, a departing employee will often argue that the "real" value they put into the business whilst employed will not become truly evident for many years and that therefore to be bought out on departure would prevent them sharing in the long-term value that he or she played a part in creating.

However, it is conventional practice in the private equity industry to cash out departing employees by acquiring their vested stock at market value upon departure, and this approach is increasingly prevalent in the VC sector. It is perhaps understandable that those remaining behind, responsible for continuing to build the company's business, would want to ensure that the departing employee does not have the right to benefit passively from their future labours to move the company on to greater things, or to use the shares and the rights associated with those shares (voting rights, veto rights, pre-emption rights, tag rights, board appointment rights, for example) to create disruption to the ongoing business – recognising that the interests of the departing employee may start to diverge materially from those remaining.

On the other hand, in the context of a high growth, venture-backed business, there is the risk that cashing out the departing employee at market value may operate materially to the disadvantage of the individual, both because of the great difficulty in determining market value for an early-stage, rapidly changing business (see Chapter 11) and because the real value inherent in the business may not be evident for some time thereafter – in direct contrast to the more mature, stable and (usually) cash-flow generative businesses that feature in the later-stage private equity market, where conventional valuation methodologies are more readily applied and step changes in value are less likely to occur in short time frames.

> *Any director, officer or employee who ceases to be employed by the Company for any reason will be required (at the option of the Company) to sell their vested Shares back to the Company (i) at par value to the Company, if the reason for the departure is fraud, theft, conviction for a criminal offence, breach of a material term of the individual's employment or service contract, or gross misconduct, or (ii) at cost, in any other case.*

Equally, in relation to such vested shares, it is also possible to differentiate between shares held by a "bad" leaver and a "good" leaver (see above discussion at 20.4.2) – for example, by differentiating between the purchase price payable by a good leaver and a bad leaver. All of the issues regarding good/bad leavers as to vesting are equally applicable in this instance.

The entrepreneur must recognise that this issue is going to be hotly debated and must be addressed in the prevailing circumstances, to understand what is fair and appropriate. Of course, the issue of disruption by ex-members of management can be addressed separately, by neutering the passive shareholder's rights (without denuding them of normal minority shareholder protections), so the key question will be whether a departing employee will be allowed to participate economically in the future of the company or not.

20.4.5   Repurchase mechanics

Part III aims to examine the underlying philosophy of a venture capital term sheet, not the specific means of implementing that philosophy in the prevailing local legal and regulatory environment, as implementation mechanisms for each component of a term sheet proposal may vary greatly, jurisdiction by jurisdiction. However, having examined the commercial issues related to vesting of shares, it is also worth recognising that there are several important technical issues that will drive the mechanics under which vesting is implemented. The purchase of shares by a corporation involves complex issues under prevailing corporation laws. Under US law, for example, the acquiring corporation will have wide powers to acquire or redeem vested and unvested shares out of capital, reserves and profits. Under UK law and the laws of most European jurisdictions, by contrast, the company may only effect such repurchase or redemption out of distributable profits (a highly technical term, but broadly meaning accrued trading profits, after deduction of accrued trading losses) or the proceeds of a fresh issue of shares made for the purpose: both core capital and share premium is inviolate under those legal systems. In the latter circumstance, if reserves, etc are not available, it may be necessary for the shares either to be neutered (by conversion to economically worthless deferred shares) or sold to a convenient third party (e.g. the VC fund) which can "warehouse" the shares pending their retransfer as part of a new incentive arrangement, or simply spread through the existing shareholder base.

Pre-emption Rights on Securities Issues

21.1 INTRODUCTION TO SHARE ISSUE PRE-EMPTION RIGHTS

Pre-emption rights are a first right for a shareholder to buy shares or other securities, usually on the same terms as a third party (e.g. a new investor) has already agreed to buy the securities. This right enables a shareholder to jump in ahead of third parties who wish to buy shares in the company – essentially a first right to protect their percentage ownership of the company and to resist the dilution that would be caused by a new investor.

Many jurisdictions regard share issue pre-emption rights as a fundamental protective mechanism for shareholders of a corporation established under the laws of that jurisdiction. This is particularly the case within the European Union and the corporations laws of many European jurisdictions have enshrined share issue pre-emption rights as a core shareholder right. Often this position is supplemented in other ways – for example, the rules of the London Stock Exchange and the regulations set by the Investor Protection Committees relating to London-listed corporations both establish the fundamental importance of pre-emption rights for investors and permit only narrow exceptions for listed companies from share issue pre-emption rights.

However, there are also many jurisdictions around the world where pre-emption rights are not embedded in the legal psyche – and the biggest and best example of this is the United States (where it is believed by many that the absence of pre-emption rights has in fact greatly facilitated the raising of finance by high-growth companies – for example the US biotechnology industry).

21.2 ATTRACTIONS OF SHARE ISSUE PRE-EMPTION RIGHTS TO A VC FIRM

The Syndicate will maintain an absolute veto over any securities offerings. However, even where the Syndicate approves the circumstances of a securities offering, except for very limited circumstances, it is vitally important that the Company does not undertake securities issues following the Initial Financing without offering the Syndicate an opportunity to participate in any such issue. Accordingly, if the Company proposes to issue any securities, it must offer the Syndicate the opportunity (but not the obligation) to purchase such securities on a pro rata basis and on the same terms as are proposed for the issue to third parties and such that following such securities issue, the Investors have the opportunity to maintain their percentage interest in the fully diluted issued share capital of the Company.

As discussed in Chapter 5, it is an important feature of the VC business model that the VC fund is able to participate fully in the upside of an investment opportunity, and it can also be attractive for the VC fund to be able to take advantage of "bumps in the road" in order to average down its overall cost on investment per share, or (if it takes a longer term view that the turnaround will be advantageous) to be able to take command opportunistically of a rescue or turnaround situation that arises. One of the principal mechanisms a VC will use to achieve this is share issue pre-emption rights.

However, it is rare that the VC firm will rely only on the protections afforded by applicable laws, not only because in some countries (e.g. the United States) no such protection will exist, but also because, even where pre-emption rights are prevalent in the applicable legal systems, they are usually seen by VC firms as inadequate to protect their interests as:

(1) they usually apply only to issues for cash – leaving a potentially large hole in the protective environment where shares are issued for non-cash consideration;
(2) they usually only apply to the issue of equity securities or rights over equity securities ("equity" being a complex defined term in corporations laws, broadly referring to securities with an uncapped right as to dividends and/or capital) – which again may leave the shareholder exposed commercially in certain situations (the issue of preference shares might not be prohibited, for example);
(3) they usually only offer a shareholder pro rata pre-emption rights (a right to maintain its percentage interest in the company) in an "all or nothing" process under which the pre-emption rights fall away unless all rights are taken up – which once again may not offer the maximum protection for shareholders (for example by determining priorities between shareholders and/ or enabling some shareholders to pick up the entitlements of others that are not taken up).

It is therefore generally seen as very important by VC firms for pre-emption rights to be addressed in detail and in a sophisticated manner in the investment documentation. The traditional pre-emption rights set out above provide the VC fund with a first right to maintain its pro rata interest in the company by taking up rights to subscribe shares at the same price and on the same terms as a third party offer (the subtext of pre-emption rights is that there *is* such a third party offer, though this may not necessarily be the case). Note that there is no *obligation* upon the VC fund to take up it's rights, merely an opportunity – there is no quid pro quo in this regard. So, a VC fund will have the opportunity to follow its investment in all cases.

21.3   THE ENTREPRENEUR'S RESPONSE

To some extent, the entrepreneur will wish to be supportive of anything that will facilitate follow-on investment by existing shareholders (including the entrepreneur), particularly if the provisions proposed by the VC firm supplement and enhance the provisions of the prevailing law. On the other hand, the entrepreneur must guard against any provisions which may, directly or indirectly, hamper external fund-raising activities by the business designed to strengthen the company's shareholder roster and/or grasp optimal capital-raising opportunities. This is against a background that there is some evidence from the public company environment that pre-emption rights can operate to frustrate access to capital and/or raise the cost of capital – which could seriously hamper the competitiveness of the business vis à vis peers who may not suffer this disadvantage (e.g. US corporations).

21.4   AREAS TO WATCH OUT FOR

An entrepreneur should be aware that there are many issues lurking in this area, which require consideration and careful negotiation. These are discussed below.

21.4.1   What triggers pre-emption rights?

> *The above provisions will not apply to the following securities issues: (i) Ordinary Shares issued as a consequence of the exercise of options under the ESOP, (ii) securities offered or sold to third parties pursuant to an IPO, (iii) Ordinary Shares issued on the conversion of the A Shares, (iv) securities issued pursuant to any group reorganisation, Merger or Sale, (v) securities issued as consideration for the acquisition by the Company of third party assets, or other business or entity, and (vi) securities issued to third parties as part of a commercial collaboration or other arm's length commercial undertaking.*

It is of course vital to identify the range of transactions which should trigger pre-emption rights, to ensure that in all cases the needs of the shareholders and the business are properly balanced. There are two key aspects of this question – "what kind of transactions should be caught by pre-emption rights?" – and – "what pricing and terms should apply in the case of a transaction that triggers pre-emption rights?".

VC firms will work from the premise that all forms of securities issue should trigger pre-emption rights. To this extent, VC firms may not differentiate between issues of equity, mezzanine (hybrid equity and convertibles, options and warrants) and debt issues: if the company is raising finance, then they will want pre-emption rights. This will require a very careful evaluation by the entrepreneur in the light of the prevailing business plan: the entrepreneur must evaluate where the financing requirements of the company lie and how the company's best interests may be properly protected. In particular:

(1) it is common for a range of conventional share incentive programmes (ESOPs, options, warrants, share grants to incoming senior executives, etc), as well as certain foreseen "technical" share issues (conversion of VC firm's shares, exercise of employee options, etc), to be excluded from the operation of pre-emption rights;

(2) the entrepreneur may wish to exclude securities issues made for the purpose of the acquisition of another company, or a business or assets – in such a case the securities issue is clearly not made for fund-raising purposes, but for strategic purposes, and the dilutive effect of the securities offering is offset by the accretion of value to the overall business;

(3) the entrepreneur may also wish to have the ability to cement a defined range of other strategic deals with third parties – for example sales and marketing initiatives, collaborations, joint ventures or partnerships – by means of equity (including cross-shareholdings) or share incentive programmes (conventionally, options or warrants) and would want these kinds of deals excluded from shareholder pre-emption rights;

(4) the entrepreneur may wish to try to negotiate a general carve-out of pre-emption rights, either in a modest annual amount for general corporate purposes, or more widely to bring in a new investor with particular complementary skills or value-add (for example a US VC for a European business, to provide the business with an entrée into the United States marketplace); and

(5) the entrepreneur will want to limit pre-emption rights so that they apply only to equity and equity-related securities issues and not to conventional banking or lease-financing transactions.

21.4.2   Reference terms of pre-emption

Having identified the range of transactions to which pre-emption rights should apply, it is then important to give careful consideration to the reference terms to which pre-emption rights will apply – in other words the terms and conditions of investment that are used as a benchmark for the pre-emption rights themselves. Obviously this issue is closely inter-linked with the agreed transactional ambit of pre-emption. For example, while it may be very simple matter to accept that a detailed term sheet, delivered by a third party aiming to subscribe equity shares for cash in a simple fund-raising, should operate as a benchmark for the pre-emption rights, conversely the terms on which equity is proposed to be issued to a business partner as part of a complex collaboration arrangement (for example a pharmaceutical company entering into a clinical development partnership with a small biotech business) may be a poor benchmark for pre-emption rights.

21.4.3   Partial pre-emption?

One important issue to understand is that pre-emption rights, in the main, do not block transactions. This is because they are required to be *taken up* – and if, or to the extent they are not taken up, new shares may then be issued free of restriction. However, this approach will often require closer scrutiny – in particular the entrepreneur should consider three important questions in designing pre-emption rights:

(1) Should the pre-emption rights be "all or nothing"? In other words, if pre-emption rights are not taken up over *all* of the shares proposed to be issued, should all pre-emption rights then drop away ("all or nothing pre-emption"), or should only those rights not taken up by shareholders, possibly pursuant to multiple rounds, be available for issue to third parties ("partial pre-emption")? This issue may be of crucial commercial importance and could, if structured inappropriately, significantly jeopardise the company's chances of procuring finance from third parties without the full support of the VC fund (which of course is precisely the position that the VC fund wishes to achieve). An "all or nothing" approach in general places the onus on the existing shareholders, as a group, to "put up or shut up" – to subscribe the entire issue or see the equity go elsewhere: conversely, a graduated approach may not be optimal for the company, because it may not be able to offer a meaningful piece of equity for an external investor at the end of the process after partial pre-emption has operated – indeed an external investor may elect not to participate in an investment process at all (which generates the benchmark term sheet used for the pre-emption process) where it cannot be guaranteed a minimum equity participation, as it may see itself as simply a stalking horse to prompt incumbent shareholders to invest. Unfortunately, this is a battle rarely won by the company, if only because, on this topic, the entrepreneur (as a significant equity holder) and the VC fund usually share the same fear of cheap equity being issued to their disadvantage to third parties.

(2) Should an individual holder of pre-emption rights be permitted to take up part of its rights, or only all of its rights? Once again, this ties into the whole question of whether the pre-emption rights should be all or nothing and of how difficult or easy it should be for a shareholder to take up pre-emption rights. It is conventional to provide that a shareholder may take up all or any part of the rights – usually driven by the fear of shareholders who are individuals that unless this is the case, they may be priced out of participation.

(3) In the event that (or to the extent that) pre-emption rights are *not* taken up, how long should the company thereafter be free to issue new shares on the prevailing benchmark terms? Usually, the parties agree that in such circumstances a transaction may progress only on the terms previously disclosed and within a relatively short timeframe (e.g. up to three months).

21.4.4   Who gets pre-emption rights?

The next question to ask is who gets the pre-emption rights? Obviously, the VC fund will be asking for the rights, but it may be reasonable to ask that the rights are extended beyond the VC fund to other constituencies – for example the founding entrepreneur – particularly where the pre-emption rights being requested go further than the prevailing legal entitlement. This will rarely be resisted by the VC firm.

However, once it has been established that more than one class of shareholders may participate in pre-emption rights, this then raises the issue of whether there should be priorities between these classes. For example, should the holders of the senior class of shares have pre-emption rights in priority to the holders of more junior classes of shares, with the junior classes only participating to the extent that senior classes of shares have not taken up their rights? Whilst at first glance this may seem illogical, it is less so in the context of a new share offering of securities which are senior to the securities then in issue – meaning that the holders of the senior securities then in issue (usually the VC fund) will not only be diluted by the share issue, but also lose their priority too (which they hold exclusively, of course). In these circumstances, the VC fund may seek to argue that they should have the option to maintain their priority exclusivity ahead of other classes of shares. So, this issue may turn on a discussion of which is more important – priority or percentage ownership in the company. Usually, if the entrepreneur presses hard enough, the argument is won on percentage ownership (as priority is fleeting in an upside scenario) and it is not unusual to see all classes granted pre-emption rights pari passu and pro rata – in other words equally and ratably between each other as to shareholding. Of course, in large capital-raisings, it may be a distinction without a difference, as smaller investors may be priced out of the majority of their pre-emption rights.

21.4.5   Pre-emption top-ups

> *To the extent that any member of the Syndicate fails to take up all or any part of its pre-emption rights in any instance (the "Pre-emption Shortfall"), other Syndicate members who have taken up their pre-emptive rights in full will have additional pre-emption rights to take up all or any part of the Pre-emption Shortfall and if more than one Syndicate member expresses such interest, then pro rata between them.*

If equality of pre-emption rights across all shareholders is accepted by the VC firm, it makes it increasingly likely that the VC firm will then press for a "top-up" right. This is a right for the VC fund to bid again for "surplus" pre-emption rights not taken up by others. It is important, inter alia because pre-emption rights may be "all or nothing" (see 21.4.3 above) and because in such circumstances a top-up right is the only way in which a VC fund can both lock out third parties from an offering and "weight-up" in a business which it's really excited about (taking advantage of its aggressive follow-on capacity planning for example).

Once again, the entrepreneur may elect to ask to participate in the second round, top-up opportunity, in order to seek to avoid dilution vis à vis the VC fund but the VC fund will require (for the reasons given above) sooner or later that it is the buyer of last resort for surplus pre-emption rights, if only as a matter of having deeper pockets.

21.4.6   Administration of pre-emption rights

Finally, it is important to ensure that the administration of the pre-emption process is managed properly, so that it does not extend endlessly through cycle after cycle, disrupting a legitimate capital-raising activity and bogging the company down in administrative niceties and risk of disputes and law suits. If at all possible, the whole process should be managed within a 30 day window and different rounds of pre-emption (priorities, cascades, top-ups, etc) should be run concurrently not consecutively through a single communication to shareholders.

22
Anti-dilution Rights

22.1 INTRODUCTION TO ANTI-DILUTION RIGHTS

Anti-dilution rights are a form of price protection, plain and simple. Unfortunately, there's nothing plain and simple about the issues which this simple concept throws up in practice. In essence, anti-dilution rights ensure that the price at which a shareholder purchased shares in a company is adjusted to take account of specified future share subscriptions at a lower price, so that the shareholder is never "embarrassed" by subsequent lower-priced share issues.

As discussed at Chapter 5, anti-dilution protection is a slightly strange item which carries little intellectual legitimacy, but which is extraordinarily prevalent in venture capital financing terms.

> *In accordance with standard market practice for investment transactions of this type, Trojan Horse requires a measure of price protection. In the event that equity securities are issued by the Company at a subscription price lower than the price per share paid by the Syndicate for the A Shares in the Financing (as adjusted to take account of any subsequent capital reorganisation) (a "Down Round"), the Company will be required either (i) to issue further A Shares to each A Shareholder by way of bonus, capitalisation or other issue for negligible consideration, (ii) to adjust the A Share conversion rights or (iii) to issue options or warrants over A Shares to the A Shareholders, exercisable for negligible consideration (the "Down Round Adjustment") so that each Investor is compensated for the dilution resulting from the Down Round on a full ratchet basis such that, irrespective of the size of the Down Round, the average subscription price per A Share for each A Shareholder following the Down Round Adjustment is equal to the price per share at which the Down Round took place.*

22.1.1 Full ratchet anti-dilution

There are two bases conventionally used to determine the nature of anti-dilution protection: the so-called "full ratchet" and the "weighted average" approaches. The full ratchet mechanism is extremely simple – this approach simply asks two questions:

(1) What is the price per share at which the down round took place?
(2) What is the number of additional shares which would have to be issued to those shareholders with anti-dilution protection in order to ensure that the entirety of their shares (or at least those classes which have anti-dilution protection) are, on average, issued at that price per share?

Where a large down round triggers anti-dilution protection, this seems an obvious and straightforward approach – and it is. However, where it starts to fail is in relation to more modest share issues, where the full ratchet mechanism makes no adjustment for *relative* dilution. At the far end of the spectrum, this can operate arbitrarily and totally without regard to the reality of the situation.

For example (using the term sheet example), if ten million A Shares are issued at $1 each for one third of the fully diluted share capital, just the issue of one ordinary share thereafter at 50 cents a share would, under a full ratchet anti-dilution rights scenario, trigger a massive recapitalisation of the share capital – doubling the A Shares in issue (bringing the average subscription price down to 50 cents) and increasing the VC syndicate's ownership to 50% from 33%...all for the cost of 50 cents to the business. Clearly, this is a ludicrous example, but it demonstrates the more profound truth that full ratchet anti-dilution protection treats harshly smaller share issues and therefore perversely drives the business towards larger dilutive issues (particularly in conjunction with pre-emption rights where shareholders without anti-dilution protection may protect themselves by participating). It is for these reasons that in general full ratchet protection should be fiercely resisted by an entrepreneur.

22.1.2   Weighted average anti-dilution

The weighted average approach deals with many of the deficiencies of the full ratchet approach. The weighted average approach examines the relative dilutive impact of the down round on the share capital with the protective rights, in the context of the overall share capital (fully diluted or undiluted). It works out the relative dilution suffered by the protected share-holders and compensates them accordingly – it is therefore focused exclusively on dilution as the factor to be protected against, rather than the average price per share. This is a far more realistic approach and ensures that smaller share issues will not give rise to disproportionate anti-dilution protection.

However, it is important to note that there are two sub-approaches within this broad mechanism that may be operated – a broad-based calculation and a narrow-based calcu-lation. The broad-based calculation will examine the relative dilution to the protected class of shareholders in the context of the *fully-diluted* share capital and the narrow-based calculation will examine the relative dilution to the protected class of shareholders in the context of the *undiluted* share capital. Therefore, because the denominator of the calculation will be greater in the case of the broad-based approach, minimising the dilutive effect of the down round to existing shareholders, it is generally to be preferred for the entrepreneur (assuming he or she will not benefit from anti-dilution protection themselves) over the narrow-based approach.

22.1.3   Mechanism of action

There are three mechanisms typically used to implement anti-dilution protection as a technical matter:

(1) Bonus share issues – some jurisdictions (including many European jurisdictions) permit shares to be issued by way of capitalisation of reserves – typically the share premium account. If reserves are sufficient and available for such purpose, this can be a very efficient mechanism to satisfy anti-dilution rights (but clearly a share issue that of itself should not trigger anti-dilution rights!), as it requires no cash subscription by the owners of the rights.
(2) New share subscriptions – where a bonus issue to a defined class of shareholders is not possible for any reason, it may be possible to structure the anti-dilution ratchet as a

subscription of new shares at par value. Sometimes this subscription right is itself issued in the form of warrants or options exercisable by the holder. The problem with this mechanism is that if the par value of the shares is significant (and many European jurisdictions have minimum par values of €1) and the number of shares required to be issued is large, it may require a substantial cash subscription to operate anti-dilution protections, which may not be satisfactory in the circumstances. The entrepreneur should also be aware that local law restrictions may limit the flexibility of certain warrant structures in their use for anti-dilution purposes (as is the case in France, for example, with bons de souscription en actions).

Each of these two mechanisms raises the question of which class of shares should be issued to the shareholder – the class he or she already holds and which have anti-dilution rights, or the class issued in the down round that triggered the anti-dilution protection, or ordinary shares? The conventional wisdom is the class he or she already holds.

(3) Adjustment to conversion rights – where neither of the above mechanisms is available, a simple adjustment to the conversion rights of the affected class of shares may suffice – neatly avoiding any new share issues for the time being. However, this will only be possible where the par value of the ordinary shares into which the shares convert is sufficiently low to permit such an adjustment.

In general, there are no adverse knock-on effects on the business or founding shareholders arising from the mechanisms chosen to implement anti-dilution, and as such it should be regarded as no more than a technical exercise.

22.2 ATTRACTION OF ANTI-DILUTION TO A VC FIRM

From a VC firm's perspective, anti-dilution protection enables it's fund to invest in a company but to be protected from subsequent share issues at a lower subscription price than that which applied to its investment. As such, anti-dilution is in theory an extremely useful tool to protect the VC fund on price – essentially enabling the VC firm to negotiate terms with the entrepreneur on the back of due diligence, etc, but pass across to the company (and other shareholder classes who do not have anti-dilution rights) the risk that the company may have to raise future equity at a lower price – for whatever reason (business failure, market recalibration, etc). It's a no-brainer protection and almost all term sheets will contain anti-dilution protection.

Obviously, the extent of the pricing risk taken on by the VC fund will vary on a case by case basis. In the case of a start-up, there may be a very small risk indeed that subsequent equity capital-raisings will ever be as low as the initial round: conversely later rounds of financing – particularly those predicated on a rapid exit (e.g. a pre-IPO round) may be very risky in terms of future price adjustments (e.g. if the IPO does not materialise and a further private financing round has to be completed). It can be seen at once that the VC firm can use anti-dilution protection as a means to claw back value from an over-priced investment transaction: accordingly an entrepreneur must recognise this fact when pressing for the highest possible pre-money valuation in a financing…the presence of anti-dilution protections may enable the VC firm to be relatively sanguine about over-paying on the way in, if the VC firm believes that there will shortly be an event which causes the anti-dilution protection to bite, redistributing the ownership of the company in the direction of the VC fund. Indeed it is even possible, in the case of an unscrupulous VC firm, for an artificially high valuation to be submitted in the knowledge that the company will require further funding in one to two years, at which point the "real" pre-money valuation will become evident. Entrepreneurs should be exceptionally cautious in this regard.

22.3   THE ENTREPRENEUR'S RESPONSE

22.3.1   Fundamental unfairness

Anti-dilution protection usually enrages entrepreneurs, who quite naturally see it as a totally egregious and unfair re-allocation of investment risk for no good reason – the VC firm essentially requiring the entrepreneur and the other founding shareholders to write an insurance policy regarding the pricing of the investment transaction. It's indeed hard to characterise the rights in any other way and it is equally hard to justify why VC firms merit this differential treatment given the amount of due diligence work they and their advisers undertake before investment, the barrage of warranties and indemnities which underpin that due diligence at the time and the close involvement with the day to day running of the business which the VC firm will have going forward. However, anti-dilution remains market standard in VC term sheets.

Accepting this fait accompli, the entrepreneur should waste no energy in bemoaning the unfairness of it all and can focus instead on the practicalities of the rights, and key areas of nuance. Indeed, in many cases, this is an area that may have no relevance to the entrepreneur at all – if the company keeps progressing operationally in a relatively stable financing environment, then subsequent rounds of financing will be done at higher prices than prior rounds and anti-dilution issues will never become relevant.

22.3.2   Limitation of anti-dilution in practice

It is also extremely important for the entrepreneur to recognise the limitations of anti-dilution protection as a mechanism – both as a practical matter and as a political matter. Fundamentally, anti-dilution protection can only work if some constituencies do not have it – so that they can be diluted – and it is both possible and practicable for those constituencies (and those alone) to be the ones out of whose "hide" anti-dilution protection is taken, for them to be diluted aggressively by the operation of anti-dilution rights against them. As such, anti-dilution protection is not so much a matter of concern for the company or the business as it is for those shareholding constituencies (typically the founders and early, non-institutional investors in the business) who either do not have anti-dilution protection themselves or who have been forced to give it up by an incoming VC investor. But even then, one often finds that the very constituencies without anti-dilution rights are those who are protected as a practical matter from anti-dilution, because they are usually the very constituencies that are delivering value to investors by growing the business – and what kind of sense does it make to savagely dilute such persons' ownership interests? An investor would be effectively "cutting off his nose to spite his face". Equally, an incoming investor in the lower-priced subsequent financing (a "down round") will not want to see key constituencies damaged or disincentivised either, and may therefore demand that prior classes of shares give up their anti-dilution rights as the price of its incoming capital. As a consequence, in many cases the operation of anti-dilution rights is either simply impracticable, or requires that (following its operation) key value-drivers in the business (essentially the senior management team) need to be made whole again by the issue of new equity or equity incentives to them.

Using the term sheet example – following the financing round, there are essentially two classes of shareholders – the A shareholders comprising the investment syndicate, holding one third of the issued share capital, and the ordinary shareholders who are the entrepreneur and other founders and the core management team, holding the remainder. In this situation, were the syndicate to invoke their anti-dilution rights, they would be destroying the equity ownership of the team that is running the company day to day, meaning that far from protecting their investment in the company, the syndicate might simply drive the management team out of the door to do other things that are more remunerative for them – a self-defeating course of action to take. But if we assume that some of the individuals in this grouping of ordinary shareholders are in fact now passive shareholders providing no future value to the development of the business, then the situation may be very different and indeed it may suit all remaining active constituencies in the company (both investors and management) to implement the anti-dilution rights in full and then award new equity or equity incentives to the sub-set of management that remain relevant to the future development of the business.

Finally, it is worth recognising that the decision to effect anti-dilution is fraught with liability risk for an investor, in the same way as with any down round. The decision to effect and support a down round, particularly one that carries with it anti-dilution rights that will essentially "wash out" other shareholders raises very real questions about whether (a) the pre-money value is really the best that can be achieved, (b) with or without share issue pre-emption rights, the interests of minority shareholders are being abused by the majority and (c) it is legal in the circumstances to operate anti-dilution rights. This creates a situation where disputes and even litigation may arise and this factor alone will cause the syndicate to implement anti-dilution very cautiously and after much debate.

In practice, therefore, anti-dilution rights may be more token than actual. However, it is certainly true that passive shareholders (angel investors, prior classes of institutional investor) are very exposed to anti-dilution rights held by holders of senior securities – as they provide the perfect "cannon fodder" against which anti-dilution mechanisms can be brought to bear.

22.3.3   Shareholder double advantage

It is also the case that a down round can generally only take place with the full support of the VC syndicate (as they would also have shareholder veto and pre-emption rights over new share issues (see Chapters 17 and 21 above). A down round therefore would only result in shares being issued to a third party if the VC syndicate had approved the issue and decided not to exercise their pre-emption rights. To some extent, therefore (although this is of course an over-simplification) down rounds are willingly embraced by shareholders and it is perfectly possible for a shareholder to "benefit" from subscribing shares in a low-priced down round and yet still have the right to anti-dilution protection (non-existent "dilution" caused by its own share subscription)! It is therefore all the more important to understand the range of transactions caught by the operation of the right – see 22.5.1 below – to ensure that this kind of mischief is curtailed, but equally, it is clear that a VC firm can benefit from a down round without activating anti-dilution protections too.

22.4 PAY TO PLAY

> *Anti-dilution protection shall only apply to the extent that the relevant Syndicate member has partic-ipated in the Down Round at least pro rata to his shareholding in the Company and in the event that any Syndicate member does not comply with such requirement, he will lose any anti-dilution rights attaching to the same proportion of his A Shares.*

22.4.1 What is "pay to play"?

One of the most unpalatable aspects of anti-dilution rights is that they can in principle be enjoyed by a shareholder passively – in other words the shareholder does not have to participate in the down round to benefit from the rights. To deal with this issue, the fight-back by entrepreneurs on anti-dilution rights began a few years ago with the development of the concept of "pay to play" – and entrepreneurs should not consider accepting any anti-dilution provision without at least arguing for the inclusion of such a provision.

Pay to play provisions are based on the assertion that a shareholder with the benefit of anti-dilution protection should not gain access to this benefit (indeed should even be penalised further – see below) unless he or she is *also* prepared to support the company "in its time of need" by participating in the down round. It is based on the doctrine that with rights should come commensurate responsibilities. This at least ensures that the several deeply unattractive aspects of anti-dilution rights will be partly offset by the positive benefits of encouraging existing shareholders to stump up to support a down round. Of course, as discussed above, it is generally advisable to have a true reference price created by a new investor, to ensure that the down round valuation is properly calibrated to the market.

In fact, the VC firm may itself not be too unhappy with such a proposal, if it is made by an entrepreneur. This is because the VC firm is likely to have a dual role to consider in this area – its fund's position as an *investor* and as *syndicate leader*. As investor, the VC fund would certainly prefer the anti-dilution rights to be unfettered by any qualification, such as pay to play, although it may not be too concerned if it has allocated sufficient follow-on capability and retains a veto – possibly even a unilateral veto – over all share issues; however, as a syndicate leader, it will be perfectly happy to see incentives that ensure that its fellow syndicate members properly reserve for follow-on investments ... and suffer the consequences for failing to do so (to the advantage of those members of the syndicate who do follow-on).

As such, pay to play provisions can prove to be an enormously useful tool to ensure that syndicate members (i) allocate sufficient reserves to continue to support the company into the future and (ii) actively commit those reserves to the company in future fund-raisings, particularly down rounds (which may be expected to be more difficult for the company to close than a conventional "up" round).

22.4.2 Determining the amount to pay

Clearly, it will be important to determine the basis on which the pay to play obligation will be calculated – in other words, how much of a participation is required by a shareholder to satisfy its obligation? The usual starting point is to require that a shareholder contributes its "pro rata" share.

However, it may be difficult to determine a shareholder's pro rata participation in advance of the financing that triggers the anti-dilution rights. In this respect it is important to consider the following:

(1) The entrepreneur may want to have the ability to get an "insider round" completed (as this will typically be quicker than a round that brings in a new investor), provided that there is a clear reference price, and in such circumstances it will be necessary to determine the level of support by the syndicate members that will trigger a pay to play ("put up or shut up") provision for those members of the syndicate who decide *not* to participate;
(2) The entrepreneur will have to consider the potential for the round to contain one or more new investors, which would mean that the concept of "pro rata" for existing shareholders would exclude the component of the down round allocated by the company to these new investors – essentially existing investors being employed to "fill the gap"; and
(3) The entrepreneur will have to consider whether the calculation of "pro rata" should be pro rata to the shareholder's proportion of the VC syndicate, or of the wider existing shareholder base.

By the same token, the VC firm will want to ensure that the pay to play provision can operate fairly, by ensuring that the concept of pro rata is as narrow as possible in all likely circumstances and that (unless it agrees otherwise) the terms and conditions of that part of any down round financing made available to it are entirely at arm's length and fair (usually by benchmarking the terms to those offered to a material new investor or by ensuring that the financing carries the approval of a significant majority of the syndicate) and that it is not being deliberately prejudiced by its syndicate colleagues.

22.4.3 Consequences of not paying...

There are two broad approaches in terms of the consequences of a shareholder failing to "pay to play":

(1) Anti-dilution rights are simply disapplied to the extent of the individual shareholder's failure to contribute new capital up to its pro rata amount (e.g. if a shareholder contributes only half of its pro rata entitlement, half of the anti-dilution rights are disapplied): this leaves the other share rights of the shareholder unaffected, but simply limits the anti-dilution protection provided to the shareholder on that share issue transaction (without prejudice to future transactions) – clearly variants to this approach would be (i) an "all or nothing" disapplication under which the shareholder would get no anti-dilution rights unless it contributed its entire pro rata share or (ii) once disapplied, anti-dilution rights would be cancelled forever; or
(2) To the extent of the individual shareholder's failure to contribute new capital up to its pro rata amount, the shareholder's shares convert to ordinary shares (e.g. if a shareholder contributes only half of its pro rata entitlement, half of its preferred shares will convert to ordinary shares): this is a much more draconian approach which offsets anti-dilution protection with a significant disincentive to doing less than pro rata of an as-yet-unidentified financing round.

Both types of provision are seen in venture financing terms. It is somewhat surprising that a more sophisticated middle way has not developed. Obviously, the latter approach is preferable for an entrepreneur, but may only be achievable with a robust syndicate leader in support.

22.4.4   New developments

Given the development of pay to play provisions in recent years, it is perhaps surprising that a "pay to avoid" variant has not also been tried out. If anti-dilution rights can be made subject to the shareholder supporting the company in its time of need, why could not a junior shareholder propose that it does not form part of the constituency diluted, to the extent that it contributes capital to the company in the down round?

22.5   AREAS TO WATCH OUT FOR

22.5.1   Carve-outs

> *Anti-dilution rights will not apply to the following securities issues: (i) Ordinary Shares issued as a consequence of the exercise of options under the ESOP, (ii) securities offered or sold to third parties pursuant to an IPO, (iii) Ordinary Shares issued on the conversion of the A Shares, (iv) securities issued pursuant to any group reorganisation, Merger or Sale, (v) securities issued as consideration for the acquisition by the Company of third party assets, or other business or entity, and (vi) securities issued to third parties as part of a commercial collaboration or other arm's length commercial undertaking.*

As with pre-emption rights, VC firms will work from the premise that *all* forms of securities issue should trigger anti-dilution rights, but this will rarely be appropriate. The entrepreneur must evaluate the range of transactions that should be carved out, both in principle and by reference to the prevailing business plan: the entrepreneur must evaluate where the financing requirements of the company are likely to lie and how the company's best interests may be properly protected. In particular:

(1) it is very common for a range of conventional and foreseeable share incentive programmes (ESOPs, options, warrants, share grants to incoming senior executives, etc), as well as certain foreseen "technical" share issues (conversion of the VC fund's shares under their conversion rights, exercise of employee options, etc), to be excluded from the operation of anti-dilution rights;

(2) the entrepreneur may wish to exclude securities issues made for the purpose of the acquisition of another company, or the business or assets of another company – because in such a case the securities exchange issue (the issue of shares in exchange for the transfer of assets or shares to the company) is clearly not made for fund-raising purposes, but for strategic purposes, and not only is the pricing of the securities exchange issue therefore in no way comparable to the prior financing issue (apples and oranges), but any dilutive effect of the securities exchange issue can be expected to be offset by the accretion of value to the overall business – in other words the company, business or assets acquired can be expected to have been acquired at their full market value in exchange for the shares issued;

(3) again, just as with pre-emption rights, an entrepreneur may also wish to have the ability to strike strategic deals with third parties – for example sales and marketing initiatives, collaborations, joint ventures or partnerships by means of an equity deal (including cross-shareholdings) or share incentive programmes (conventionally, options or warrants) and would want these kinds of deals excluded from anti-dilution rights;

(4) the entrepreneur may wish to try to negotiate a general carve-out from anti-dilution rights in a modest amount for general corporate purposes (where the dilutive potential is not significant);

(5) the entrepreneur may try to resist the application of anti-dilution to early-stage financings, where the risk of share price volatility remains extremely high but the expectation of significant upward movement over the medium term (provided the business performs) can also be expected; and

(6) the entrepreneur should seek to exclude financings which are entirely subscribed by existing shareholders, at least unless the pricing of such transactions is validated by an external reference point (for example, a third party term sheet), because of the arbitrary nature of any such financing and the significant benefit already gained by the syndicate of investors through the internal financing.

22.5.2 Pricing considerations

Anti-dilution mechanisms operate solely by reference to price. Stating the obvious – if the price per share of the subsequent new issue is not lower than the price of the previous round, then the anti-dilution protection will not be triggered at all in such circumstances. So, lowering the price per share at which shares are issued in a financing will reduce the prospect that anti-dilution rights in the future could be triggered. At the margins of term sheet negotiation, therefore, the entrepreneur should recognise that anti-dilution rights are part of the suite of downside protection rights that a VC firm will insist upon, and the entrepreneur should make a conscious decision where he or she is happiest granting the lion's share of that protection. If an entrepreneur feels comfortable about pushing for the highest possible share price in a fundraising, then this will ratchet up the risk of anti-dilution occurring in the future. But if an entrepreneur is less willing to take that risk, then a modest price reduction will do the trick.

Taken to the next level, the entrepreneur may find that it is possible to improve the quality of other downside protection mechanisms elsewhere in the term sheet in order to gain a better position on anti-dilution rights – for example it might be possible to flex the terms of the equity instrument being issued by trading a reduced share price for reduced downside protection, which will reduce the risk that anti-dilution rights will become exercisable – e.g. a convertible preference share (single dip, 1× preferred return and an interest coupon) issued at 50 cents a share might be preferable to a double dipping convertible preferred share issued at $1 (the additional downside protection warranting the increased subscription price).

To some extent, an entrepreneur must gauge which kinds of risk he or she feels most comfortable with and appreciate that, in the term sheet, there is an inter-related package of downside protections and upside participation mechanisms that, together, catalyse the valuation at which the deal can be done.

22.5.3 Proxies for value

As discussed elsewhere in this book, one of the most annoying features of anti-dilution protection is that the protection may apply where the business has performed admirably, but the inevitable cycles of the fund-raising market have moved against the business to ensure that, regardless of operational achievements, the business may be "worth" less at its next financing than previously. If ever there were a risk that it should be unfair for the VC firm to offload onto the company and its shareholders, this is it. The obvious solution would be either to find a proxy for "the market" and exclude down rounds caused solely by market movements, or to disapply down round protections when the company has performed to an agreed business plan. Unfortunately, this is an innovation yet to be seen in term sheets.

22.5.4   Price benchmarks

An entrepreneur should also give careful consideration to the reference terms to which anti-dilution rights should apply – in other words the terms and conditions of investment that are used as a benchmark for the anti-dilution rights themselves. Obviously this issue is closely inter-linked with the agreed applicable transactions (see 22.5.1 above). For example, while it may be a very simple matter to accept that a detailed term sheet, delivered by a third party aiming to subscribe equity shares for cash in a simple, arm's length fund-raising, should operate as a benchmark for the anti-dilution rights – conversely the terms on which equity is proposed to be issued to a business partner as part of a complex collaboration arrangement (for example a pharmaceutical company entering into a clinical development partnership with a small biotech business) may be a poor benchmark for anti-dilution rights and, in particular, an "insider round" funded entirely by those to whom anti-dilution rights will apply anyway, has so many inherent conflicts of interest that either such a transaction should have anti-dilution disapplied (see above) or there should be some kind of referencing procedure to ensure that the price provided by the insiders is sufficiently robust against market metrics.

22.5.5   Who squeezes who?

As mentioned above, anti-dilution rights only work when there are other shareholder constituencies which can be squeezed. However, often these constituencies are the very persons who are primarily responsible for developing the business and delivering the core value to investors (founders and management). Clearly, it would be wholly counter-productive to operate anti-dilution rights to penalise such persons significantly and in consequence, where the ordinary shares or junior securities are held primarily by founders and senior management (which is very often the case) anti-dilution rights end up either being waived or operated only on a very limited basis, or the rights are operated in full but the key value-drivers are then "made whole" by means of new share incentives such as share option grants.

To some extent, this means that the most dangerous place to be is as a legacy founder who is no longer crucial to the future of the business, or an unprotected "angel" or other early stage passive investor. Just like pre-emption rights, such constituencies are cannon-fodder for anti-dilution rights.

22.5.6   Differential pricing

It is not uncommon for a high growth company to go through two or three rounds of venture funding in half a dozen years. That can lead to a situation where several classes of shares have anti-dilution rights – often triggered at different prices. The entrepreneur should simply note that anti-dilution protection can be almost impossible to operate where more than one class of shares has anti-dilution protection that may be triggered at the same time but at different trigger prices. In the end, this is usually to the entrepreneur's benefit – but it may equally be true that this kind of confusion can be very damaging to a company as it tries to close a down round. It would be better to plan for this issue in advance and either to resist anti-dilution rights altogether, or organise a common low watermark for the rights to be exercisable, or demand that earlier classes of equity forfeit their anti-dilution rights in favour of the latest class of securities to be issued.

22.5.7 Syndicate dangers

As mentioned above, operating anti-dilution rights in an insider or insider-led round can be dangerous and there have in recent years been a number of court cases in the United States seeking to test the limits of an investment syndicate's powers to effect low-priced investment rounds into an existing investment: anti-dilution protection adds insult to injury in this regard.

In essence, a VC fund looking to contribute capital to its portfolio company faces a clear conflict of interest – on the one hand it would like the company to raise funding on the best possible terms and at the highest possible pre-money valuation, to demonstrate growth in value since the last financing. On the other hand (and remember that shareholder vetos can be used to prevent a company taking funding from external sources), the VC fund would also like the opportunity to contribute further capital into the company at the lowest possible price, to secure the maximum ownership of the business for the least amount of money, possibly also triggering anti-dilution protection to boot. The constituencies that suffer most are passive minority shareholders who have no effective measure to protect themselves. These constituencies may feel that their interests are not even protected by the board, if the VC syndicate has effective control of the board (notwithstanding fiduciary duties). This situation is a recipe for litigation in extreme cases. Accordingly, VC syndicates can be expected to be scrupulous in price formation in difficult cases and a measured approach on anti-dilution protection may be expected as part of this approach.

To some extent, therefore, anti-dilution protection may be seen as no more than a negotiation "counter" in the process that leads to formation of a down round financing on generally agreed terms.

Provisions Relating to Share Transfers

23.1 INTRODUCTION TO SHARE TRANSFERS

A high degree of control over the share capital of its portfolio companies is a fundamental component of a VC fund's investment approach. Not only is it essential, as we have seen, for the VC fund to retain tight control over new securities issues and to protect itself from dilution arising on the issue of new equity shares (by means of techniques such as pre-emption, anti-dilution, etc), but the VC fund's desire to control matters extends also to transfers of shares.

There are three distinct reasons for this:

(1) Firstly, maintaining a tight grip on who owns shares in its portfolio company enables a VC firm to ensure not only that the shares are held only by a defined set of value-drivers in the business (financiers, management, founders, employees, etc), but also that potentially disruptive interlopers are not admitted without their permission. Both of these factors are risk management issues – put simply, it matters very much to a VC firm that it knows who it is dealing with in an investment situation.

(2) Secondly, transfers of shares are of interest to a VC firm because it presents an opportunity for its fund to acquire further shares opportunistically, weighting-up its investment in a performing company, or equally opportunistically averaging-down the overall cost per share of its investment (if the VC firm takes a long term favourable view on the company and believes that it is at present undervalued).

(3) Thirdly, transfers of shares may represent liquidity (sale) opportunities, in which the VC may wish to participate.

The various features of share transfer provisions found in venture capital term sheets can variously be explained by one of these reasons above.

23.2 TRANSFER RESTRICTIONS

23.2.1 General restrictions

> *It is very important to Trojan Horse and the Syndicate that securities issued by the Company are locked-up for a protracted period. Therefore, Ordinary Shareholders may not transfer any interest in their shares except for the purpose of normal tax and estate planning purposes (including on the death of any member of management), or with the consent of 75% of the Syndicate (by shareholding), in each case provided that the transferee accedes to the Financing documentation. A Shares held by the Syndicate will be freely transferable. Transfer restrictions will not apply to the transfer of Shares following or pursuant to the operation of the pre-emption, tag-along and drag-along rights described below.*

It is extremely common, for the reasons given above, for severe transfer restrictions to be placed on the shares held by the founders, management and employees, and potentially also all holders of securities junior to the VC fund's class of shares. Typically, a term sheet will provide for a blanket prohibition on any form of transfer (which will include the alienation of any interest in the shares – catching sales of rights over the shares, security interests, etc), occasionally with limited exceptions for tax and estate planning purposes.

The key question for the entrepreneur is whether he or she should seek to extend the no-transfer prohibition to the VC syndicate as well. This has become more important as a consideration in recent years, as the "secondaries" market for VC fund investments has grown enormously – this is a market in which specialist buyers seek to acquire LP interests in VC funds, entire LP portfolios, VC fund investments, or entire VC fund portfolios. Unless a portfolio company (and indeed other members of the VC syndicate) are properly protected against secondary transactions of this kind, it can be very destabilising suddenly to find that a significant shareholder has departed and that the owner of a chunk of your share capital is a new entity unknown to you. Not only does this raise the question of the departing share-holder's view on the company's prospects, but it also raises concerns about the investment strategy, reputation, behaviour and follow-on capability of the new shareholder. Of course, the specialist secondary buyers will argue that they bring new skills, a new investment horizon and most of all a refreshed investment capacity which together will greatly benefit the company, but these things are not a given and it is usually better for the entrepreneur to judge these facets from a position of strength than weakness. As such, prima facie an entre-preneur should seek to lock up the investment syndicate just as he or she is locked up, so that there is reciprocity. After all, the identity of the entrepreneur's investors is at least as important to him or her as the identity of fellow shareholders is to the VC firm.

However, a VC firm will often resist such restrictions, taking the view that it should be free to explore any and all liquidity events for its VC fund. Indeed the rapidly growing secondaries market for VC fund portfolio interests may well encourage the VC firm, particularly an early-stage investor, to hold out for this kind of flexibility. But if pressed hard, a VC firm will usually agree to be bound by lock-up provisions, at least for a defined initial period and subject to perfectly acceptable carve-outs to permit the small range of circumstances in which a transfer would be permissible (e.g. a fund reorganisation, or change of trustee or administrator). This can be valuable for the entrepreneur, safe in the knowledge that the VC fund will not spring a sale transaction upon the company at short notice, potentially destabilising the business. In drafting such restrictions, the entrepreneur should ensure that the agreement captures not only a direct sale of the company's shares by the VC fund, but also an indirect change of control of the VC fund through a change of manager or adviser (the VC firm), or change of control at the fund level. Once again, the active secondaries market operates at the fund level: equally it is becoming increasingly common for VC firms to undergo changes of control – which in either case effectively changes the entity the entrepreneur is working with in the same way as a share transfer.

23.2.2 IPO restrictions

> In the case of an IPO by the Company, all shareholders and optionholders will agree to an appropriate lock-up period in terms agreed between the Company, Trojan Horse and the relevant underwriters, but being no longer than the shorter of (i) six months and (ii) the period ending on the date of publication of the Company's half year or full year (as applicable) financial results next following the IPO.

It is extremely common in term sheets to see an early commitment among the shareholders to agree to a common approach on lock-ups in an IPO scenario. These provisions typically commit the shareholders in advance to agree to a lock-up (a restriction on them selling shares into the secondary market in the aftermath of an IPO to prevent a collapse in the share price caused by a flood of shares being sold) for a period not longer than six months on commonly applicable terms (the latter issue ensuring that the institutional investors are not able to garner a better deal for themselves in an IPO than the other shareholders). This is conventional stuff, which should not be resisted by the entrepreneur and indeed it can often be very valuable for the shareholders to be commonly committed not to disrupt the trading market in the company's stock immediately post IPO by "running for the exits". However, the entrepreneur should be aware that:

(1) it will often be the case that the IPO book-runners will insist that members of management be locked up either for a more protracted period or on more onerous terms, and so the lock-up provisions in the term sheet must simply set a minimum floor on lock-ups; and
(2) institutional shareholders, particularly VC funds with chunky shareholdings post IPO, are often in an excellent position post flotation (notwithstanding the lock-up, which may be waived by the book-runners) to work collaboratively with the book-runners and/or the company's corporate brokers in a placing of their stock into the market – therefore the entrepreneur should try to position the other shareholders to be able to benefit from any such lock-up release.

23.2.3 Mandatory sales

> Any director, officer or employee who ceases to be employed by the Company for any reason will be required (at the option of the Company) to sell their vested Shares back to the Company (i) at par value to the Company, if the reason for the departure is fraud, theft, conviction for a criminal offence, breach of a material term of the individual's employment or service contract, or gross misconduct, or (ii) at market value, in any other case.

As discussed above in Chapter 20, there are circumstances in which the company will want to insist on the mandatory disposal of shares by a shareholder. The provisions set out above merely implement the disposal in such circumstances.

23.3 TRANSFER PRE-EMPTION RIGHTS

As discussed above, it is an important feature of the VC business model that the VC fund is able to participate fully in the upside of an investment opportunity, and it can also be attractive for the VC fund to be able to take advantage of "bumps in the road" in order to average down its overall cost of investment per share, or (if it takes a longer term view that the turnaround will be advantageous) to be able to take command of a rescue or turnaround situation that arises.

As in the case of new share issues, one of the principal mechanisms to achieve this in relation to share transfers is the use of pre-emption rights. Transfer pre-emption rights are a first right to acquire shares being transferred, on the terms upon which a third party has agreed to purchase them. This right enables a shareholder to jump in ahead of third parties who wish to buy shares in the company. Unlike share issue pre-emption, transfer pre-emption rights are not concerned about protection from involuntary dilution, but about opportunistic buying. Unlike share issue pre-emption, local laws usually do not provide for pre-emption protection on share transfers.

23.3.1   Nature of Pre-emption

> *Even where the Syndicate are prepared to approve of a transfer of securities to a bona fide third party purchaser, it is vitally important that a transfer takes place only after Syndicate members have been offered the opportunity to acquire the shares proposed to be sold. Accordingly, if any shareholder proposes to transfer any securities, it must offer the Syndicate the opportunity (but not the obligation) to purchase such securities on a pro rata basis and on the same terms as are proposed for the sale to a bona fide third party purchaser.*

The traditional pre-emption rights set out above provide the non-transferring shareholders with a first right to acquire the shares being sold, at the same price and on the same terms as the third party offer (like share issue pre-emption rights, transfer pre-emption rights are triggered by a third party offer). Note that there is no obligation upon the shareholders to take up their rights, merely an opportunity.

23.3.2   Partial pre-emption?

> *Unless all transfer shares are taken up under the transfer pre-emption process, the sale may proceed free of transfer pre-emption rights on the same price and terms as notified to shareholders within 90 days from the end of the 30-day pre-emption period.*

One important issue to understand is that transfer pre-emption rights, in the main, do not block transactions. This is because they are required to be *taken up* – and if, or to the extent they are *not* taken up, the shares may be transferred free of restriction. However, this standard approach will often require closer scrutiny – in particular the entrepreneur should consider three important questions in designing transfer pre-emption rights:

(1) Just as with share issue pre-emption rights, should the pre-emption rights be "all or nothing" – in other words, if pre-emption rights are not taken up over *all* of the shares proposed to be transferred, should *all* pre-emption rights drop away ("all or nothing pre-emption"), or should only those shares not "taken up" by existing shareholders, possibly pursuant to multiple rounds, be available for sale to the third party ("partial pre-emption")? Again, an all or nothing approach places the onus on the existing shareholders, as a group, to "put up or shut up" – to buy all the shares proposed to be sold, or see the equity go elsewhere: conversely, a graduated approach allowing partial pre-emption gives the non-transferring shareholders more flexibility to pick up only those shares they want, but is far from optimal for the transferring shareholder, because it may not be able to guarantee a meaningful piece of equity to the third party transferee at the end of the process after pre-emption has operated – indeed the third party potential acquirer may elect not to participate in the transaction at all without a guaranteed minimum participation, and if the acquirer drops out of the transaction at the end of a partial pre-emption process, the transferor shareholder may even be left with a "stub" piece of equity that may be unsaleable on its own, unless in such circumstances the pre-emption rights fall away too. This is a classic example of a different answer being optimal depending on whether the entrepreneur believes he or she will be a seller, a buyer or a passive spectator in a transfer situation. One approach would be to allow pre-emption rights to be exercised in part – and accept that this de facto may operate as a complete fetter on share transfers. However, unlike share issue pre-emption rights, it is usually accepted by shareholders that the price and terms

generated by a third party is underpinned by the size of the stake proposed to be transferred – and therefore an all or nothing approach is the most common approach adopted in investment terms. The consequence of this is that it makes additional rounds of pre-emption, top-up rights, etc all the more important to ensure that the buying demand of the current shareholders under their pre-emption rights is fully tapped.

(2) Should a holder of pre-emption rights be permitted to take up part of his or her rights, or only all of them? This ties into the whole question of whether the pre-emption rights should be all or nothing and of how difficult or easy it should be for a shareholder to take up his pre-emption rights. It is conventional to provide that a shareholder may take up all or any part of his or her transfer pre-emption rights – usually driven by the fear of smaller shareholders that an all or nothing approach would cause them to be priced out of participation.

(3) In the event that (or to the extent that) pre-emption rights are *not* taken up, how long should the transferring shareholder be free to transfer the shares to the identified third party? Just as with share issue pre-emption, the term sheet will often provide that the third party sale transaction may progress only on the terms previously disclosed and within a relatively short timeframe (e.g. up to three months).

23.3.3   Who gets pre-emption rights?

As with share issue pre-emption, the next question to ask is who gets the transfer pre-emption rights. Obviously, the VC fund will be asking for the rights, but it may be reasonable to ask that the rights are extended beyond the VC fund to other constituencies – for example the entrepreneur, and again this will rarely be resisted by the VC fund.

The question arises once more whether there should be priorities between different classes of shares in terms of transfer pre-emption. For example, should the holders of the senior class of shares have pre-emption rights in priority to the holders of more junior classes of shares, with the junior classes only participating to the extent that senior classes of shares have not taken up their rights? Unlike share issue pre-emption rights, there is no issue about a holder of a senior class of securities maintaining its priority over other classes in new share issues – conversely an issue that raises its head in transfer pre-emption (and not share issue pre-emption) is the question of maintaining the equilibrium between share classes, which may be important in areas such as veto rights, etc. For this reason, it is not unusual to see a first pre-emption right given to shareholders within the same class of shares being transferred and thereafter to other classes (usually the VC syndicate first) although often all classes are granted transfer pre-emption rights pari passu and pro rata – in other words equally and ratably between each other as to shareholding.

23.3.4   Pre-emption top-ups

> *To the extent that any member of the Syndicate fails to take up all or any part of its pre-emption rights in any instance (the "Transfer Pre-emption Shortfall"), other Syndicate members who have taken up their pre-emptive rights in full will have additional pre-emption rights to take up all or any part of the Transfer Pre-emption Shortfall and if more than one Syndicate member expresses such interest, then pro rata between them.*

In an all or nothing scenario, particularly if equality of pre-emption rights across all shareholders is accepted by the VC firm, it makes it increasingly likely that the VC firm will then press for a "top-up" right. This is a right for the VC fund to bid again for "surplus" transfer pre-emption rights not taken up by others and in circumstances such as an all or nothing or class-based pre-emption, a right of top-up may be the only way that a VC fund can lock out third parties from becoming shareholders, or increase its holding in a business which it believes has great potential.

Once again, the entrepreneur may elect to ask to participate in the second round, top-up opportunity, in order to seek to avoid a change in the equilibrium in his or her relationship with the VC fund, but the VC fund will require, sooner of later, that it is the buyer of last resort for surplus pre-emption rights.

23.3.5   Buyer of last resort

Finally, one sometimes sees the company itself being given a "buyer of last resort" right, enabling it to retire securities that are not taken up under the pre-emption process (or direct that they are acquired by another third party). This is obviously commercially significant in the context of an all or nothing approach to the pre-emption rights, because it enables the remaining constituencies to use the company's resources (subject to stringent requirements of applicable company law) to shrink the capital base to avoid having to take in new shareholders, or to find a more attractive buyer than the one proposed by the transferring shareholder.

23.3.6   Administration of pre-emption rights

In order to ensure that the above pre-emption process does not derail the sale opportunity for the transferring shareholder, the process will be operated under a 30 day fast-track procedure under which Syndicate members will elect both for core and additional pre-emption rights in one round. In addition, unless all the shares to be sold are taken up under such pre-emption process, the sale may proceed free of pre-emption rights on the same price and terms as notified to shareholders within 90 days period from the end of the 30-day period.

As for share issue pre-emption rights, it is important to ensure that the administration of the transfer pre-emption process is managed properly, so that it does not extend endlessly through cycle after cycle, disrupting a legitimate share transfer transaction. If at all possible, the whole process should be managed within a 30 day window and different rounds of pre-emption (priorities, cascades, top-ups, etc) should be run concurrently not consecutively through a single communication to shareholders.

23.3.7   Exclusion of certain transactions

Pre-emption rights on transfer will not apply to (i) transfers by management shareholders for the purpose of normal tax and estate planning purposes (including on the death of any member of management), (ii) transfers by Syndicate members, in each case provided that the purchaser accedes to the Financing documentation or (iii) transfers of Shares pursuant to the operation of pre-emption, tag-along or drag-along rights.

Just as for share issue pre-emption, it will be important to prescribe certain types of transaction to which share transfer pre-emption rights should not apply. Usually these will be very limited exceptions – typically tax and estate planning and administration, transfers required to be made pursuant to the shareholders agreements and transfers pursuant to permitted transfer transactions such as the exercise of tag-along or drag-along rights, or the transfer pre-emption rights themselves.

23.4   DRAG-ALONG RIGHTS

> *It remains vital that the Syndicate are, with sufficient shareholder support, able to initiate and complete an IPO, Sale (including a sale of business for such purpose) or Merger transaction, to carry out an exit of their investment in the Company. Accordingly, a majority of the Shareholders (by shareholding, on an as-if-converted basis) may, with the prior written consent of 75% of the Syndicate (by shareholding), require the initiation of an IPO, or a Sale or Merger of the Company or of all or substantially all of its business or assets, and in such circumstances all shareholders will be obliged to do all things as may be necessary and desirable to permit the flotation, sale or merger of the Company or its business or assets.*

23.4.1   What are drag-along rights?

A "drag-along" right (often referred to less pejoratively as a "take-along" right) is a right to require other shareholders to sell their shares (or take advantage of any quasi-exit opportunity, such as an IPO) alongside the initiator(s) of the transaction. As discussed in some detail at Chapter 5 above, a VC firm regards it as essential that it is able to get everyone associated with an investment to work together to secure an attractive exit opportunity. Drag-along powers are axiomatic in creating such an effect and ensure that, once a sale or other exit opportunity has been identified and has the support of a sufficient majority of the shareholders, the company or its shares can be delivered into the transaction.

23.4.2   Why is drag-along needed?

Most entrepreneurs assume that if an exit opportunity emerges that is sufficiently attractive, it will be straightforward to get all shareholder constituencies behind the sale transaction. In fact, this is rarely the case in venture capital transactions, for commercial and prosaic reasons. Commercially, the existence of differential share rights may give rise to anomalies among the different classes of shareholders, such that some constituencies may find a particular exit opportunity highly attractive and others may be motivated to hold on for a better offer or even a different form of exit (e.g. IPO versus trade sale). Equally, some shareholders (notably employees and sometimes the entrepreneur) may simply be reluctant to sell at all at the particular time on the basis that, whatever the price on offer, the "time is not right". Rather more prosaically, as the shareholder roster gets larger and more diverse as the company grows and develops, some shareholders may lose contact with the company, either generally, as they move away (or even die, with their shares transferring to the beneficiaries of their estate) or specifically in the context of an exit opportunity, when they may be travelling, on vacation or unreachable for some reason.

Assuming that in a particular exit scenario there will always be some reluctant or absent shareholders, does this matter? Unfortunately, in the absence of drag-along rights, it does. Without each and every shareholder voluntarily signing up to a binding agreement to sell their shares, it may not be possible to transfer their shares to the transferee purchaser of the company. Selling shares is inherently a voluntary act in the absence of binding contractual provisions to the contrary (a drag-along right in the investment documentation) or some form of compulsory buy-out provisions under the applicable law. Therefore, the first place that the selling shareholders will want to look, in the absence of drag-along rights, is to any rights they may have under applicable laws to compel dissenting or absent shareholders to sell their shares or effect the necessary corporate actions or approvals. Many legal systems have compulsory acquisition procedures that will assist – for example in both France and Germany a shareholder holding 95% of the issued share capital may compulsorily acquire the minorities and in the US and the UK similar "squeeze-out" provisions apply following takeover offers – but unfortunately almost invariably these legal systems cannot be relied on, inter alia because:

(1) almost without exception these legal routes require the shares compulsorily acquired to be acquired for cash at their fair value – and this may not work in the context of a complex acquisition of several different classes of share (with differential sale consideration between classes), perhaps for a mix of cash and shares (or even wholly for shares), and where therefore there is a real prospect that the fair value of the shares (as determined by applicable law) is different from the value placed on the shares in the acquisition;
(2) shares compulsorily acquired may be transferred under applicable laws without the benefit of key warranties or undertakings, and almost certainly without being fully dove-tailed into the terms of the acquisition itself, which may be materially unattractive for the buyer;
(3) those jurisdictions which employ the concept of a takeover offer to trigger compulsory squeeze-out mechanisms, often do not coalesce all share classes into their required trigger thresholds (for example acceptance of the takeover by 90% of *each* class separately is required under UK law, although a scheme of arrangement under UK law would require only acceptances from a majority in number of the class together holding 75% or more of the voting rights of that class) and so a large number of dissenting shareholders in a single class (even one which is economically insignificant) can foil the use of the squeeze-out mechanics under applicable law;
(4) statutory squeeze-out mechanisms rarely deal with options and warrants – which must accommodate terms relating to sale transactions, etc in their constitutive documents;
(5) invoking applicable laws requires a significant amount of time, cost and complexity and the prospect of litigation is ever-present – this has pricing implications for the buyer and may be sufficient to deter a buyer entirely.

In the absence of being able to deliver the entirety of the issued share capital of the company, the selling shareholders only have two strategies to fall back on:

(1) Sell the business, not the company itself (i.e. an assets sale not a share sale) – although this may be prima facie attractive to a purchaser (which will only acquire those past liabilities it specifically agrees to purchase), more usually difficulties associated with the transfer of intellectual property rights and the benefit of contracts (high growth technology-based companies tend to have intangible, not tangible assets), together with the value of tax losses generated in the early years of development and probably not yet utilised (which would be lost on a business sale), will mean that the optimal approach for a buyer will be a share sale. For the sellers, a share sale is usually greatly to be preferred, as it is cleaner and simpler, and avoids leaving the sellers with a corporate shell whose only asset is cash and which then needs to be wound down and liquidated

before the cash can be paid to investors in a liquidation distribution – a process that is costly and time-consuming and always subject to the risk of unforeseen liabilities emerging. In addition, a liquidation distribution will often be treated as income in the hands of many investors, potentially significantly less attractive than the capital gains treatment on a share sale.

(2) Sell only some of the share capital, leaving the buyer with a small piece of stub equity. Clearly, this is highly unattractive for the buyer who inherits a recalcitrant minority shareholder group, possibly with special share rights, limiting the buyer's ability to assimilate the business with its own group and impacting in a whole series of ways on the buyer's freedom of action going forward. At the very least, this will have a significant negative price impact.

For these reasons, although applicable laws may offer a modicum of protection in the circumstances, it is usually optimal for the VC fund to have specific contractual powers to drag dissenting shareholders into an exit opportunity.

23.4.3 Drag-along implementation

Once the concept of a drag-along has been agreed, certain key features of the right need to be considered. Obviously, the single most critical feature is the shareholder approval threshold at which the drag-along power can be invoked. From the VC fund's perspective, it will want to ensure that it has (at least) unilateral powers to block a drag-along being invoked and sometimes (at most) unilateral power to force through a drag-along. Conversely, the entrepreneur will want the same power to block a drag-along. In fact these desires are not, for once, mutually irreconcilable, although it is certainly the case that the more "special interest groups" which have been created by many layers of share classes in the company's share capital, the more difficult it is going to be to settle upon an agreed constituency to trigger the drag-along rights. There are three particular approaches to defining this constituency that are often seen in venture capital term sheets:

(1) A super-majority of all shares in issue, without discrimination between share classes – this has the benefit of simplicity and, so long as the threshold is high enough, ensures that in practice there needs to be sufficient representation from every class of shares (even if the representation may only be low among the most junior classes of shareholder)

(2) A defined majority of the VC syndicate – again, this has the benefit of simplicity and recognises what may be economic reality: that the economics of the transaction to the VC syndicate may be substantially driving the exit process. It is probably the mechanism which is easiest to achieve, as the syndicate is likely to hold one class of shares and to be motivated to exit their investments at above broadly the same exit valuations (conversely, the situation may become much more complicated if there are multiple classes of VC equity)

(3) A combination approach, which requires separate approvals both of the VC syndicate and of all shareholders, possibly at slightly lower levels than as single constituencies.

Which option feels right will depend on the circumstances. It may even be that the approval thresholds should change over time. Note in particular that it is rare that majority constituencies are specified to require a minimum number of *shareholders* (as opposed to a minimum number of *shares*) – meaning that smaller shareholders are often effectively disenfranchised by this approach, as they carry little weight in shares, merely as numbers of human beings. If the entrepreneur is determined that these small shareholders are adequately represented in the required threshold, he or she may seek to include an additional qualification regarding the number of shareholders required to consent to the sale (for example, "a majority in number holding not less than X% of the issued share capital").

23.4.4   Further issues to consider

There are certain classic issues regarding drag-along rights which constantly come up in term sheet negotiations, including the following:

(1) Many entrepreneurs will feel extremely nervous about vesting drag-along powers in third parties without some kind of benchmarking on exit value, at least in the early years, to avoid the chance that their business may be sold out from under them before it has had the opportunity to reach its true potential. On the other hand, if the opportunistic exit price is above a rigorous benchmark, even the entrepreneur may be prepared to sell the business for a good price!

> *Shareholders together holding 60% or more of the issued share capital may, with the consent of the VC syndicate, require the initiation of a flotation or a sale of the entire issued share capital of the Company or of all or substantially all of the assets of the Company (1) after one year and within three years following Completion, in the event that the exit value for the Company is not less than $200 million and (2) after three years following Completion, in any event.*

In this kind of situation it may make sense to impose a timing and value threshold, so that the bar is set high in the early years and the VC syndicate is dissuaded from trading the business quickly for a small exit multiple but a high IRR.
(2) It is often a matter of great concern how warranties and indemnities will affect persons who are "dragged" into sale transactions by the exercise of drag-along rights. In particular, it may be highly advisable for selling shareholders to make it clear in the shareholder documentation that, as the price of granting a drag-along right in advance of a specific transaction, they expect to be treated in the same manner as the VC syndicate – giving them the certainty that they will be treated in the same manner as the constituency with the most experience and negotiating power in any M&A, exit or IPO scenario.

> *It is accepted that selling shareholders will only provide warranties and indemnities to a buyer on the same terms as provided by the VC syndicate to any such buyer and that all selling shareholders shall have limits of liability under such warranties and indemnities proportionate to their respective holdings of shares in the Company.*

(3) Finally, it is of course necessary to stipulate that while the fundamental premise of the drag-along power is that the sale terms apply equally to all shareholders – this does not

mean that the net proceeds of sale will be allocated on an equal basis, but in line with the underlying share rights or shareholders agreement.

> *In the case of a sale, the above drag-along right shall be subject to apportionment of the sale proceeds in accordance with the preference provisions set out above.*

Without this specification, the drag-along right is susceptible to challenge on the basis that it is not intended that all shareholders be treated equally (one of several flaws in the squeeze-out mechanisms in many jurisdictions).

23.4.5 Enforcement of drag-along rights

Practical enforceability of drag-along provisions remains an issue of concern in venture capital investment terms. While no one doubts that properly drafted drag-along provisions are fully enforceable through the appropriate dispute resolution forum (e.g. arbitration or litigation), by the time that this process has wound its way to conclusion (arbitral award or judicial decision) the purchaser of the company is probably long gone (having lost interest) and so the purpose of enforcement has gone – all that is left is a claim for damages for the lost opportunity. As such, the normal avenues of enforcement of a contractual provision (which is what a drag-along right is, whether or not the drag-along rights are entrenched in the company's by-laws or are in a shareholders or investment agreement) are not necessarily the way to go, and the focus instead is usually on developing mechanisms that can provide a measure of *practical* enforcement of the drag-along, by enabling the company or the selling shareholders effectively to gain control of non-assenting shareholders' shares and deliver them to the buyer.

This is not an easy matter to achieve, but it often begins with provisions purporting to empower the company or named individuals with irrevocable power to act as the attorney of the non-assenting shareholders to carry out certain basic acts, including:

(1) delivering the shares to the buyer, together with duly signed stock transfer forms, and (as share certificates or other documents of title will often in such circumstances be missing) cancelling the old documents of title and issuing new documents of title for the purposes of the transfer;

(2) executing on behalf of the non-assenting shareholder all of the sale documentation required to be signed by a shareholder, including the sale agreement; and

(3) receiving the sale consideration from the buyer on behalf of the non-assenting shareholders and releasing such funds to the non-assenting shareholders (possibly upon a defined form of release and acceptance being delivered by the non-assenting shareholder).

So far, this is the best solution available. Unfortunately, in many jurisdictions even so-called "irrevocable" powers of attorney may be revoked by the grantor of the power and so the powers under which the company and its majority shareholders attempt to take control of the drag-along process may not work if the non-assenting shareholder is smart enough to purport to revoke the power of attorney at the outset of his or her dissenting action and then take out an injunction against the company to prevent enforcement via the revoked power.

23.5 TAG-ALONG RIGHTS

23.5.1 Introduction to tag-along rights

> *In the event that the Syndicate are prepared to permit another Shareholder to transfer its shares to a bona fide third party purchaser, nonetheless we propose that all other Shareholders should have the right to participate in such a liquidity opportunity. Therefore, upon any transfer of Shares to a third party, pro rata "tag-along" rights in favour of the other Shareholders will apply to ensure that no such transfer will be permitted unless the purchaser acquires an equivalent proportion of Shares from the Shareholders on the same terms.*

The final element of the provisions dealing with the transfer of shares is the area of tag-along rights (also known as "come-along" rights). These are the exact opposite of drag-along rights. Tag-along rights apply in the event that someone *else* is able to sell shares (in other words a putative selling shareholder has been through both the threshold approval process for sale and the transfer pre-emption process and has emerged unscathed with a parcel of shares to sell to a third party, or to an existing shareholder outside the pre-emption process) – and in such circumstances tag-along rights grant a pre-emptive right to the other shareholders in the company to *participate* in that sale transaction alongside, or partly instead of the selling shareholder, on a pro rata basis.

Tag-along rights are therefore rights to "piggy-back" on someone else's liquidity event. It is founded in the VC fund's obsession with being able to grab every opportunity to head for the exit, where attractive. However, because it is often the smaller, junior classes of shareholders who will find it hardest to generate liquidity in their shareholdings while the company remains private (in contrast to the VC funds, which typically have larger share stakes with attractive terms – senior preferences, board rights, etc – plus the expertise and networks to find interested buyers), in fact a tag-along right is usually of most benefit to these smaller, junior shareholders rather than the VC funds and for this reason the initiation of tag-along discussions is often made by the entrepreneur.

However, for the reasons discussed in detail below, the use of tag-along rights, whether by a VC fund or by an entrepreneur, should be treated with extreme circumspection. They are not at all what they first appear to be, and their operation is fraught with difficulty, complexity and unintended consequences. Handle with care.

23.5.2 Nature of tag-along rights

Traditional tag-along rights provide the non-transferring shareholders with a pro rata and proportional right to elect to participate in the sale transaction, at the same price and on the same terms that the selling shareholder has agreed with the buyer. There is no obligation upon the shareholders to take up their rights, merely an opportunity. There are two ways in which tag-along elections can as a practical matter be accommodated in the sale – either by the buyer agreeing to enlarge his or her acquisition to accommodate the additional "tag-along shares" (i.e. shares elected to be sold into the acquisition pursuant to the tag-along rights), and/or, to the extent the buyer is not prepared to enlarge his or her acquisition further, by "cutting back" the number of shares to be sold by the initiating selling shareholder (but not below its pro rata participation overall) to accommodate all tag-along shares.

For example (using the worked example in which Trojan Horse has purchased 5 000 000 shares in the company), if Trojan Horse finds a buyer for its 5 000 000 shares in the company (20.83% of the issued share capital – note that holders of options will not generally be taken into account in determining tag-along rights), and pre-emption rights are not exercised over those shares by the other shareholders, then up to 79.17% of those sale shares (3 958 500 shares – the other shareholders' pro rata share of the 5 000 000 sale opportunity) would be susceptible to being replaced in the sale transaction by the shares of the other shareholders who elect to have them "tagged-along" into the sale. For example, the next most senior syndicate member (holding 8.33% of the issued share capital) could elect to sell up to 416 500 shares to participate pro rata in the sale transaction (note that generally holders of options do not have participation rights in such circumstances, unless they exercise their options first) and the buyer could not acquire Trojan Horse's shares without also buying the shares elected in the tag-along process. To the extent that either tag-along elections are not made, or the buyer that Trojan Horse has found is happy to acquire more than 5 000 000 shares in aggregate, Trojan Horse will be able to get closer to selling the entirety of its 5 000 000 shares.

It can immediately be seen that tag-along rights operate as a very significant brake on liquidity for shareholders – and this is the reason why they are often both supported vehemently by some VC firms and entrepreneurs (those who "see the glass as half empty" and whose focus is on preventing others from selling their shares) and fought against by other VC firms and entrepreneurs (those who "see the glass as half full" and whose focus is on reducing the restrictions on them selling their shares in bona fide transactions). Indeed, an entrepreneur who receives a term sheet which contains no reference to tag-along rights faces an interesting choice – does he or she broach the subject or not? It depends on the relative importance he or she places on liquidity versus maintaining the status quo.

Fundamentally, once a selling shareholder triggers the tag-along process, it may have no idea whether it will be possible to sell all the proposed shares or only a small percentage of them, and consequently what size of stub equity in the company, if any, it will come to hold following the completion of the sale. This is anathema to most professional investors. There are some ways to manage these issues in the design of the tag-along rights (discussed below), but the best way is simply to pre-wire the desired result in the sale terms agreed with the third part buyer at the outset by:

(1) agreeing with the purchaser the extent to which it will take up additional shares that are tagged into the sale process, thereby providing the seller in advance with a better picture of the likelihood that it will be able to sell the entirety of the shares it wishes to sell; and/or
(2) providing in the purchase agreement that the sale transaction will not complete in the event that tag-along elections are above a specified threshold in aggregate (which could be the maximum level of additional shares that the purchaser has agreed to acquire, if tag-along elections are made).

At least in such a situation, the selling shareholder will have ensured that, whatever the tag-along terms may say in the company's articles of association or other constitutive documents, the selling shareholder will not be obliged to sell only some of the shares it intends to sell (which might dilute the value either of the piece being sold, or the piece being retained) – although the consequence will be that the sale transaction will fail instead: it's an "all or nothing" outcome. Sometimes, that very level of strategic clarity is enough to dissuade the other shareholders from electing to tag along, thereby facilitating the transaction (although many shareholders can be somewhat "dog in the manger").

23.5.3   Partial tag-along?

There is no such thing as an "all or nothing approach" to tag-along rights, as they simply operate up to a pro rata participation in the underlying sale transaction. However, it is important for the entrepreneur to take a view on whether a shareholder should be permitted to take up part of its tag-along rights, or only all of such rights (i.e. its full pro rata participation). Clearly, the latter approach in theory makes it much less likely that rights will be exercised: however, it is conventional to provide that a shareholder may take up all or any part of its tag-along rights.

23.5.4   Timing of subsequent sale

Just like for both issue and transfer pre-emption rights, in the event that tag-along rights are not taken up, the entrepreneur will need to consider how long the transferring shareholder should have in order to transfer the shares to the identified third party buyer. Usually, the term sheet will provide that the third party sale transaction may progress only on the terms previously disclosed and within a relatively short timeframe (e.g. up to three months).

23.5.5   Different classes of shares

One of the most difficult issues to get right in relation to tag-along rights is how to make the concept apply to a company which has different classes of shares (as is extremely common for venture capital-backed companies) and it is here that tag-along rights fundamentally fall down. If the tag-along rights are genuinely to generate liquidity both for the larger institutional share-holders such as the VC syndicate (who will tend to hold senior preference or preferred shares) and for minority shareholders (who will tend to hold junior, ordinary shares) then presumably there has to be some kind of mechanism to enable shareholders in one share class to tag-along into sale transactions involving shares in another class. But how is this to be achieved?

Trying to apply tag-along rights to different classes of shares at the same time – and still preserve the underlying economic rights of each share class – presents almost insuperable problems. For example, it would be possible for shareholders of different classes to elect to participate pro rata and equally in the sale transaction, with the proceeds of sale then re-allocated among the selling shareholders in accordance with the preference cascade – however, the problem with this is that it would mean that some holders of senior securities (the sellers) would have received differential distributions on their shares to other holders of the same class (the non-sellers), which would either have to be reflected in subsequent distributions or give rise to an immediate re-allocation among the members of the same class to maintain parity (essentially putting everyone on the same footing as though all had tagged pro rata) with a right between the selling and non-selling preferred shareholders to a re-allocation of subsequent distributions to reflect the giving up of value on the initial sale. By the same token, ordinary shareholders involved in the sale would probably receive nothing (at least until all preferred shareholders had received the entirety of their preference), but despite having sold their shares would presumably have to retain some kind of a deferred entitlement against the selling (and possibly non-selling) preferred shareholders to eventual recovery of the economics once the preference has been satisfied in subsequent transactions. It's so complex that it is completely unworkable ... and we haven't even thought about how the buyer would fit into that equation!

Alternatively, tag-along rights could simply be allocated pro rata and ratably across all shareholders, irrespective of class, but the right would simply be to participate in the sale on the same terms as the selling shareholder (including as to price). Although this approach is often seen in term sheets (see the term sheet example) and sounds terrific at first blush, in fact it is an extremely rough and ready approach. It requires the VC firm potentially to be prepared to give up value and to be treated as fully pari passu with the ordinary shares on a sale transaction, whether it initiates a sale of preferred shares and permits ordinary share-holders to tag-along on the same terms, or whether it faces the option of tagging-along its preferred shares into a sale of ordinary shares on the same terms. It's an effective conversion of the preferred shares to common, as the price of tag-along. When push comes to shove, this is something that many VC firms will not be willing to accept. Of course, if the fundamental goal of the entrepreneur in proposing tag-along rights is effectively to shut down opportunities for the VC firm to generate early partial liquidity, then this may be the preferred approach! Another major flaw in this approach that is rarely considered is the impact on the purchaser of the shares – in each case he or she pays for one class of shares and is then asked to acquire a mix of preferred and ordinary shares pursuant to tag-along rights, in each case without adjustment to the sale terms! It's a non-starter.

As a final alternative, tag-along rights could be allocated and operated exclusively class by class, so that the right to participate only applies to those shareholders who hold the same class of shares as are proposed to be sold in the sale transaction. This approach is by far the most common and the only one that genuinely works, even though, in the context of the multi-class share structures that are so prevalent in venture capital financings, it essentially means that the VC syndicate's rights will be limited to tagging along on each others' sale opportunities and, similarly, the founders' rights will be limited to tagging along on each others' and on management's sale opportunities. However, there is nothing to prevent tag-along working in relation to several share classes being sold at the same time – for example where a shareholder who holds more than one class of shares agrees with a buyer to sell all of his or her shareholding in the company. In that situation, tag-along would operate in parallel for each class of shares the selling shareholder proposes to sell. The issue for the entrepreneur in such a situation is to ensure that there are protective provisions making it difficult for the seller artificially to allocate the sale consideration across the different share classes (to which the buyer may be indifferent) in a manner which has the practical effect of frustrating the tag-along process.

23.5.6   Who gets tag-along rights?

The next question to ask is who gets the tag-along rights. A VC fund may ask for the rights, taking the view (somewhat erroneously, as discussed above) that it will increase its liquidity, but as discussed above an entrepreneur will often believe that it is in his or her interest to ask that the rights are extended beyond the VC fund to other constituencies – for example the founding management team and the entrepreneur. Indeed, some firms do not raise the question of tag-along rights at all in their term sheets, for fear that by raising the issue they will open Pandora's Box and the entrepreneur will immediately ask for equivalent rights! Indeed, they are right – and once the issue of tag-along rights has been brought out into the open, it may be very difficult to resist extending the rights to all shareholder constituencies.

Once it has been established that more than one class of shareholders may participate in tag-along rights, this then raises the issue of whether there should be priorities between these classes. For example, should the holders of the senior class of shares have tag-along rights in priority to the holders of more junior classes of shares, with the junior classes only participating to the extent that senior classes of shares have not taken up their rights in full? It is not uncommon to see priorities negotiated into tag-along rights, but for the reasons discussed in 23.5.5 above it is rare that this priority is in fact meaningful.

23.5.7 Pre-emption top-ups

As for issue and transfer pre-emption rights, it is perfectly possible to apply "top-up" rights to the tag-along process. This would be a right for a defined group of shareholders to have the right to bid again for "surplus" tag-along rights not taken up by others. However, it is rarely seen in practice.

23.5.8 Administration of pre-emption rights

Such rights will operate on a 30-day fast-track procedure which will run simultaneously with the transfer pre-emption rights described above. In such a case, the purchaser will be at liberty to elect either (i) to increase the size of the purchase transaction to accommodate all elections for tag-along rights or (ii) to maintain the size of the purchase transaction, in which event the selling shareholder's participation in the transaction will be scaled back to accommodate tag-along elections.

As for issue and transfer pre-emption rights, it is important to ensure that the administration of the tag-along process is managed properly, so that it does not extend endlessly through cycle after cycle, disrupting a legitimate share transfer transaction (unless the entrepreneur believes that this is strategically attractive). If at all possible, the whole process should be managed within a 30 day window contemporaneously with the transfer pre-emption process (see the term sheet example) and different rounds of tag-along (priorities, cascades, top-ups, etc) should be run concurrently, not consecutively, through a single communication to shareholders.

23.5.9 Exclusion of certain transactions

Tag-along rights will not apply to (i) transfers by management shareholders for the purpose of normal tax and estate planning purposes (including on the death of any member of management), (ii) transfers by Syndicate members, in each case provided that the purchaser accedes to the Financing documentation or (iii) transfers of Shares pursuant to the operation of pre-emption, tag-along or drag-along rights.

Just as for share issue and share transfer pre-emption, and drag-along rights, it will be important to prescribe certain types of transaction to which tag-along rights should not apply. Usually these will be very limited exceptions – typically tax and estate planning and administration, transfers required to be made pursuant to the shareholders agreements and transfer pursuant to permitted transfer transactions such as the exercise of pre-emption or drag-along rights, or the tag-along rights themselves.

24

Deal Management Terms

24.1 INTRODUCTION

Many of the remaining features in a venture capital term sheet relate to deal management issues. Deal management is discussed in detail in Chapter 11 above, but three additional areas are covered below – being the ones usually explicitly dealt with on a binding basis in a term sheet: conditions precedent to closing, exclusivity and cost reimbursement.

These three areas seem relatively insignificant and they are often the parts of a term sheet which are not closely negotiated in the venture capital deal process. However, each of these areas contains significant traps for the unwary entrepreneur and needs to be considered carefully before a term sheet is agreed.

24.2 CONDITIONS PRECEDENT

Implementation of the above-described Financing will be conditional upon:

(i) *completion by Trojan Horse of its remaining items of due diligence, to its full satisfaction and sign-off by the incoming members of the Syndicate. Trojan Horse will agree with the Company a plan for the completion of outstanding items of due diligence and will manage the process of ensuring that incoming members of the Syndicate complete their own due diligence requirements in a timely manner. The Company will provide all reasonable assistance and access to Trojan Horse, potential members of the Syndicate and their legal and other professional advisers for such purpose.*

(ii) *the grant of all approvals and the waiver of share issue pre-emption rights by the Company's current shareholders and the completion of any and all other necessary corporate formalities to permit the Financing (including the Reorganisation) to be completed. Trojan Horse will agree any and all such approvals, waivers, etc, in advance with the Company.*

(iii) *no material adverse change in the Company's position or prospects having occurred or having become likely to occur between the date of this term sheet and completion of the Financing. In the event that any such event does occur or becomes likely to occur, the Company must notify Trojan Horse immediately.*

(iv) *Trojan Horse investment board approval and such investment, advisory board or other required entity approval(s) as may be required to be obtained by other members of the Syndicate as a pre-condition to their participation in the Financing. The Company agrees to provide Trojan Horse and each member of the Syndicate with all such assistance as they may reasonably require for the purposes of seeking and obtaining any such consents or approvals, etc.*

(v) *the Reorganisation is completed in a manner satisfactory to Trojan Horse.*

(vi) *the Company puts in place (i) key man insurance on the senior management team in an amount and (ii) patent litigation insurance (covering pursuit, defence and commercial agreements), in each case in an amount and on terms and to an extent agreed with Trojan Horse.*

Every term sheet will contain conditions precedent to the closing of the financing, identifying issues which are on the critical path to completion of the transaction.

24.2.1   VC firm's strategy

It is absolutely in the interests of the VC firm to have as long a list of conditions as possible, to provide it with the maximum flexibility to terminate the transaction for a pre-defined reason (ideally an entirely subjective reason). Usually, the conditions proposed by a VC firm will fall into five different categories:

(1) Due diligence conditions – recognising that the term sheet triggers the third phase of the investment transaction, which includes the final phase of due diligence by the VC firm and its advisers and consultants. As can be seen above, the condition is usually highly generalised and personalised (satisfaction of the condition is *subjective* to the VC firm).
(2) Technical conditions itemising matters legally required in order to effect completion – for example necessary shareholder consents, completion of a group reorganisation, tax clearances etc.
(3) VC firm approval (as discussed above, final sign off under the VC firm's own investment procedures is a sine qua non of completion).
(4) Specific deal conditions that are of particular relevance to the deal in question and which underpin the price at which the VC fund is prepared to commit funds – usually these conditions are commercially-oriented (for example, final agreement on the business plan and budget; recruitment of a key member of senior management; conclusion of a specific supplier, customer or collaborator contract, etc).
(5) A sweeper-up "no material adverse change" condition, giving the VC firm an exit from the transaction should circumstances change materially for any reason during the final phase of the investment transaction (given the due diligence condition, which also provides a huge ability for the VC firm to walk away for almost any reason, this additional layer of protection is fairly academic).

24.2.2   Entrepreneur's strategy

It is absolutely in the best interests of the entrepreneur to reduce the number of conditions precedent and narrow down the scope of those which remain, thereby minimising transaction risk. As such:

(1) Due diligence conditions – the entrepreneur should not accept a generalised due diligence process at face value, but should identify in detail the exact scope of the VC firm's due diligence plan, to make sure that the plan itself is reasonable and to ensure that the roll out of this plan is accomplished in a cost- and time-efficient manner. This will require extensive planning with the VC firm in advance of the roll-out of the plan, and regular monitoring of and involvement with the various teams involved in the due diligence exercise as it rolls forward. The net result may be an ability to narrow the due diligence condition materially, and if not, at least the practical pathway to satisfaction of the condition will be both identified and properly managed, with the full involvement of the entrepreneur.

(2) Technical conditions – clearly the entrepreneur should ensure that there are as few technical conditions as possible, that these conditions are fully capable of being satisfied in the required timeframe (as far as possible in the hands of the entrepreneur and his management team alone) and that their satisfaction is objectively measurable.

(3) VC firm approval – in practice, there is little that can be done to subvert the sometimes laborious process of internal approvals that may be required by VC firms to commit their managed funds unconditionally to an investment, but the entrepreneur should at least understand the exact process lying ahead very clearly, as well as the likelihood of an about-turn on the decision-making process.

(4) Specific deal conditions – ideally there should be *no* additional closing conditions, but those that are difficult commercially to reject should, like milestones, be fully capable of being satisfied in the required timeframe (as far as possible in the hands of the entrepreneur and his management team alone) and their satisfaction should be objectively measurable and not subject to the whim or interpretation of the VC firm. Once these have been identified and drafted then, in the same way as for the due diligence work, it is very important that a programme of action to nail the conditions is agreed in advance between the VC firm and the entrepreneur and that when the plan rolls out, the entrepreneur is fully engaged in regular monitoring of and involvement with the various teams involved in the programme.

(5) No material adverse change condition – as in banking documentation, it is extremely unlikely that a VC firm will invoke a "no material adverse change" condition (known as a "MAC clause") alone in order to kill a deal – except in the extremely rare situation that fully fits the definition – because of the risk of litigation that would flow from such action, so it may not be worthwhile making a big deal of seeking to have this condition thrown out. However, it's worth a try. If it's in – then it's important to make sure the test of a "material adverse change" is completely objective and *not* subjective in any way to the views of the VC firm.

In addition to narrowing down the closing conditions and making sure that they are as objective and deliverable as possible, the entrepreneur (who should always retain a "weather eye" for plan B in the event of transaction failure) should try as far as possible to avoid an all or nothing situation on the day of completion: instead the entrepreneur should ensure that he or she and the VC firm are ticking off closing conditions as the transaction progresses and ideally the entrepreneur should identify a series of specific break points for the transaction when a go/no go evaluation can be made on the back of specific, measurable and agreed progress on the transaction. This enables the entrepreneur to be more in control of the progression of the financing transaction through to completion and in particular (a) to retire transaction risk as the work progresses (narrowing the "outs" for the VC firm) and (b) maintain a plan B scenario and if necessary bring that scenario live at the earliest moment that the financing starts to slew off the track. It is not always possible to achieve this gradual process of firming up the deal, but proactive and aggressive deal administration of this type will greatly strengthen the entrepreneur's hand in most deals.

24.3   EXCLUSIVITY

> It is vital that Trojan Horse be granted a reasonable period of exclusivity, during which it may commit the potentially significant resources (including the incurral of costs) necessary to progress the Financing to completion. Therefore, in consideration of Trojan Horse committing such resources, the Company grants Trojan Horse the exclusive right (together with the Syndicate chosen by Trojan Horse) to invest in the Company on the terms set out in this term sheet (as varied by agreement) for a period of three months from the date of this term sheet (the "Exclusivity Period"). During the Exclusivity Period, neither the Company, nor any director, officer, employee nor shareholder of the Company will, directly or indirectly, without Trojan Horse's prior consent (i) share any information regarding the Company, or its business or financial affairs, with another potential investor or lender, whether strategic or financial, or (ii) issue or agree to issue any Company securities (including securities having rights over the Company's capital or assets), in each case without Trojan Horse's prior written consent.
>
> If within twelve months following the later of (i) the breakdown of negotiations between the Company and Trojan Horse relating to the Financing and (ii) the expiry of the Exclusivity Period, the Company enters into negotiations with a third party with respect to the raising of equity or debt financing for the Company (the "New Financing"), the Company will give Trojan Horse an opportunity to participate in an amount of up to $5 000 000 in the New Financing on the same terms as are made available to other third party institutional investors.

The provisions granting exclusivity to the VC firm in relation to the financing are one of the few parts of the term sheet that are legally binding. Indeed, as discussed in detail at Chapter 12 above, one of the major purposes of the term sheet in a venture capital transaction is to get the entrepreneur sufficiently comfortable to grant exclusivity to the VC firm, following which the VC firm has sufficient confidence to start to spend money more freely on completing its evaluation of the investment opportunity and driving the deal to completion.

24.3.1   VC firm's strategy

As discussed above, time is generally on the VC firm's side in an investment transaction, as the company's financial position may be expected to worsen materially through the deal process and particularly if the investment transaction becomes extended (unless the entrepreneur has planned accordingly), changing the balance of power just at the time the company can least afford it. There is always a temptation therefore for the VC firm to spin out an investment transaction, and the entrepreneur must guard against any delay or inefficiencies, as well as plan for contingencies.

In this context, the grant of exclusivity to a VC firm to pursue a specific transaction carries even more strategic importance, because not only does it focus all of the company's efforts upon bringing the VC firm to completion of the transaction, but the exclusivity terms also seek to prevent the company from exploring any *other* opportunity that might be competitive or antipathetic to the investment transaction. Whilst this might not be of material significance if the exclusivity period is short, the longer the exclusivity period runs on, the more likely it is that other financing opportunities previously available to the company (other potential investors, etc) will "wither on the vine" and no longer be available – particularly at short notice – should the current transaction fail, but also that the company's "plan B" options will also narrow appreciably as it runs out of resources and time to implement any such plan. In other words, by using exclusivity cleverly, not only can the VC firm lock out any competition, but it can also actually destroy the viability of any alternative strategy for the company. This, from the VC firm's perspective (a) minimises the chances of the management team proposing changes to the deal terms at a late stage and (b) strengthens the VC's hand in any negotiations about proposing its own changes to the financing terms away from the term sheet (e.g. if a major issue is discovered in due diligence) and therefore greatly enhances the likelihood that the proposed transaction will close successfully, repaying the VC's significant investment in progressing the deal. VC firms are not over-resourced and they really want deals that have been progressed to a signed term sheet rapidly to close.

So, a VC will naturally wish to gain an extended period of exclusivity at the outset which will:

(1) permit a thorough and professional due diligence exercise, as well as the chance to see the company trade over a protracted period; and
(2) strengthen the VC firm's negotiating power as the transaction progresses, as the company's financial position and plan B options will erode significantly.

24.3.2 Entrepreneur's strategy

Not surprisingly, the core of the entrepreneur's strategy in this area will be to agree a short period of exclusivity, tied in closely to the agreed transaction work plan, to take the transaction swiftly and efficiently to completion. In fact, there are four key elements for an entrepreneur to develop an effective strategy to deal with exclusivity:

(1) Detailed term sheet – it is the purpose of the term sheet to generate sufficient confidence in the entrepreneur that the deal is likely to happen and that the VC firm genuinely wishes to close the transaction on the terms proposed (as opposed to delivering a skeleton term sheet as a "sighting shot" in order to gain exclusivity, do due diligence and then come up with revised deal terms). Therefore, the entrepreneur should be satisfied before signing the term sheet and granting exclusivity that (i) the term sheet is sufficiently detailed to cover adequately every major point of substance and (ii) the VC firm has invested sufficient time, energy and money into the preliminary phase of the investment transaction and the negotiation of the term sheet itself to indicate that the agreed term sheet genuinely represents a tipping point, following which the VC firm becomes truly committed to doing the deal.
(2) "Manage" the exclusivity period – it is also vital that the entrepreneur actively manages the exclusivity period. This is more than simply ensuring that the exclusivity period is as short as is reasonable in the circumstances – it means that the entrepreneur should seek to agree specific break, review or progression points at which the company will review or renew exclusivity on the basis of the completion of defined work products. The entrepreneur should not be shy of asking the VC firm to progress the transaction *outside* exclusivity if it cannot make sufficient progress on the transaction by the defined break points. Exclusivity, if properly managed, then can become a "two-way street". The key to this is the development of an agreed workplan with the VC firm which identifies the different workstreams and their timing (as well as the prioritisation of resources against them) and the extrapolation from this plan of key "gates" at which exclusivity may end and the entrepreneur may start to pursue other options – perhaps allowing the VC firm to regain exclusivity by catching up again on progress or even deciding to waive closing conditions.

(3) Plan B – clearly, it is important for the entrepreneur to keep in mind the need for a plan B at all times and if at all possible to keep his options alive. There are three possible approaches in this regard, some of which may be run in parallel:

    (a) The entrepreneur should try to ensure that the exclusivity clause only prohibits a narrow range of transactions which are truly competitive with the financing (another venture capital financing, for example) but leaves open other plan B alternatives (such as a strategic or insider financing, a sale or merger of the business, etc). Even in terms of potentially competitive transactions, the entrepreneur should try to maintain maximum freedom for the company to keep existing relationships alive on the back burner: for example exclusivity might only prohibit the *initiation* of discussions, thereby permitting the continuation of existing discussions with other potential financiers, or the *closing* of an alternative transaction – thereby permitting all plan B options to be progressed to the point at which they could be closed immediately upon plan A transaction failure. The entrepreneur might also consider restricting only the *company and management* from entertaining other strategic opportunities, leaving the path open for shareholders to do so.

    (b) As discussed above, the company should work carefully through different scenarios under which it can maintain control of its destiny and capture other strategic alternatives in an iterative fashion upon the failure of the investment transaction – this might include an aggressive culling of the cost base, a re-prioritisation of the company's immediate ambitions, the ring-fencing of a war chest, the pre-commitment of limited bridge financing from current investors, or any number of possibilities that retain the company's freedom of action in the circumstances.

    (c) The entrepreneur should consider what the company will get in return for exclusivity – the quid pro quo – should the deal founder for any reason. This might be anything, but the entrepreneur should consider in particular the following ideas: (a) a break fee from the VC firm, (b) an unconditional working capital infusion (essentially a bridge loan – but potentially a "pier" financing with no end to the "bridge" in sight if the deal fails) to tide the company through the transaction period and/or (c) the agreement of the VC firm to hand over its work product (due diligence reports, legal documentation, internal market analyses, etc) for the company to use in subsequent financing opportunities. The first two concepts would soften the cost to the company of a failed exclusivity period and the latter could greatly facilitate the re-emergence of a plan B option.

       The stakes are very high in this area. If the entrepreneur fails to negotiate an exclusivity clause which allows the effective management of the progress of the transaction and the maintenance of reasonable plan B options, the company will genuinely be in a life or death scenario should plan A fail. Accordingly it is a real gamble for the entrepreneur to put all the eggs in one basket (or hand the chicken coop over to the fox!). It is only wise in such a situation for the company's directors to take legal advice concerning the enforceability of the exclusivity clause and the consequences of the company breaching it, so that, as the company's fiduciaries, they can weigh each option and decide upon the "least worst" option. In some jurisdictions, enforceability of exclusivity clauses is questionable and even where enforceable; sometimes recovery of damages can equally be problematic.

(4) Duty of good faith negotiation – as discussed above, the key fear for the entrepreneur when exclusivity is granted to the VC firm is that the VC firm will demonstrate bad faith and use the exclusivity period unfairly for its own ends – to manufacture spurious reasons to

re-negotiate the terms and generally to use the final phase of the investment transaction to back the company into a corner and then dictate terms mercilessly. It should be stressed that this is very unlikely to occur in practice if the entrepreneur is dealing with a reputable VC firm – for the leading VCs, the spirit of the term sheet is at least as important as its words.

However, there is one avenue that should be explored to provide the company and the shareholders with ammunition should this start to occur: some jurisdictions (notably the Netherlands, France and Germany) incorporate a duty of good faith into negotiations, which would apply in the final phase of the investment transaction. If the governing law of the term sheet could easily be one of those jurisdictions, then the VC firm will find that its room for manoeuvre may have narrowed perceptibly. Indeed, given the existence of this approach, there can be no harm in trying to draft and incorporate the equivalent concept in a contractual term (essentially a best endeavours covenant to progress the transaction in line with the term sheet) where the term sheet is governed by a legal system that does not incorporate a civil law duty of good faith (e.g. US law and UK law). But remember, good faith works both ways...

24.4 COST REIMBURSEMENT

The Company agrees to be responsible for Trojan Horse's and the Syndicate's legal and other professional fees and expenses (including the fees and expenses of legal counsel, accountants, and any and all consultants employed in the conduct of technical, commercial and regulatory due diligence) incurred by them in connection with the closing of the Financing, whether or not the Financing closes. These fees and expenses will be reimbursed in full by the Company monthly not more than 10 days following the delivery of monthly invoices by Trojan Horse to the Company.

Apart from exclusivity, the other principal area of the term sheet which is likely to be contractually binding (all of the investment terms are non-binding and statements of intent only) is the section on cost reimbursement. As soon as the term sheet is signed, the VC firm will start to spend serious money on a range of professional advisers and consultants, to conduct the final stages of the due diligence process, and of course the VC firm will instruct legal counsel to commence the drafting, negotiation and finalisation of the investment documentation. These costs can be very significant – $30–50 000 on due diligence and another $50–150 000 on legal expenses is not uncommon, particularly in regions (outside the US and UK) where the venture capital process has not yet been highly commoditised and challenging work is required to fit the business model to the prevailing legal system.

24.4.1 VC firm's strategy

There are three ways that the VC firm can deal with these costs:

(1) The VC firm can recover these costs from its VC fund, with the fund capitalising the expenses as part of the cost of the investment. This will mean that the benchmark cost of the investment will increase modestly (against which performance will be driven) and the cash resources of the fund available for genuine new investment will shrink slightly (for example, 20 investments which each cost $100 000 in deal expenses to close will mean that $2 000 000 will have been taken out of the fund's resources that would otherwise be available for new investment).

(2) The VC firm can take the expenses onto its own books, essentially netting them off against its management fee from the VC fund. This will sustain the capital in the VC fund available for new investment, but at the cost of reducing the VC firm's own resources for operating expenditure (almost all of which will be allocated to partner and staff remuneration, travel and office infrastructure).

(3) The VC firm can offload the expenses on the company which constitutes the investment opportunity – sometimes whether or not the opportunity progresses to completion. This frees up management fees for the VC firm and ensures that no dent is made in the VC fund's resources – but at a potentially significant cost to the company in which the VC firm is investing (or not, as the case may be). In our term sheet example ($10 M in), $100 000 would effectively be deducted by the VC syndicate before or contemporaneously with the contribution of funds (and all from the $5 M first tranche) – meaning that 1% of the overall funds will be deducted and 2% of the first tranche alone. Although this can be seen as a relatively conventional "corporate finance fee" (indeed extremely low, by reference to the charges of professional intermediaries for raising private equity finance – typically 5–7%), nonetheless the impact on the company may be meaningful – perhaps a month's cash flow taken out of the business plan – and effectively the pre-money valuation for the company has just been reduced. If the transaction doesn't even go ahead, the impact on the business may be even more serious, adding insult to the injury of a broken deal and further damaging the prospects of the company being able to stay alive long enough to secure a plan B alternative.

Clearly, in the case of a broken deal, the VC firm's desire to palm off its deal costs on the investment opportunity is not unexpected – at the point that the deal fails, the VC firm will cease to care anything for the business and will be motivated to get what it can from the opportunity and move swiftly on. However, it may seem slightly bizarre to the entrepreneur that the VC firm will also prefer strongly to palm off the company with its deal costs even where a transaction closes successfully: surely the best place for the VC fund to leave its money will be in the investment, where it can be put to work actively and multiplied many-fold, as opposed to taking it away from the company's high-growth business and using it to pay lawyers and accountants instead? Nonetheless, to the VC firm, the alternatives (use of management fee or capitalisation in the VC fund) are often even less palatable.

There is an additional reason why the VC firm will see cost reimbursement provisions as a good idea – they can add value to the VC firm strategically. As discussed above, if the escalating costs of an investment transaction are laid at the door of the investment opportunity itself, there may come a point at which the costs of *not* closing the transaction become deeply damaging to the continuing business or even prohibitive – and at that point the negotiating power between the parties shifts subtly, as the company will be less and less motivated to fight hard over any remaining issues between the parties and the VC firm by contrast may feel able successfully to introduce valid new issues into this changing environment.

24.4.2 Entrepreneur's strategy

Given the above, the issue of deal costs and cost reimbursement is an extremely important issue for the entrepreneur to consider at the time of term sheet negotiation. Unfortunately, it is an issue that often gets little consideration.

Fortunately, in this area the entrepreneur will in fact find that it has significant practical means to engineer an optimal end result on costs. Obviously, the starting point will be for the entrepreneur to take a robust stance and require that:

(1) in the case of a completed transaction, deal costs are borne by the VC fund and capitalised as part of the cost of investment – the entrepreneur can rightly argue that if the company retains 100% of the VC fund's share subscription proceeds, then that money will work much harder than if it is paid away in satisfaction of deal costs; and

(2) in the case of a broken deal, costs ("broken deal costs") should "fall where they lie", meaning that each party will bear their own respective costs. This is highly attractive for the entrepreneur and the investment opportunity, because the lion's share of deal costs under this approach will fall on the VC firm (which is commissioning the due diligence exercise and which will almost certainly insist on its own legal counsel leading on the documentation process). Under this scenario, the entrepreneur will be left only with the fees of its own legal counsel.

However, for most transactions this position is unlikely to be fully achievable – particularly as regards completed transactions – and the entrepreneur will have to consider a number of different fall-back positions in each material area. The following are key criteria for consideration in developing any strategy in this area:

(1) It is essential that deal expenses are properly planned, estimated and managed, to ensure that, whoever bears them, they are objectively reasonable and efficiently incurred. The entrepreneur should insist on a transparent and detailed planning process in advance of the term sheet being signed, giving rise to a transaction plan (essentially three streams of work – due diligence, documentation and satisfaction of conditions precedent) that is agreed by both parties. The entrepreneur can then feel confident in agreeing a cost-sharing arrangement based on delivery against that plan – with costs incurred in excess of or outside that plan falling to the account of the VC firm or to the adviser, unless agreed by the entrepreneur.

(2) To the extent that the entrepreneur is agreeing that the business will pick up some costs, he or she should be deeply involved in the development of the action plan and the allocation of resources against that plan. It may be possible to lower the cost of action items materially, for example by allocating internal resources, using the company's own counsel, or some other clever approach.

(3) It is also vital to recognise that if the entrepreneur is paying for certain work to be carried out, then he or she should get the full benefit and use of the work product. For example, if the entrepreneur reimburses the VC firm for its due diligence exercise, the entrepreneur should insist on full rights to receive and use all due diligence reports and paperwork generated in that exercise. Not only can this prove to be very illuminating for the business, but it can significantly shorten the time for the business to secure its plan B should the financing transaction fail – as it will in effect have in its possession an independent audit of the business, allowing it both to fix perceived problems in advance of the next financing transaction and/or expedite the implementation of that transaction on the back of a detailed and (hopefully) highly professional set of due diligence papers. As such, reimbursement of expenses to the VC firm should be made only against release of such paperwork to the entrepreneur.

(4) The entrepreneur should also push hard for an arrangement under which the VC firm and the company *share* deal costs – the ratios may be different in various scenarios, e.g. (a) a

successful deal, (b) a deal terminated by the company, (c) a deal terminated by the VC firm for good reason and (d) a deal terminated by the VC firm for no good reason.

(5) Reimbursement should only be required to the extent that costs are "reasonable" both as to nature and quantum – this concept can subsequently be used to challenge expenses successfully.

(6) Come what may, whether there is an agreed implementation plan or not, the entrepreneur must insist on a cap on reimbursable expenses, ensuring that the exposure of the business to costs are limited, or at least that there will be a vigorous debate when the costs approach the cap. With or without a cap, the entrepreneur *must* also retain at all times the ability to require the VC firm and its advisers to stop work and to cease to incur further expenditure.

(7) The entrepreneur must factor into the financing itself the business's obligation to reimburse expenses, to ensure that the business still has enough money to meet its objectives. It is surprising how often this is forgotten until an enormous reimbursement request comes winging in from the VC firm – at which point it can become an unpleasant debate. Clearly, given that the cost reimbursement will be a binding legal obligation in the term sheet, the directors of the business will have to monitor the situation from the perspective of applicable insolvency laws also.

(8) The entrepreneur should consider carefully whether it is better to reimburse the VC firm at regular intervals or in one lump sum at the end of the transaction. Almost invariably, the entrepreneur will be better off, strategically, allowing expenses to accrue until the end of the transaction (which is why VC firms increasingly are asking for their deal expenses to be reimbursed on a rolling basis), for two key reasons. Firstly, if broken deal costs are not to be reimbursed or are to be shared on a different basis than for a completed transaction, then a one-off approach is required. Secondly, there will come a point where the VC firm faces a large exposure to expenses, if the transaction collapses (either because it bears the lion's share of broken deal costs, or because in the absence of funding, the company simply cannot effect the reimbursement), at which point the balance of negotiation power may shift subtly towards the entrepreneur, as the VC firm may want to get the deal completed in order to avoid taking the accrued expenses onto its own book. The entrepreneur should also recognise that it is not uncommon in broken deals for a pragmatic solution to be employed – in other words the business will often make a payment of an amount it believes is reasonable (sometimes nothing) in full and final settlement of its obligation, and it is exceptionally rare that a VC firm bothers to sue a business for recovery of remaining deal expenses in such a situation.

24.4.3   Financial assistance

An entrepreneur should recognise that expense reimbursement arrangements may have to be carefully structured, to avoid tripping over local legal requirements. For example, in many European jurisdictions maintenance of capital rules (designed to ensure that creditors can have confidence in a company's stated balance sheet) prohibit any kind of "financial assistance" by a company relating to the acquisition or subscription of its shares and, although different safe harbours apply in different jurisdictions, the reimbursement of a subscriber's deal expenses can often fall foul of these rules, requiring that the effective reimbursement is carefully structured to avoid these rules (for example the reimbursement is effected by means of a reduction in the subscription price for the shares, or certain expenses are charged directly to the company, etc).

Index

3i   15–16
active participation, VC firms   60–1, 139–46, 147–67
administrative infrastructure   11, 190, 208, 218
  see also portfolio reporting software
advisory boards
  brainstorming sessions   12
  LPs   11–13
agency costs   9–10
"all or nothing" pre-emption rights   188–9, 206–7
Amazon.com   27
ambitions, entrepreneurs   53–7, 59–64, 65–70, 72–4, 220–5
American Research and Development (ARD)   16
"angels"   66, 177, 200
anti-competition laws   80
anti-dilution protection   41–3, 59–61, 97–8, 104, 114, 153–4, 165–7, 171–3, 185–90, 191–201
  attractions   193–5
  bonus shares   192–3
  concepts   191–201
  conversion rights   193
  dangers   194, 198–201
  entrepreneurs   194–201
  "full ratchet" approach   191–2
  mechanism of action   192–3
  new developments   198
  new share subscriptions   192–3
  "pay to play" concepts   196–8
  payment determination   196–7
  performance issues   199–200
  practical limitations   194–5
  pricing considerations   199–201
  proxy for value   199–200
  shareholders   195–201
  squeezers/squeezed   200

syndication practices   196, 201
  unfairness   194
  "weighted average" approach   191–2
ARD *see* American Research and Development
articles of association   78
Asia   8, 63
"asset class", over-allocation problems   12
assets
  asset-based valuations   84
  register   91
  spring cleaning   91–2
attrition rates
  concepts   31–2
  statistics   32, 40, 46, 51, 55
audit committees   109, 142–3

"bad leaver" provisions, vesting of management equity   180–1, 184
banks   9–13, 18–23, 61, 97–8
  see also institutional investors; limited partners
"battle of the term sheets"   28
benchmarks, performance issues   12, 25–9, 31–2, 36, 85–6, 200, 212
Bermuda   15, 93
"big idea", teaser documents   69, 72–4
biotechnology sector   3–4, 26–7, 55, 65
Birley, Sue   5
Black/Scholes pricing model   86
"bleeding edge", proprietary deal-flow   33–4
blocking minorities, veto rights   45, 141, 143–4, 145–6, 148, 149
boards of directors   9, 44–5, 60, 104, 108–9, 129–38, 139–46
  composition   108–9, 139–41
  meetings   109, 142–4
  nominations   108–9, 140–5
  observer rights   140–1
  process considerations   142–4

boards of directors (*Continued*)
  quorum   142
  regulations   140, 143
  term sheets   108, 129–38
  veto rights   110, 141, 143–4, 145–6, 148, 149
"boiler plate" term sheets   8
bonus shares, anti-dilution protection   192–3
Boston   28
brainstorming sessions, advisory boards   12
branding significance, VCs   13, 28
breaches of confidence   95–6
British Venture Capital Association   101–2
broken deals   21–2
"bumps in the road"   44, 185–6, 205–9
business "angels"   66, 177, 200
business creation, entrepreneurs   3–4, 16–17,
    69–70
business models   7, 28, 39–45, 49–98, 101–18
business plans
  see also private placement memorandum
  concepts   10–11, 67, 69
  teaser documents   69, 72–4
business premises, site visits   97
business risk, volatility   85–6
businesses   8, 53–7
  see also entrepreneurs
  grooming   81, 88–92
  positioning   8, 54–7
  valuations   8, 81, 82–8, 89–92, 104, 106–7,
    120–1, 153–4, 166, 176, 194
"buy low, sell high" golden rule   6
buy-backs   56–7, 112, 163–5
buy-outs   56–7
"buyer of last resort" rights   208
BVCA   51

Cambridge, UK   26
Cambridge MA   26, 28
Cantillon, Richard   4
capital
  competition concepts   25–9
  cost of capital   151–2
  debt finance   41–5, 153–6, 165–7, 187
  distributions   111
  dynamic capital allocation   45–6, 59–61, 101
  entrepreneurs' needs   4–6, 13, 22–3, 28–9,
    53–7, 81–98
  equity finance   6, 41–5, 53–7, 81–98, 147–67
  fund sources   10–13, 20, 22–3, 41–2, 51–2,
    53–7, 60–1, 81–98, 106–18, 133–8,
    147–67
  fund-raising cycle   8, 10–13, 20, 22–3, 41–2,
    60–1, 81–98, 106–18, 129–38, 147–67
  human capital   46–8, 63, 71, 76–80, 92,
    94–5, 98
  intellectual capital   46–8, 71, 76–80, 92

  LP commitments   10–13, 20–2
  market volatility   3, 85–6
  supply chains   9–13
capital gains, VC aims   6–7, 22–3, 29, 169
carried interest vehicle, concepts   18–19, 23
carve-outs   198–9
cash flows
  free cash flows   56–7, 84, 89
  management importance   6
  new ventures   4–6, 22–3, 41–2, 56–7,
    84, 89
cash management, spring cleaning   91–2
cash-on-cash metrics, concepts   27–9, 31–2
cashing-out treatment, vesting of management
    equity   183–4
"catch-up" approach, "high watermark" preferred
    shares   158–9
Cayman Islands   15, 93
CEOs *see* chief executive officers
change agents, entrepreneurs   4
chief executive officers (CEOs)   55–6, 66–70,
    141, 177
chief financial officers (CFOs)   177
children's-schooling analogy, VCs worries   13
clauses, term sheets   8
clawback   21
"cliff" period   175–84
CMO   55
co-investment rights, LPs   12–13
cold calling   67
collaboration relationships   62–4, 97–8, 198
come-along rights *see* tag-along rights
commitments, LPs   10–13, 20–2
committees   11, 37–8, 109, 142–4
common law   104–5, 161–2
  see also legal…
communications sector   3, 26–7
company by-laws   78
Compaq   27
competitive environment   22–3, 25–9, 36, 40,
    42–3, 54–7, 59–64, 70
  see also capital competition; deal competition
completion, investment process step   71, 76–80,
    108, 129–38
compulsory conversion rights   166–7
computing sector   3–4, 26–7
conferences, personal contacts   68–70
confidentiality issues   95–8, 106, 117
consensus to proceed, investment process step
    71–4
consultants   11–13, 66–7
contributed capital, management issues   20–2
controls   44–5, 55–7, 76–80, 81, 91–2, 97–8,
    141–6, 147–67, 177, 203–18
conversion rights   112, 155–6, 165–7, 193
corporate finance boutiques   11–13, 66–7

corporate governance   36–8, 104, 108–9, 139–46
    see also boards...
    committees   109, 142–4
    concepts   36–8, 104, 108–9, 139–46
    shareholder information rights   110, 144–5
    shareholder veto rights   110, 141, 143–4,
        145–6, 148, 149
    term sheets   104, 108–9, 139–46
corporate lawyers   8
cost of capital   151–2
cost-sharing arrangements, term sheets   102,
    117–18
"cottage industry"   7
creative destruction   4, 53–4
creditors, spring cleaning   91–2
crossover points, concepts   153–62
CSO   55
CTO   55, 178
cultural issues   15–17
cumulative dividends   151–2
customer contracts, term sheets   79–80, 97–8
"cut and run" rights   45

"dazzling the LPs" preoccupation, VCs   11
DCF-based valuations   84
deal champions   72–80
deal competition, concepts   25, 28–9
deal management terms
    concepts   116–17, 219–28
    conditions precedent   219–21
    exclusivity conditions   117–18, 222–5
    financial assistance   228
    reimbursement of costs   117–18, 225–8
    term sheets   104, 116–17, 219–28
deals
    see also term sheets
    broken deals   21–2
    concepts   7–8, 11, 16–17, 21–2, 28–9, 72–80,
        86–8, 93–5, 98–105, 116–17, 219–28
    proprietary deal-flow   33–4, 65–6
    terms   11–12, 16–17, 28–9, 37, 75–80, 93–5,
        98–105, 116–17, 219–28
    US influences   16–17, 28
    VCs/entrepreneurs   7–8, 16–17, 28–9, 72–80,
        86–8
debt finance   41–5, 153–6, 165–7, 187
debtors, spring cleaning   91–2
decision-making processes
    redemption features   163–4
    VCs   8, 36–8, 163–5
default, redemption features   162–5
deferred shares   184
Delaware law   17, 92
derivatives   85–8, 97–8, 187, 193
    options   85–8, 97–8, 127, 187, 193, 198
    warrants   98, 187, 193, 198

dilution   41–3, 59–61, 84–8, 97–8, 104, 114,
        121, 153–4, 165–7, 171–3, 185–90, 191–201
    see also anti-dilution protection
directors
    boards of directors   9, 44–5, 60, 104, 108–9,
        129–38, 139–46
    non-executive directorships   12, 64, 108–9,
        139–46
disclosures, confidentiality issues   96
dishonourable behaviour, VC firms   60
disputes, milestones   136–7
distributions
    see also capital...; dividends
    term sheets   110–11
diversification see portfolio diversification
dividends   90, 110–11, 150–62
    concepts   150–62
    taxation   156
documentation
    legal documentation   77–80, 101–5, 117
    term sheets   117
Doriot, George   16, 69–70
"double-dipping" preferred shares   154–6
    see also preferred shares
"down round"   43
downside risk management   31, 32, 35–48,
        59–61, 97–8, 104, 114, 153–4, 159–60,
        191–201
    anti-dilution protection   41–3, 59–61, 97–8,
        104, 114, 153–4, 165–7, 171–3, 185–90,
        191–201
    concepts   40–8
    human capital   46–8
    protection tools   41–5
drag-along rights, share transfers   116, 166–7,
        209–14, 218
DRI-WEFA   51
drip-feed investment approach, risk management
        35, 41–5, 129–38
"drop-dead" rights   45
drug products, regulatory pre-clearance   94
due diligence   21–2, 34–5, 37–8, 43, 44–5, 59–64,
        71–80, 92, 97, 101–18, 193–4, 220–8
    concepts   34–5, 37–8, 43, 44–5, 59–64, 71–2,
        74–80, 92, 97, 101–18, 193–4, 220–8
    conduct   118
    downside risk management   34–5, 37–8, 43,
        44–5
    final due diligence   71, 76–80
    focus areas   74–5, 76–7
    investment process step   71–2, 74–80
    legal due diligence   77–80, 92, 97–8
    preliminary due diligence   71, 74–6, 101–18
    site visits   97–8
    streams   74–6
    "two way street"   59, 223–4

dynamic capital allocation, concepts   45–6,
    59–61, 101
dynamics, VCs   7, 8, 45–6, 59–61, 85–6, 101

early warning systems   11
earn-ins   137–8
EBITDA   84, 89
ejection, GPs   20
"elevator pitch"   69
EMEA IND   94
employees
    see also human capital
    non-solicitation covenants   96–8
    share ownership programmes (ESOPs)   94,
        104, 113, 120, 169–73, 187–90, 198
    termination of employment   180–1, 183–4,
        205
England   15
    see also UK
entrepreneurs
    see also businesses; new ventures
    advice   98, 127
    ambitions   53–7, 59–64, 65–70, 72–4, 220–5
    anti-dilution protection   194–201
    business creation   3–4, 16–17, 69–70
    capital needs   4–6, 13, 22–3, 28–9, 53–7,
        81–98
    capital supply-chain cycle   13, 22–3
    change agents   4
    concepts   3–8, 16–17, 22–3, 28–9, 33–48,
        49–98, 101–5, 127
    confidentiality issues   95–8, 106, 117
    controls   44–5, 55–7, 76–80, 81, 91–2, 97–8,
        141, 147–67, 177, 203–18
    creative destruction   4, 53–4
    deals   7–8, 16–17, 28–9, 33–4, 65–70, 72–80,
        86–8, 93–5, 98–105
    definitions   4
    dividend rights   151–2
    due diligence reports   34–5, 44–5, 59–64,
        71–2, 74–80, 92, 101–18, 220–8
    entry point   65–70
    evolution   4
    exclusivity conditions   34, 102, 117–18,
        222–5
    exit attitudes   56–7, 181–3
    external finance   4 6, 28–9
    failure statistics   32, 40, 46, 51, 55, 65, 81
    fit needs   57, 59–64, 71–4, 169–73
    fund sources   10–13, 20, 22–3, 41–2, 51–2,
        53–7, 60–1, 81–98, 106–18, 133–8,
        147–67
    individuals   4, 91
    innovators   4, 53–7
    investment process   36–8, 49–98
    key questions   53–7

liquidations   29, 159–60
management teams   47–8, 54–7, 69–70,
    73–80, 90–2, 157–8, 169–73
meetings   8, 68–70, 71–4, 95, 97–8
milestone attractions   132–4
owner-management aims   55–6, 141, 177
personal contacts   63–4, 66–7, 68–70
personality traits   4
plan B   54, 70, 82, 121, 221–2, 224–5
poison pills   97–8
positioning   8, 54–7
pre-emption rights   186–90
preparations and management   81–98
product needs   54–7, 69–70
profitability potential   54–7
proprietary deal-flow   33–4, 54, 65–6
quality-of-life considerations   56
risk takers   4, 53–4
side-by-side "Entrepreneurs' Funds"   12
site visits   97–8
statistics   32, 40, 46, 51, 55
strategy   54–7, 70, 84, 88–92, 94–5, 98,
    116–18, 220–2, 226–8
successful entrepreneurs   3–5, 32, 53–5, 87
succession planning   56, 141
teaser documents   69, 72–4
types   65
valuation perspectives   84–8, 89–92
VC access considerations   49–98
VC relationships   6–8, 9–13, 28–9, 33–48,
    49–98, 101–18
VC selection criteria   59–64, 65–7, 69–70, 88
venture capital   3–8, 28–9, 53–98
vesting of management equity   176–8
voting-rights attractions   149
word origins   4
work-life balance   56
entry point
    see also qualified access
    CEOs   66–70
    concepts   65–70
    industry gurus   66–7, 68–70
    initial message   69
    meetings   8, 68–70
    personal contacts   63–4, 66–7, 68–70
    portfolio community   62–4, 66–70
    route selection   65–7
equities   6, 38, 41–5, 56–7, 70, 78, 90, 94, 104,
    106–18, 147–67, 169–73
    see also shareholders
    bonus shares   192–3
    complexity   171, 186
    conversion rights   112, 155–6, 165–7
    dividends   90, 110–11, 150–62
    exit options   56–7, 85, 159–62, 181–3,
        209–10

IPOs   6, 38, 56–7, 70, 112–14, 133, 143, 151,
    161, 165–6, 181–2, 187–90, 193–4, 198,
    204–5, 212–13
  pre-emption rights   44, 104, 114, 115–16,
    185–90, 205–9
  preference/preferred shares   147–62, 167
  redemption features   112, 162–5
  share incentives   94, 104, 113, 169–73,
    175–84, 187–90, 198
  share transfers   45, 104, 115–16, 203–18
  VC   6, 41–5
  vesting of management equity   104, 113,
    175–84
  voting rights   110–11, 141, 147–50
equity finance   6, 41–5, 53–7, 81–98,
    147–67
equity participation, term sheets   104, 110, 111,
    147–67
equity syndication see syndication practices
ESOPs see employees, share ownership
    programmes
Europe   8, 16–17, 19, 28, 63, 93–4, 104, 167,
    184–5
  see also individual countries
  historical background   16–17
European Union, Directives   19
European Venture Capital Association   101–2
evaluations
  investment process step   71, 74–6,
    101–18, 121
  skills, VCs   9–10, 22–3, 37–8
evolution, entrepreneurs   4
exclusivity conditions
  deal management terms   117–18, 222–5
  risk management   34, 102, 117–18, 222–5
executive summaries   69
existing shareholders
  see also shareholders
  fund-raising cycle   10–13
exit
  concepts   31–2, 38–9, 45, 56–7, 62, 79–80,
    85–8, 98, 149–50, 159–62, 172–3, 181–3,
    209–10
  entrepreneurs   56–7, 98
  IPOs   56–7, 161, 181–2, 193–4, 209–10,
    212–13
  methods   56–7, 159–62, 181–2, 209–10
  obsessions   38–9
  potential   31, 32, 38–9
  trade sales   56–7, 160–2, 181–2, 209–10
  vesting of management equity   181–3
expenses, reimbursement   117–18, 225–8
experience
  learning   32
  VC firm selection   61–2
experiential learning, risk   32

expertise, VCs   9, 61–2
external due diligence   74–6
  see also due diligence
external finance
  see also capital…
  entrepreneurs   4–6, 28–9
extreme caution, investment   31, 33–8

facets, LPs   17–19
failures   4, 31–2, 40, 45–6, 65, 81
  statistics   32, 40, 46, 51, 55
  success aspirations   4, 31–2, 40,
    45–6, 55
FDA IND   94
fees, management issues   18–19, 20–2
fiduciary duties, VCs   10
final due diligence, investment process step   71,
    76–80
financial controls   44–5, 55–7, 76–80, 91–2,
    97–8, 141–6, 147–67, 177, 203–18
financial instruments   6
financial intermediaries   9–10, 66–7
financing conditions, deal management
    terms   116–17, 219–28
first right of refusal, deal management
    terms   117–18
fit needs, relationships   57, 59–64, 71–4,
    169–73
fixed assets and inventory, spring cleaning
    91–2
"flat round"   43
"flip-flop" approach, "high watermark" preferred
    shares   158–9
flotations   6, 38, 56–7, 161, 167, 181–2
  see also initial public offerings
follow-on investments   21–2, 42–5, 59–61, 186
  downside risk management   42–5
France   93–5, 193, 225
free cash flows   56–7, 84, 89
  see also cash flows
Freedom of Information Act, US   25
FTSE 100   51
"full ratchet" approach, anti-dilution
    protection   191–2
fully diluted valuations, concepts   84–8,
    121, 192
fund managers   6–7, 9, 11–13, 18–19
  see also venture capital
fund sources   10–13, 20, 22–3, 41–2, 51–2,
    53–7, 60–1, 81–98, 106–18, 133–8,
    147–67
fund-raising cycle, concepts   8, 10–13, 20,
    22–3, 41–2, 60–1, 81–98, 106–18,
    129–38, 147–67
"funds of funds"   11–13
further funds, partnership agreements   22

Genentech   27
general partners (GPs)
   see also partnership agreements; senior
      partners
   concepts   17–23, 61–2, 63–70, 71–4
   definition   17–18
   ejection   20
   kick-off meetings   71–4
   LPs   18–23
   presentations   71–4
geographic performance   26–9, 32
Germany   16, 93, 225
golden rule, investment   6
Good Clinical Practices   77
"good leaver" provisions, vesting of management
      equity   180–1, 184
Good Manufacturing Practices   77
Google   27
GPs see general partners
grooming the business, investment process
      preparations   81, 88–92
guarantees   21
Guernsey   15

"halo effect", VC brands   28
"high watermark" preferred shares   157–9
   see also preferred shares
"hopeful achievers"   65
"hot deal"   86
human capital
   see also employees
   concepts   46–8, 63, 71, 76–80, 92,
      94–5, 98
   employee share ownership programmes   94,
      104, 113, 120, 169–73, 187–90, 198
hurdle rates   21, 151–2

IASs   169
identity, LPs   11–13
IFRSs   169
individuals, value-dependency
      considerations   91
industry events, personal contacts   68–70
industry gurus, qualified access point   66–7,
      68–70
inflection points, concepts   42–3, 59–61,
      86–7, 179
information
   asymmetries   9–10
   protection   44–5
   shareholder rights   110, 144–5
   VC firms   59, 69–70
initial engagement, investment process step
      71–4
initial message, communication   69, 71–4
initial presentations   69, 73–4, 95

initial public offerings (IPOs)   6, 38, 56–7, 70,
      112–14, 133, 143, 151, 161, 165–6, 181–2,
      187–90, 193–4, 198, 204–5, 212–13
   see also flotations
innovators   4, 53–7, 62
   see also entrepreneurs
"insider rounds"   197, 201
institutional investors   9–13, 18–23, 117–18
   see also banks; insurance companies; limited
      partners; pension funds
   types   9–13
insurance companies   9, 11–13
   see also institutional investors
intellectual capital, concepts   46–8, 71,
      76–80, 92
internal due diligence   74–6
   see also due diligence
internal investment process, concepts   36–8,
      49–98
internal rates of return (IRRs)   26–9, 31–2, 38,
      70, 131–4, 137
international capabilities, VC firms   63
Internet sector   3
inventory, spring cleaning   91–2
investment
   attrition rates   31–2
   "buy low, sell high" golden rule   6
   committees   11, 37–8
   concepts   6, 21–2, 31–48
   downside risk management   31, 32, 35–48
   drip-feed investment approach   35, 41–5,
      129–38
   due diligence   21–2, 34–5, 37–8, 43, 44–5,
      59–64, 71–2, 74–80, 92, 101–18, 193–4,
      220–8
   dynamic capital allocation   45–6, 59–61, 101
   exclusivity conditions   34, 102, 117–18,
      222–5
   exit   31, 32, 38–9, 45, 56–7, 62, 79–80, 85, 98,
      149–50, 159–62, 172–3, 181–3, 209–10
   extreme caution   31, 33–8
   follow-on investments   21–2, 42–5, 59–61,
      186
   golden rule   6
   human capital   46–8, 63, 71, 76–80, 92,
      94–5, 98
   internal investment process   36–8, 49–98
   leverage   35–6, 59–61
   portfolio diversification   33–4, 45–6, 62–4
   proprietary deal-flow   33–4, 54, 65–6
   restrictions   21–2, 34
   risk management   6, 7, 29, 31–48, 102–4
   syndication practices   35–6, 62, 76–80, 97–8,
      103–4, 107, 120, 125–7, 148–67
   tranching an investment   35, 41–5, 59–61,
      119–20, 129–38

Investment Advisors Act, US   140
investment banks   8, 11–13, 15–16
investment commitments, term sheets   104, 107,
     125–7
investment milestones *see* milestones
investment model, VCs   31–48
investment process
   concepts   36–8, 49–98
   phases   71–80, 101–2
   preparations   81–98
investors
   see also institutional investors; limited partners;
        shareholders
   liability risks   195
   types   9, 11–13, 15–23, 61–2, 92–5
involvement levels, LPs   11–13, 17–19
IPOs *see* initial public offerings
Ireland   93, 104
IRRs *see* internal rates of return
Israel   93
Italy   16

J.H. Whitney and Co.   16
J-curves   42, 87
Jersey   15, 17, 93
joint ventures   198–9

kick-off meetings, investment process step
     71–4, 95
Kleiner Perkins Caulfield & Byers (KPCB)
     27–8
KPCB *see* Kleiner Perkins Caulfield & Byers

lead equity syndicates   36, 62, 107, 125–7, 196
leadership concepts, VC firms   62, 72–3, 126
leaver provisions, vesting of management
     equity   180–1, 183–4
legal documentation   77–80, 101–5, 117
   concepts   77–80, 101–5, 117
   key contents   78
legal due diligence   77–80, 92, 97–8
   see also due diligence
legal instruments   6, 15
legal issues   15–22, 71, 76–80, 92–5, 97–8,
     101–5, 161–4, 184–90, 210, 225, 228
legally-binding elements
   investment process step   71, 76–80
   term sheets   102, 136–7, 161–2, 213
leverage, syndication practices   35–6, 59–62,
     76–80
liabilities, LPs   17–19
liability risks, investors   195
life assurance companies   11–13
lifespan, VC funds   19–22
limited liability companies (LLCs)   92–5
limited liability partnerships (LLPs)   92–5

limited partners (LPs)   6, 9–13, 15–23, 145,
     147–8
   see also partnership agreements; shareholders
   advantages   17
   advisory boards   11–13
   capital commitments   10–13, 20–2
   co-investment rights   12–13
   concepts   6, 9–13, 15–23, 147–8
   definition   17
   facets   17–19
   "funds of funds"   11–13
   further funds   22
   GPs   18–23
   historical background   15–17
   identity   11–13
   interests (LPIs)   22
   investment restrictions   21–2
   involvement levels   11–13, 17–19
   liabilities   17–19
   loyalties   10–11
   major players   11–13, 15–17
   management issues   15–23
   minimum-investment levels   12
   primacy   15–17
   profit shares   21–2
   reports   11
   risk-averse attitudes   12
   transaction costs/fees   21–2
   transfer of LP interests   22
   US origins   15–17
   VC relationships   9–13, 17–23, 145
"line", vesting of management equity   179
"liquidation preference"   159–60
   see also preference cascade
liquidations, entrepreneurs   29, 159–60
LLCs *see* limited liability companies
LLPs *see* limited liability partnerships
"lock-ups"   204–5
logistics, investment process preparations   81, 95
London Stock Exchange   143, 185
losses   29
loyalties, LPs   10–11
LPs *see* limited partners

M&As *see* mergers and acquisitions
MacMillan, Ian   5
management issues
   concepts   15–23, 47–8, 54–7, 60–4, 69–70,
        73–80, 90–2, 104, 116–17, 169–73, 219–28
   deal management terms   104, 116–17, 219–28
   fees   18–19, 20–2
   share incentives   94, 104, 113, 169–73,
        175–84, 187–90, 198
   termination of employment   180–1, 183–4, 205
   vesting of management equity   104, 113,
        175–84

management teams
    entrepreneurs   47–8, 54–7, 69–70, 73–80,
        90–2, 157–8, 169–73
    grooming the business   90–2
marked to market values   12
market needs, recognition   4, 54, 70, 76–80
MBA students   8
mechanism of action, anti-dilution
        protection   192–3
meetings   8, 68–70, 71–4, 95, 97–8, 109
    boards of directors   109, 142–4
    entry point   8, 68–70
    kick-off meetings   71–4, 95
    site visits   97–8
mergers and acquisitions (M&As)   81, 93,
        160–1, 187–90, 198, 212–13
mezzanine securities   97–8, 187
milestones   41–5, 88–92, 104, 108, 129–38
    alternatives   133–4, 137–8
    attractions for the parties   131–4
    careful drafting   135
    concepts   41–5, 88–92, 104, 108, 129–38
    danger areas   134–8
    definitions   129–30
    disputes   136–7
    earn-ins and ratchets   137–8
    syndication practices   135–6
    term sheets   104, 108, 129–38
    waivers   130–1
minimum-investment levels   12
Minute Maid   16
"Miser's Axiom"   5
mistakes   32–48
MIT   16
monitoring, early warning systems   11

Nasdaq   143
National Venture Capital Association   101–2
negotiations
    investment process step   71, 74–6, 101–18
    term sheets   71, 75–80, 98, 101–5, 220–8
net present value (NPV)   83–4
Netherlands   93, 225
new ventures
    see also entrepreneurs
    cash flows   4–6, 22–3, 41–2, 56–7, 84, 89
    "Promised Land"   5–6
    "Valley of Death"   5–6, 87–8
"no material adverse change" condition   220–1
nominations, boards of directors   108–9,
        140–5
nominations committees   109, 142–3
non-cumulative dividends   151–2
non-executive directorships   12, 64, 108–9,
        139–46
non-solicitation covenants   96–8

Norburn, David   5
notional value   83–4
NPV see net present value

observer rights   140–1
opportunities
    business creation   3–4, 16–17, 22–3, 32,
        69–70
    resources   4–5
options   85–8, 97–8, 127, 187, 193, 198
    poison pills   97–8
    pricing   85–8
other people's money   9–13
over-allocation problems, VC "asset class"   12
"over-deliver" problems, valuations   89–90, 130
over-trading dangers, VC firms   65
overview   3, 8, 48, 104–5
owner-management aims, entrepreneurs   55–6,
        141, 177

partial pre-emption rights   188–9, 206–7
partial tag-along rights   216
partnership agreements
    capital commitments   20–2
    concepts   19–23, 29
    further funds   22
    investment restrictions   21–2, 29
    lifespan   19–22
    management issues   20–2
    profit share   21–2
    transaction costs/fees   21–2
    transfer of LP interests   22
partnership relationships, VCs/entrepreneurs
        6–8, 9–13, 28–9, 33–48, 49–98, 101–18
partnerships
    see also general…; limited…
    concepts   6–8, 9–13, 17–19, 28–9, 33–48,
        49–98, 101–18
    terms   19–23
    types   17–18
"pay to play" concepts, anti-dilution
        protection   196–8
pension funds   9–13, 16, 18–23, 25
    see also institutional investors; limited partners
performance issues   10–13, 25–6, 31–2, 39–45,
        46–8, 51, 85–6, 88–92, 104, 108, 129–38
    see also returns
    anti-dilution protection   199–200
    benchmarks   12, 25–9, 31–2, 36, 85–6, 200,
        212
    cash-on-cash metrics   27–9, 31–2
    failure statistics   32, 40, 46, 51, 55
    geographic factors   26–9, 32
    human capital   46–8, 63, 94–5
    IRRs   26–9, 31–2, 38, 70, 131–4, 137
    lifecycles   26

milestones   41–5, 88–92, 104, 108,
    129–38
relative performance   25–6, 31–2, 40
sectors   26–9, 32, 55
statistics   32, 40, 46, 51, 55
transparency   25–6
upside potential   31, 32, 46–8, 53–7, 183–4,
    185–6
VC-backed companies   51
vintage years   25–9
personal contacts, relationships   63–4, 66–7,
    68–70
personality traits, entrepreneurs   4
phases, investment process   71–80, 101–2
"piggy back" rights   45, 214
plan B, entrepreneurs   54, 70, 82, 121, 221–2,
    224–5
poison pills   97–8
Polo, Marco   16
portfolio community, VC firms   62–4,
    66–70
portfolio diversification, concepts   33–4, 45–6,
    62–4
portfolio reporting software   11
    see also administrative infrastructure
positioning, businesses   8, 54–7
post-money valuations, concepts   83–8, 121,
    153–4, 176
"potential achievers"   65
power-point presentations   73–4
    see also presentations
powers of attorney   213
PPM see private placement memorandum
PR   91
pre-emption rights
    administration   190, 208, 218
    attractions   185–6
    concepts   44, 104, 114, 115–16, 185–90, 198,
        205–9, 214–18
    dangers   186–90
    obligations   186
    partial pre-emption   188–9, 206–7
    recipients   189, 207, 217–18
    reference terms   188
    share transfers   115–16, 205–9, 214–18
    term sheets   104, 114, 115–16, 185–90, 198,
        205–9, 214–18
    top-ups   189–90, 207–8, 218
    triggers   187–8
pre-money valuations, concepts   83–8, 90,
    120–1, 166, 194
preference cascade, concepts   152–62, 167
preference shares   151–62, 167
preferred shares   147–62, 167
preliminary due diligence, investment process
    step   71, 74–6, 101–18

preparations, investment process   81–98
presentations   37, 69, 71–4, 95
    concepts   37, 69, 71–4, 95
    confidentiality issues   95–6
    guidelines   73
    initial presentations   69, 73–4, 95
price protection
    downside risk management   41–5
    milestone advantages   133
private placement memorandum (PPM)
    see also business plans
    concepts   10–11
pro forma example, term sheets   8, 103–18
products, VC requirements   54–7, 69–70
professional advisors, qualified access   66,
    102–3
professional intermediaries, qualified
    access   66–7
profit share, partnership agreements   21–2
profitability potential, entrepreneurs   54–7
"Promised Land", new ventures   5–6, 88
proprietary deal-flow, risk management   33–4,
    54, 65–6
proprietary networks, VC firms   62–4, 65–70
proxies   147–50, 199–200
"put up or shut up" pre-emption   188–9,
    206–7

qualified access
    see also entry point
    concepts   65–70
    generation   67–70
    route selection   65–7
Qualifying Stock Exchange Flotation   167
quality-of-life considerations, entrepreneurs   56
quorum, boards of directors   142

R&D   62, 89–90
raising VC finance   8
ratchets
    anti-dilution protection   191–2
    complexity   172–3
    milestones alternative   137–8
    term sheets   112–13, 137–8, 161, 167, 172–3,
        191–2
recapitalisations   56–7
recessions   25
recycling options, VC funds   20–2
redemption features   112, 162–5
    alternatives   164–5
    concepts   162–5
    decision-making processes   163–4
    legal issues   164
reference terms, pre-emption rights   188
register, assets   91
registration rights agreements   78, 118

regulations   15–22, 71, 76–80, 92–5, 97–8,
    101–5, 161–4, 184–90, 210, 225, 228
    see also legal…
    boards of directors   140, 143
    drag-along rights   210
    pre-clearance factors   80, 94, 104, 118, 140
    pre-emption rights   185–6
    vesting of management equity   184
reimbursement of costs, term sheets   117–18,
    225–8
relationships
    see also partnership agreements
    collaboration relationships   62–4, 97–8, 198
    deals   7–8, 11, 16–17, 21–2, 28–9, 33–4,
        65–70, 72–80, 86–8, 93–5, 98–118
    entry point   65–70
    exclusivity conditions   34, 102, 117–18, 222–5
    fit needs   57, 59–64, 71–4, 169–73
    information asymmetries   9–10
    long-term resources   59–64, 81–98
    personal contacts   63–4, 66–7, 68–70
    VCs/entrepreneurs   6–8, 9–13, 28–9, 33–48,
        49–98, 101–18
    VCs/LPs   9–13, 17–23, 145
relative performance   25–9, 31–2, 40
    see also performance…
    benchmarks   12, 25–9, 31–2, 36, 85–6,
        200, 212
    IRRs   26–9, 31–2, 70, 131–4, 137
    sectors   26–9, 32
    vintage years   25–9
remuneration committees   109, 142–3
reorganisations   79–80, 111–12, 187
"repeat performers"   65
reports   11
repurchase mechanics, vesting of management
    equity   184
reputations
    valuations   86
    VCs   11, 13, 22–3, 28, 32, 62, 63, 86–8, 102
resources
    limited resources   4–5
    opportunities   4–5
returns   26–9, 31–2, 38, 41–2, 70, 131–4, 137,
    151–62
    see also performance issues
    hurdle rates   21, 151–2
    IRRs   26–9, 31–2, 38, 70, 131–4, 137
    lifecycles   26
    preference cascade   152–62
    risk   39–40
    shareholders   6, 151–62
reverse take-overs   160–1
rewards
    risk   39–40, 57
    syndication leadership   126

rights issues   44, 104, 114, 115–16, 185–90, 198,
    205–9, 214–18
    see also pre-emption rights
risk
    concepts   4, 6, 7, 9–13, 27–8, 29, 31–48,
        53–7, 102–4, 129–38
    experiential learning   32
    exposure   4, 6, 9–13, 27–8, 31–48
    fundamentals   31–2
    rewards   39–40, 57
    takers   4
    volatility   85–6
risk management
    basic themes   32–48
    concepts   6, 7, 29, 31–48, 102–4, 129–38
    downside risk management   31, 32, 35–48,
        159–60
    drip-feed investment approach   35, 41–5,
        129–38
    due diligence   21–2, 34–5, 37–8, 43, 44–5,
        59–64, 71, 74–80, 101–18, 193–4, 220–8
    dynamic capital allocation   45–6, 59–61, 101
    exclusivity conditions   34, 102, 117–18, 222–5
    exit   31, 32, 38–9, 45, 56–7, 98, 149–50,
        159–62, 172–3, 181–3, 209–10
    extreme caution   31, 33–8
    internal investment process   36–8
    portfolio diversification   33–4, 45–6, 62–4
    proprietary deal-flow   33–4, 54, 65–6
    syndication practices   35–6, 62, 76–80, 97–8,
        103–4, 120, 125–7, 148–67
    term sheets   102–4, 129–38
    tranching an investment   35, 41–5, 59–61,
        119–20, 129–38
    VCs   6, 7, 29, 31–48, 102–4
    veto rights   44–5, 110, 141, 143–4, 145–6,
        148, 149
risk-averse attitudes, LPs   12
"rubber stamping exercise"   37

sales pipeline, spring cleaning   91–2
salvage, "Miser's Axiom"   5
San Francisco Bay   28
Sarbanes Oxley Act   143
Say, Jean Baptiste   4
Scandinavia   93
Schumpeter, Joseph   4
Scotland   15
    see also UK
screening, investment process step   71–4
SEC   143
sectors
    performance issues   26–9, 32, 55
    types   3–4, 26–7, 32, 55
selection criteria, VC firms   59–64, 65–7,
    69–70, 88

senior partners
  see also general partners
  concepts   18–23
services provided, VCs   6–7
share incentives   94, 104, 113, 169–73, 175–84,
    187–90, 198
  attractions   169
  concepts   169–73, 175–84, 198
  dilution factors   171–2
  size issues   170–1
  vesting of management equity   104, 113,
    175–84
share ownership programmes, employees   94,
    104, 113, 120, 169–73, 187–90, 198
share transfers
  "buyer of last resort" rights   208
  concepts   45, 104, 115–16, 203–18
  drag-along rights   116, 166–7, 209–14, 218
  excluded transactions   208–9, 218
  IPO restrictions   204–5
  mandatory sales   205
  pre-emption rights   115–16, 205–9, 214–18
  restrictions   203–5
  tag-along rights   45, 115–16, 214–18
  term sheets   104, 115–16, 203–18
shareholders   6, 9–13, 15–23, 78–80, 97–8, 104,
    108–9, 139–46, 147–67, 195
  see also equities; investors; limited partners
  anti-dilution rights   195–201
  bonus shares   192–3
  conversion rights   112, 155–6, 165–7
  corporate governance   104, 108–9, 139–46
  dividends   90, 110–11, 150–62
  drag-along rights   116, 166–7, 209–14, 218
  existing shareholders   10–13
  fund-raising cycle   10–13, 20, 22–3, 41–2,
    147–67
  information rights   110, 144–5
  legal documentation   78
  pre-emption rights   44, 104, 114, 115–16,
    185–90, 205–9, 214–18
  preference/preferred shares   147–62, 167
  redemption features   112, 162–5
  returns   6, 151–62
  share transfers   45, 104, 115–16, 203–18
  veto rights   44–5, 110, 141, 143–4, 145–6,
    148, 149
  voting rights   110–11, 141, 147–50
shares *see* equities
short-form term sheets
  see also term sheets
  dangers   103
short-termism   90–2
side-by-side "Entrepreneurs' Funds"   12
signed term sheets, investment process step   71,
    74–6, 101–18

site visits   97–8
size issues
  share incentives   170–1
  tranching an investment   134–5
  VC trends   54–5
skills   9–10, 22–3, 37–8, 47–8, 63
"smart-money"   6
software sector   3–4, 26–7
special exit rights, downside risk
    management   45
special situations, term sheets   79–80, 111–12
special-purpose vehicles, concepts   18–19
spin-outs   79–80
spring cleaning, grooming the business   91–2
start-ups *see* new ventures
Stevenson, Howard   4
strategy
  entrepreneurs   54–7, 70, 84, 88–92, 94–5, 98,
    116–18, 220–2, 226–8
  VC firms   116–18, 219–28
structural issues
  investment process preparations   79–80, 81,
    92–5
  term sheets   104, 107, 110–11, 123, 147–67
subordinated preference certificates   155–6
success aspirations
  failures   4, 31–2, 40, 45–6, 55
  statistics   32, 55
successful entrepreneurs   3–5, 32, 53–5, 87
  see also entrepreneurs
succession planning, entrepreneurs   56, 141
Sun Microsystems   27
supplier contracts, term sheets   79–80, 97–8
supply chains, capital   9–13
"sweat equity"   176
Switzerland   93
syndication practices   35–6, 62, 76–80, 97–8,
    103–4, 107, 120, 125–7, 148–67
  anti-dilution protection   196, 201
  concepts   35–6, 62, 76–80, 97–8, 103–4, 107,
    120, 125–7
  lead equity syndicates   36, 62, 107, 125–7,
    196
  milestones   135–6
  term sheets   104, 107, 120, 125–7

tag-along rights, share transfers   45, 115–16,
    214–18
take-along rights *see* drag-along rights
Tanaka Business School   65
taxation   17, 92, 94–5, 156, 169, 209
  dividends   156
  investment process preparations   92, 94–5
  share incentives   169
  spring cleaning   92
  transparency   17

teaser documents
  see also business plans
  concepts   69, 72–4
technology-based companies   41–2, 54
term sheets   8, 37, 71, 74–80, 98–118, 121, 123,
    125–7, 129
  anti-dilution protection   104, 114, 153–4,
    165–7, 171–3, 185–90, 191–201
  boards of directors   108, 129–38
  clauses   8
  concepts   8, 37, 71, 74–6, 98–118, 121, 123,
    125–7
  conversion rights   112, 155–6, 165–7
  corporate governance   104, 108–9, 139–46
  cost-sharing arrangements   102, 117–18
  customer contracts   79–80, 97–8
  deal management terms   104, 116–17, 219–28
  definition   101–2
  dividends   110–11, 150–62
  documentation production   117
  equity participation   104, 110, 111, 147–67
  examples   101, 104–5, 121, 123, 125, 129,
    139, 147, 185, 191, 203, 219
  investment milestones   104, 108, 129–38
  key areas   101–5
  legally-binding elements   102, 136–7, 161–2,
    213
  length   101, 103
  life cycle   104–5
  negotiations   71, 75–80, 98, 101–5
  pre-emption rights   104, 114, 115–16, 185–90,
    198, 205–9, 214–18
  preference cascade   152–62, 167
  pro forma example   8, 103–18
  purposes   101, 102–5
  ratchets   112–13, 137–8, 161, 167, 172–3,
    191–2
  redemption features   112, 162–5
  registration rights agreements   78, 118
  regulatory requirements   118
  reimbursement of costs   117–18, 225–8
  risk management   102–4, 129–38
  share ownership and incentives   104, 113,
    120, 169–73, 175–84, 187–90, 198
  share transfers   104, 115–16, 203–18
  short-form term sheets   103
  signed term sheets   71, 74–6, 101–18
  special situations   79–80, 111–12
  structural issues   104, 107, 110–11, 123, 147–67
  supplier contracts   79–80, 97–8
  syndication practices   103–4, 107, 120, 125–7
  valuations   104, 106–7, 121
  VC policy   103
  vesting of management equity   104, 113, 175–84
  veto rights   141, 143–4, 145–6, 148, 149
  voting rights   110–11, 141, 147–50
terms
  "battle of the term sheets"   28
  deals   11–12, 16–17, 28–9, 37, 75–80, 93–5,
    98–105, 116–17, 219–28
  partnership agreements   19–23, 29
"tied VCs"   16
timing needs, investment process
    preparations   81–2, 88–92
"tipping points"   179, 223
top-ups, pre-emption rights   189–90, 207–8, 218
trade sales   56–7, 160–2, 181–2, 187–90, 209–10
tranching an investment   35, 41–5, 59–61,
    119–20, 129–38
  downside risk management   35, 41–5
  size issues   134–5
transaction costs/fees, partnership
    agreements   21–2
transaction logistics, investment process
    preparations   81, 95
transaction size, term sheets   104, 106–7, 121
transaction structure, investment process
    preparations   79–80, 81, 92–5, 107, 123
transfer of LP interests, partnership
    agreements   22
transparency   17, 25–6
  performance   25–6
  taxation   17
trusts   11–13, 209
turn-around potential   45–6
"two way street", due diligence   59, 223–4

UK   15–17, 51, 93–5, 104, 161–2, 169, 184–5, 210
  see also England; Scotland
UK GAAP   169
undiluted valuations, concepts   84–8, 121, 192
unlimited liability, concepts   17–19
upside potential   31, 32, 46–8, 53–7, 183–4, 185–6
US   8, 15–17, 25–9, 51, 63, 92–5, 104, 140–3,
    161–2, 167, 169, 184–6, 201
US GAAP   92, 169

"Valley of Death", new ventures   5–6, 87–8
valuations
  businesses   8, 81, 82–8, 89–92, 104, 106–7,
    120–1, 153–4, 166, 176, 194
  entrepreneur's perspective   84–8, 89–92
  importance   86–8
  introduction   82–4
  investment process preparations   81, 82–8
  "over-deliver" problems   89–90, 130
  post-money valuations   83–8, 121, 153–4, 176
  pre-money valuations   83–8, 90, 120–1,
    166, 194
  reputations   86
  term sheets   104, 106–7, 121
  VCs   12, 85–8, 89–92

value-added   6–7, 12–13, 28, 47–8, 62–4, 91,
    153–4
value-drivers   85–8, 89–92, 169–73, 194–5
VAT   92
VC firms (VCs)
    see also term sheets
    active participation   60–1, 139–46, 147–67
    administrative infrastructure   11
    advisory boards   11–13
    aims   6, 9–10, 22–3, 29, 31–3, 53–7, 59–64,
        69–70, 103, 179, 220–8
    anti-dilution attractions   193–5
    branding significance   13, 28
    capital gains   6–7, 22–3, 29, 169
    capital supply chains   9–13
    challenges   3–4, 13
    children's-schooling analogy   13
    competitive environment   22–3, 25–9, 36, 40,
        42–3, 59–64, 70
    concepts   3–8, 9–13, 15–23, 25–9, 31–48,
        53–98, 103–5, 139–46
    corporate governance   104, 108–9, 139–46
    "dazzling the LPs" preoccupation   11
    decision-making processes   8, 36–8, 163–5
    dishonourable behaviour   60
    dividend rights   150–1
    due diligence   21–2, 34–5, 37–8, 43, 44–5,
        59–64, 71–2, 74–80, 92, 101–18, 193–4,
        220–8
    dynamics   7, 8, 45–6, 59–61, 85–6, 101
    early warning systems   11
    entrepreneurs   3–8, 9–13, 16–17, 28–9,
        33–48, 49–98, 101–18
    entry point   65–70
    experience criteria   61–2
    expertise   9, 61–2
    extreme caution   31, 33–8
    fiduciary duties   10
    fund-raising cycle   8, 10–13, 20, 22–3,
        41–2, 60–1, 81–98, 106–18, 129–38,
        147–67
    information   59, 69–70
    internal investment process   36–8
    international capabilities   63
    investment model   31–48
    leadership concepts   62, 72–3, 126
    LP relationships   9–13, 17–23
    milestone attractions   129–38
    needs   5–6, 69–70, 87–8
    over-trading dangers   65
    partnership agreements   19–23, 29
    performance issues   10–11, 12–13, 25–6
    personal contacts   63–4, 66–7, 68–70
    policy   103
    portfolio community   62–4, 66–70
    PPM   10–11

pre-emption rights attractions   185–6
proprietary networks   62–4, 65–70
raising finance   8
redemption features   162–3
reputations   11, 13, 22–3, 28, 32, 62, 63,
    86–8, 102
research   59, 69–70
risk exposure   4, 6, 9–13, 27–8, 31–48
risk management   6, 7, 29, 31–48, 102–4,
    129–38
roles   6, 9–10, 22–3, 29, 33, 53–7, 59–64,
    69–70, 103, 179
selection criteria   59–64, 65–7, 69–70, 88
services provided   6–7
share incentives   169–73, 187–90, 198
skills   9–10, 22–3, 37–8, 47–8, 63
strategy   116–18, 219–28
successes/failures   4, 31–2, 40, 45–6, 53–5,
    65, 81, 87
syndication practices   35–6, 62, 76–80, 97–8,
    103–4, 107, 120, 125–7, 148–67
value-added   6–7, 12–13, 28, 47–8, 62–4,
    153–4
vesting of management equity   175–84
veto rights   44–5, 110, 141, 143–4, 145–6,
    148, 149
voting-rights attractions   147–9
VC funds
    see also venture capital
    concepts   15–23, 40, 54–7
    size trends   54–5
VC *see* venture capital
VCs *see* VC firms
Venture Capital Operating Company, US
    Investment Advisors Act   140
venture capital (VC)
    access considerations   49–98
    capital commitments   10–13, 20–2
    complexity   6, 17
    concepts   3–8, 9–13, 15–23, 25–9, 33,
        40, 53–98
    deals   7–8, 11, 16–17, 21–2, 28–9, 33–4,
        65–70, 72–80, 86–8, 98–105
    definition   6
    equities   6, 41–5
    historical background   3, 15–17, 25–6, 54–5
    lifecycle   19–23
    lifespan   19–22
    management issues   15–23, 60–4, 104,
        116–17, 175–84, 219–28
    minimum-investment levels   12
    over-allocation problems   12
    overview   3, 8, 48, 104–5
    recessions   25
    recycling options   20–2
    reports   11

venture capital (VC) (*Continued*)
  size trends   54–5
  suitability considerations   53–7
  taxation   17
  term sheets   8, 37, 71, 74–80, 98–118
  US origins   16–17
  valuations   12, 85–8, 89–92
  vintage years   25–9
venture capitalists *see* VC firms
vesting of management equity   104, 113,
    175–84
  attractions   175–7
  cashing-out treatment   183–4
  complexity   178
  concepts   175–84
  danger areas   178–84
  definition   175
  entrepreneurs   176–8
  exit events   181–3
  leaver provisions   180–1, 183–4
  pace and level   178–9
  regulations   184
  repurchase mechanics   184
  term sheets   104, 113, 175–84
  treatment of shares   183–4

veto rights, downside risk management   44–5,
    110, 141, 143–4, 145–6, 148, 149
vintage years   25–9
vision   4, 64–70, 71–4
volatility
  business risk   85–6
  problems   12
voluntary conversion rights   165–6
voting rights
  attractions   147–9
  concepts   110–11, 141, 147–50
  dangers   148–50
  shareholders   110–11, 141, 147–50
VP BusDev   55

waivers, milestones   130–1
"warehoused" shares   184
warrants   98, 187, 193, 198
"weight-up"   189–90
"weighted average" approach, anti-dilution
    protection   191–2
Wharton Business School   5
wine analogies   25–6
work-life balance, entrepreneurs   56
World War Two   16

Index compiled by Terry Halliday